LEHMAN BROTHERS'
DANCE WITH DELUSION

Wrestling Wall Street

by Stanley J. Dziedzic, Jr.

ISBN: 1453791566
ISBN-13: 9781453791561

PREFACE

O ur narrative begins in the mid 1980s with Salomon Brothers' storied training class, proceeds through the demise of the savings and loan industry, and ends with a damning chronicle of Lehman's slide into disgrace—all witnessed and illustrated by an ex-managing director and former mortgage-bond salesman who had a unique bird's-eye view of events. Along the way it takes an interesting and provocative route through the global securities and derivatives evolution, Long Term Capital Management's (LTCM) implosion, the government's intrusion into the mortgage market, and the destructive and irresponsible failure of Lehman Brothers' management to rein in risk. The journey supplies a slew of frank and sometimes ironic anecdotes that bring clarity to Lehman's descent into obscurity. These first-person accounts supply potential restructuring routes for global policymakers to dampen the irrational swings currently associated with financial crises, a virtual curriculum vitae with which to survey *Lehman Brothers' Dance with Delusion!*

Unique international wrestling experiences provide a vivid lens through which to view the evolution of the capital markets as well as apt lessons to ease the exposition. In the world of sports, international wrestling is the most egalitarian and democratic: no refined fields, courts, courses, or specialized equipment are needed. Wrestling does not require rackets, apparatus, balls, or even gloves, just a twelve-meter by twelve-meter mat and three judges. Two equal-sized wrestlers—armed with nothing more than their individual physical abilities, wit, arsenal of techniques, and most importantly, their will to win—step onto the mat to determine who the best is. Much like the capital markets, international wrestling is designed to be a massive meritocracy.

In August 1984, the Los Angeles Olympic Games had just ended and I was en route to Wall Street, to Salomon Brothers' training program, to be exact. I had just completed a six-year stint as a United States National Team wrestling coach, a pilot program funded by Sun Oil to determine the efficacy of National Team coaches at the Olympic level. Sun Oil's original commitment to the grant had been for three years. Yet in 1980, shortly after President Carter decided to respond to the Soviet Union's invasion of Afghanistan by boycotting the 1980 Olympic Games in Moscow, for the first time the United States wrestlers defeated the USSR national team in the World Cup. At that juncture, with the unprecedented success of the program, Sun Oil decided to renew the grant through the 1984 Olympic Games in Los Angeles.

The 1984 USA Olympic freestyle wrestling team had performed exceptionally well. Out of ten weight classes, U.S. wrestlers won seven gold medals and two silver medals. The only freestyle wrestler not to medal was injured during the early rounds. For me it was a somewhat bittersweet victory. It would have been far more rewarding had the Soviet Union not boycotted. They were clearly the preeminent wrestling team and the ones we sought to dethrone.

Nonetheless, in a dramatic personal change, my attention would now be devoted to Wall Street, a substantially different culture from the one I had grown accustomed to—international sports. My immediate focus would be Salomon Brothers' training class and later it would turn to the mortgage-backed securities market as an institutional salesman* at Salomon Brothers and Lehman Brothers.

From 1984 through 1991, my primary responsibility was the financial industry, mostly savings and loan companies and banks, in Salomon's Atlanta office. In 1991 that all changed. When the pay package of Salomon's Larry Hilibrand surfaced, Salomon's head of government trading Paul Mozer was enraged. Apparently in a fit of moral amnesia, Mozer submitted a bid to the U.S. Treasury that exceeded the then authorized amount in any government-bond auction. Mozer previously had worked in the arbitrage group** where Hilibrand now toiled. The attendant scandal would force the resignation of Salomon's chairman John Gutfreund, President Thomas Strauss, and Vice Chairman J. M. Meriwether. Mozer was suspended and sentenced to four months in a minimum-security prison and fined $30,000.[1] Hilibrand, despite his intellect and intense work ethic, eventually faltered in tandem with LTCM.

Fortunately for Salomon, Warren Buffett, with a substantial preferred convertible investment at stake, took the reins as interim CEO, and in his own inimitable manner saved Salomon from the regulators. Yet repairing the confidence in Salomon's credit and returning it to its once formidable standing would prove to be a much tougher task.

Lehman Brothers, then part of American Express, was at that time in the process of building its Atlanta presence and asked if I would consider moving. Salomon Brothers had mutated into small fiefdoms replete with discontent, disappointment, and disillusionment, so the time seemed right for a change. For the next thirteen years I would be a mortgage-backed-securities salesman and eventually would manage Lehman's Atlanta office. During my tenure with Lehman Brothers, I covered banks, insurance companies, and hedge funds. In 1996, I was promoted to managing director. Until I retired in 2005 I managed Lehman's Atlanta office, but always kept a hand in selling. I found it easier to manage and recognize risk when I remained close to the markets.

My position, first as a mortgage salesman covering the thrift industry at Salomon Brothers and later as a salesman and managing director of Lehman's southeast region, provided me a panoramic perspective: a front-row seat to witness the systemic changes that led to Lehman's self-destruction, which took our global financial system to the edge. What began as a quest to profit from allocating global capital more efficiently lapsed into an overreach for profits. The tasks drifted from having intrinsic purpose to solely seeking extrinsic reward. And the cast of those complicit in the odyssey goes beyond Wall Street.

Lehman, more clearly than anyone, should have understood how fragile our financial system had become. Following the LTCM debacle, the banking sector took measures to put in place a sounder credit structure. The changes were necessary but were, as we now know, insufficient. Let us hope this time more meaningful changes are incorporated and that global policymakers do not fail again to adequately alter the structure of risk in our capital markets.

Unless policymakers review our capital market structure carefully and incorporate the necessary changes, they will again squander an opportunity to right the ship, leaving the global financial system vulnerable. Today, global financial assets are increasingly more concentrated and money managers are often measured by similar metrics. Managers' successes are most often measured relative to a bench mark or peer group, not to absolute performance, which has a tendency to exacerbate volatility.

U.S. financial systems senior executives, especially those at Lehman, failed miserably in adequately heeding the warnings from past crises. The bailout of the thrift industry and the havoc created by Russia's default which led to the looming failure of LTCM should have served as wake-up calls. It is not the first time regulators have faced the dilemma of either bailing out financial entities or taking the risk of bringing the system crashing down.

As far as ethical underpinnings go, I do my best here to re-create facts accurately while trying to avoid moralizing. It would be easy to jump onto the political populism bandwagon and bash the "selfish banksters," but my intention is to defer to the reader's judgments of right and wrong. Nonetheless, I do not shy away from directing blame at management for their unbounded overconfidence, miscues, omissions, incompetence, and sheer negligence. The populist ire toward the tainted industry is justified, but focusing on issues of morality, injecting accusations of malfeasance, or dousing the banking sector with contempt only distracts from what should be the principal debate: how do we create a structure resilient enough to avoid a repetition of the recent "great recession"? Painting everyone in the industry with the same brush does little to establish a sound banking system and stands in the way of effective reform.

In *Liar's Poker*, the author Michael Lewis provided the following explanation for writing his book:

> "It should be said that I was, by the standards we use to measure ourselves, a success. I made a lot of money. I was told often by people who ran our firm that I would one day join them at the top. I would rather not make this boast early. But the reader needs to know that I have been given no reason to feel bitterly toward or estranged from my former employer. I set out to write this book only because I thought it would be better to tell the story than go on living the story."[2]

It is unfortunate, given Lewis's talent as a writer that he did not choose to live the story longer before telling it. Perhaps given more time, and with his talent to entertain his readers with his eloquent prose, he could have gone deeper, captured the flaws in the system, and exposed the inadequate risk management.

I feel no compulsion to make any such proclamations. As I have often said, there is little socially redeeming about investment banking, but no one needs to apologize for a career in the capital markets. The financial system, including the capital markets, is both an essential and vital part of our country's economy. Without access to capital, the economy ceases to function efficiently.

In stark contrast to Michael Lewis, I would rather not be telling this story. Instead, my visceral anger at Richard "Dick" Fuld and his loyal lieutenants for failing to ensure Lehman's viability and my frustration at Wall Street's unwillingness to address the fundamental structural flaws in its risk management compels me.

* An institutional **salesman**, unlike a retail salesman, maintains a comprehensive dialogue with an assigned list of sophisticated, mostly large active accounts to ensure that material strategic changes in their respective market are communicated in a timely manner.

** Loosely speaking, **arbitrage** means to take advantage of price differentials among markets, with the aim of creating a nearly risk-free return.

INTRODUCTION

This is a story of how skewed incentives, dysfunctional regulatory and risk management structures, and a concentration of risk imperiled the global financial system. It is not a chronicle of unscrupulous or greedy traders, though these exist. Most of the anecdotes that follow are based on my recollection of misguided confidence, incompetence, hubris, and management's failure to recognize defects in an evolving financial system. More importantly, it is a candid depiction of how Lehman Brothers' management ignored the lessons from previous market dislocations—which led to its demise.

Although America's archaic regulatory structure needs repair, this is not a call for intrusive government regulation. Rather it is an attempt to identify and assign risk which will require a higher quality of supervision of our financial system, coupled with an expanded authority to intervene. Those who shoulder the cost, including the taxpayer, should reap the markets' rewards for such risk. Where systemic risk is introduced, it needs monitoring. In a market-oriented economy, the more assets become concentrated within financial institutions, the more vital the need for quality supervision with independent statutory powers.

The Federal Reserve and other central banks took aggressive policy actions to help the financial system mend itself. The Fed lowered the federal-funds rate to near zero and expanded the volume of its balance sheet via the capital markets. Most notably, it purchased long-term securities and introduced lending programs to restart the flow of credit. For the moment, it appears that these actions by the Federal Reserve, the U.S. Treasury, and other world central banks collectively averted a more vicious financial crisis and augmented the functioning of several key markets.

An important question we must ask as the Federal Reserve is becoming increasingly preoccupied with developing and enunciating its monetary and macroeconomic policies, is this: Are policymakers sacrificing an opportunity to remodel financial markets and revitalize the banking sector? So far no one, not even the financial institution's management, has been able to identify potential bubbles or implement changes to thwart them. This may be too much to expect of gifted theorists and may divert their attention from practical components of monetary policy.

Economic theorists may be highly capable of determining when the nation's economy is expanding and of formulating the most effective policies to drain excess liquidity in order to avoid inflation. At the same time, they may not be capable of effectively regulating today's vast financial institutions. Given the extension of banks and nonbanks by consolidation of financial activities into comprehensive financial institutions and their exposure to complex securities,* the task of identifying people who embody the requisite skills and industry knowledge, then providing them with statutory authority to intervene, appears daunting.[1]

Clarity about who is in charge does not necessarily require consolidating authority. Sufficient broad-based participation, along with delineation of responsibility, may be more effective. More often, seeking multiple views, fostering healthy debate, and convening a consensus generate superior ideas.

What the American public knows is that reverting to the risky behavior of "heads I win, tails you lose" is irresponsible. It should be unacceptable to taxpayers, who are saddled with the risk of subsidizing purchases while others stand to reap most, if not all, of the profit. This is not only rigged but will not stabilize the banking system. A bolder reworking of the risk/reward balance is prudent. The option to access the discount window, like FDIC deposit guarantees, should have a cost, preferably market-based.

When the taxpayers' money stands behind bets, risky behavior is encouraged and illusory performance is rewarded. Allocating capital efficiently is not accomplished by using taxpayers' money to guarantee against solvency. Policymakers are being remiss if they fail to assign a market-based cost to the options. The capability to determine market pricing is available. The term "free markets" should not be interpreted to mean "without cost."

Long-term sustainability of our financial system requires more substantive changes that isolate or at least contain the risk at a cost to those responsible. This may be at the holding company level, within business units, on individual desks, or with all of the above. Free-marketers should insist on utilizing markets to price this stopgap option. Should lawmakers solve these structural problems, the world may find a more stable financial system that allocates capital more efficiently and effectively.

The prevalent thinking seems to be that our current financial crisis is a once-in-a-lifetime event. But viewing the current crisis through the prism of conventional wisdom may prove to have dangerous consequences. Relying on the past as a predictor is just another misguided idea of what the future may hold. An inaccurate diagnosis or a misinterpretation may lead policymakers and business leaders to neglect the infrastructure reform on which the entire financial system's welfare may depend.

The Federal Reserve, Treasury, and Wall Street should know the perils of depending on historical norms as a guide to the future. Consolidation of assets should continue to be viewed as a harbinger of greater risk. Prudence suggests that the escalating severity of consecutive crises signals a need to recalibrate risk models to a new financial paradigm of higher volatility.

This means modifying financial models to accurately price risk and then determine where it is best accommodated. This does not mean avoiding risk. The venture capital industry is a poignant example. Their mission is to take risk. In their current form, venture capital firms are mostly small, not highly leveraged, and pose little threat to the financial system. No venture capital firm has required government bailout funds or has been deemed too big or interconnected to fail. Their investors are screened and meet strict suitability requirements.

More important, venture funds provide vital money to start-ups considered too risky by other investment vehicles. Any regulation to rein in venture capitalists may stymie entrepreneurship and lead to less innovation in the United States. A brief review of history shows a large portion of venture-supported firms go belly-up, making them best suited for partnerships. Burdening venture funds with additional regulation, when no federal dollars are at risk, would increase the cost to the small businesses the economy depends on for much of its growth.[2]

As financial crises unfold there are no watershed events that are easily recognizable; rather, they are like symptoms which become clearer once the disease is diagnosed. The financial system is like an obese smoker recovering from a massive heart attack. He has received the requisite emergency care and is recuperating, but unless the core causes of obesity and hypertension are addressed, the likelihood of another heart attack in the foreseeable future is high.

Efficient marketers, whose arguments I generally support, would contend the patient will certainly adopt a healthier lifestyle since any rational person would not put his life (or his capital) in mortal danger. Unfortunately the argument assumes that in addition to the obvious and powerful incentive of survival, each individual has the requisite fortitude, intelligence, and discipline to implement a rational, healthy regime.

Too many times, though, such is not the case. We all recognize the patient: the recalcitrant relative or friend, maybe even educated and productive in other aspects of his life, who time and again ignores the doctor's warning of the critical need to adopt a healthier lifestyle. "If I can't enjoy a cigarette or a hamburger and fries, life isn't worth living. Life is too short to count calories." And like the prescription for managing obesity, the process of reorganizing our financial system will not be easy to digest.

When the taxpayers' money is at risk, financial markets require the proper incentives (alignment of risk with reward), fortitude (transparency/disclosure), and discipline (structural guidelines) to live a healthy lifestyle. In addition, competent doctors (supervisors), regular check-ups (risk reviews), and vital-sign bench marks (leverage limits) are necessary disciplines to ensure survival. In the long run, financial markets may very well digest the requisite information and price assets appropriately, but the challenge today is to structure a system with the necessary safeguards that will ensure its survival in times of short-term dislocations.

At the time of this writing, the patient is still dependent upon drugs (government support). Innovation continues to be stifled and access to credit for many consumers still impaired. Market participants' demands may very well obviate the need for government reform as to transparency and disclosure. Nonetheless, side by side with transparency must be confidence in the integrity of the information.

Submitting false or inaccurate data and improperly withholding information from the market should have repercussions and consequences. Those responsible for misdeeds, regardless of the financial entity—bank or non-bank—should be held accountable. Competent oversight with adequate discretionary powers and supervision regarding the content of information are paramount. Qualified and dedicated supervision within the structure of the financial institutions is necessary to restore confidence in our tainted markets.

Furthermore, I must warn the reader and ask for indulgence for the liberal use of acronyms and complex anecdotes to explain the financial components of my story. Also, I frequently illuminate my story with wrestling analogies that illustrate some of the guiding principles. The analogies from wrestling are a convenient medium of comparison because my life outside of Wall Street influenced my approach to the business. The acronyms are a kind of shorthand that has become part of everyday Wall Street. These reflect a natural tendency to find a less time-consuming terminology to recognize and retain.

It is far more efficient to say, "Freddie 7s are up a 32nd overnight" as opposed to, "The Federal Home Loan Mortgage Corporation's 7 percent coupons' price increased by .03125 of 1 percent in London and Tokyo trading last night." Nonetheless, for the reader some of these dialogues may conjure up some strange thoughts. An early-morning conversation on the trading desk may go as follows: "When I woke up this morning I panicked. I realized I did not cover my position and I was long. How did Fannies do over night? The Fannies were flat in Tokyo but firmed nicely in London. You should be happy you were long. I am short."

Similarly, the complex nature of securities is an integral component of the financial industry and its anecdotes. I attempt, as best I can, to simplify their complicated nature and make them more understandable for the reader. When possible, I attempt to provide a condensed *Readers Digest*-type version.

The stories in this book reflect my notes and my best recollection from more than twenty-one years' experience as a Wall Street professional—some from a very long time ago and others more recent. The recent insights in many cases are those of former colleagues and acquaintances who are still employed in the industry. They are talented, qualified, and intensely devoted individuals who I count as my friends and whose confidence I wish to keep.

---

* Financial **securities** are obligations; for instance corporate debt or mortgage loans packaged and issued in a standardized, marketable form.

1

SALOMON BROTHERS' TRAINING CLASS

"Doubt yourself and you doubt everything you see. Judge yourself and you see judges everywhere. But if you listen to the sound of your own voice, you can rise above doubt and judgment. And you can see forever." Edmund Hoyle

On the plane from Los Angeles to New York I was filled with conflicting emotions. I was leaving what had consumed my life, the sport of wrestling. For the past twenty years, wrestling had been my passion. After graduation from college, I was hired as the assistant wrestling coach and part-time instructor at Michigan State University (MSU). While assistant at MSU, I continued to compete for the United States national wrestling team. In the 1976 Olympic Games I won a bronze medal, and in 1977 I ended my competitive career and became the sixth American wrestler to win the World Championships in Lausanne, Switzerland.

In 1978 I turned my efforts fulltime to become wrestling's United States national coach. During my tenure as wrestling's national coach, it became increasingly clear that it would be difficult for me to return to a coaching position at the university level. My international wrestling experiences and the difference between the commitments of the Olympic athletes versus those of college wrestlers compelled me to make a change. The amount of focus and effort to prepare and succeed as an Olympic wrestler overshadows the dedication needed to win as a collegiate wrestler.

More important to the decision process, however, was the international travel—often to remote areas of the world such as Chechnya, Dagestan, Iran, or Azerbaijan—where wrestling intersected with economic and social authoritarianism. The experience afforded me an opportunity to witness firsthand the shackles of communism and to appreciate the gift of freedom, both economic and political. I could no longer see myself returning to the relative simplicity of college coaching. It was time to seek a new career.

In preparation for the career shift, I took classes and earned an MBA during my six-year tenure as national coach. Yet now that the time had arrived for my new challenge, I had a sense of anxiety, not dissimilar to the feeling I had had the morning after I earned a spot on the Olympic team. My elation and sense of accomplishment from winning the wrestle-offs had quickly turned to a feeling of urgency. I realized that in the next few months I needed to prepare to wrestle Olympic and world medalist Jan Karlsson of Sweden, Olympic champion Jiichiro Date of Japan, world champion and Olympic silver medalist Monsoor Barzegzar of Iran, and two-time world champion Rouslan Ashuraliev of the Soviet Union. Then as now, the jitters did not make me withdraw emotionally, but rather led to an inner determination. I promised myself that I would not fail through a lack of focused effort.

It was not the competitive aspect of Salomon Brothers that gave me pause. There is nothing more fundamentally competitive than international wrestling. The pay-for-performance attracted me, but the conventional opinion of Wall Street's manner of achieving success tugged at me. My perception of the primary difference between Wall Street and the Olympic movement worried me. Yet this was certainly not from the wide-eyed innocent view of an amateur athlete. The Iron Curtain countries, ironically communists, took Ayn Rand's "morality of rational self-interest" to new heights. Think Ayn Rand on steroids!

One of my first exposures to this attitude as a coach came during the 1979 World Championships. At the time, the international rules employed a round-robin format. In the first of the three round-robin matches in the eighty-two-kilogram weight class the Hungarian wrestler pinned the Soviet wrestler. In the second of three, the U.S. wrestler John Peterson, the '76 Olympic champion, defeated the Hungarian by points. Since the

Soviet wrestler lost by fall against the Hungarian, he could defeat John by a decision and still not win the gold medal.

The Soviets viewed this situation as an opportunity to improve their future tally of gold medals. One of their coaches approached me with a proposition: "We are willing to allow Mr. Peterson to win the match and gold medal." His perverse justification or moral logic was, "The round-robin format provides this circumstance and we are only availing ourselves of the situation." To the Soviets, the "spirit of the rule" was merely an abstract concept and viewed as a weakness. Not ever having lived under the heavy hand of a totalitarian regime and its cultural influences, I hesitated to make a judgment of his personal morality.

Of course there were conditions. Not to offend his sense of morality I explained, "There are two things you may not understand. First, if John Peterson ever found out I was complicit in arranging his victory; he probably would never speak to me again. Second, you would require us to reciprocate at some time under similar circumstances."

He responded, "Of course," as if this were an everyday occurrence.

I tried to explain. "Even if I wanted to, I would never be able to pay you back."

"But you are the national coach," he emphasized, with a quizzical look on his face.

In a gracious tone and manner, striving not to convey even a hint of condescension, I responded, "Yes, maybe someday I will be able to explain it to you." Grabbing his hand to shake it, I said, "Let Arazilov and Peterson determine who wins, okay?" With a somewhat puzzled look on his face, he turned and walked away.

Peterson and Arazilov tied, and the Hungarian wrestler Kovacs won the gold medal, John the silver, and Arazilov the bronze. Kovacs is now an accomplished international referee. On the occasions when I see him, I often wonder if he is even faintly aware of the behind-the-scenes negotiation that played out in his world championship.

Given the publicity surrounding Olympic athletes testing positive for performance-enhancing drugs and the bidding history by those who hoped to be selected as the Olympic host city, I run a risk of straining the reader's incredulity by citing the fundamental principles that govern the noble idea of Olympic spirit. But most of the Olympians strive to abide by the ideals of the Olympic movement. Also the U.S. wrestlers take pride in the fact that no American wrestler has ever tested positive for a performance-enhancing drug at any Pan American, World, or Olympic games.

My next claim may draw even more suspicion, but I hope no guffaws. My concerns about a moral cavity at the core of Wall Street were mistaken. The media's depiction of shady dealings and insider trading did not hold true. Salomon's training class made it clear that there were distinct rules of engagement and protocol—with no lack of moral clarity. "When you don't know the answer, don't bluff it, just say you don't know but that you will learn the answer, and then find out." This was Salomon's creed. Withholding information was tantamount to lying. It was the responsibility of the sales-person to uphold the reputation of the firm and to deliver information.

The storied history of Wall Street established a tradition of open markets that most adhered to. While self-interest and profit motives drove trading, untrammeled greed was mostly absent. Adam Smith and our forefathers described greed as "the motor that powers capitalism." They understood—and the collapse of the Soviet Union validated—the pursuit of self-interest as a necessary ingredient in a successful democratic society. Yet they also understood that it was more complicated. Adam Smith's greed (or self-interest) requires boundaries—a set of rules or protocols to keep it from drifting into unscrupulousness.[1]

Although too often characterized by the public as greedy, most traders, even if gruff and foul-mouthed, did not fit the image of the scalawag, scrambling for the bounty. Normally, they were talented, decent, hardworking individuals dedicated to earning or advancing self-interest. They were skilled professionals who felt their work made the capital allocation process more efficient and who thrived on the energy, competitiveness, and discipline that was required to succeed on Wall Street. When trading desks wandered from this precept and got caught up in unexpected or perilous risk taking, it was the responsibility of management to rein in the practice. As revealed in the recent crisis, artfully demonstrated by Lehman, management missed the mark wretchedly.

What was most refreshing, when accurately measured, was the respect for performance. As in wrestling, when management did its job, you were measured by how well you competed, irrespective of your race, nationality, or religion. In consecutive seats you might find an Irish Catholic, Iranian Muslim, Indian Hindu, and Russian Jew, and no one gave it a moment of thought. If it were not for the suits and ties, you would think you were at a weigh-in for the World Wrestling Championship. The only thing that mattered was how well you did your job.

Because of my responsibilities as the Olympic freestyle manager, I entered Salomon's training late. Knowing I would miss the first section of the class, Leo Corbett, the man at Salomon responsible for overall recruiting and the training class, suggested I spend time reviewing the section I would miss. So between the Olympic trials and the start of our U.S. training camp I spent several days holed up in Salomon's media room reviewing the previous year's training-class videos. This also gave me the opportunity to move most of my personal belongings. I was fortunate enough to be assigned to one of Salomon's efficiency apartments in Battery Park while most of the training class stayed in an uptown hotel.

On the first morning I arose before dawn, as I suspect is customary for most trainees. By choice I walked from my apartment to Salomon's offices at One New York Plaza via Wall Street. The only time I had seen Wall Street was in a cab going to my final interviews; now I wanted to sense the energy from the ubiquitous rickety yellow cabs and the mass of people as they rushed from the subways to their offices. As I walked toward the center of the world's largest financial market, with the sun peeking thru the skyscrapers, I began to wonder why Salomon chose me. What set me apart from the thousands of other Ivy-League educated MBAs?

The competition had been fierce, at least that is what they told me, and I was not your typical Salomon trainee. I lacked a pedigree MBA and it was not my life's passion to be in the investment business. Though finance classes were more appealing to me than accounting, the first time I had given such a career any serious consideration was after one of many wrestling trips to the Soviet Union.

Each winter the U.S. sent a team to Tbilisi, the capital of the Republic of Georgia, for a tournament followed by three dual meets. In exchange, the USSR National Team traveled to the United States each spring for the World Cup and a series of three dual meets here. On several occasions in the Soviet Union there were hints of restrictions. One such incident that comes to mind occurred during my second trip as a competitor.

Most of our U.S. teams had at least one wrestler who was a member of Athletes in Action's (AIA) team. The AIA is a ministry of Campus Crusade for Christ. They utilize the platform of sport to extend Christ's message to the world. And what more fertile audience than an atheistic state whose propaganda discouraged any religious worship? More importantly, because the U.S. wrestlers were guests of the Soviet sports minister, the team was subjected to far less scrutiny than in the normally intrusive customs process. The AIA athletes knew this, of course, and used the opportunity to smuggle in a few cases of Bibles translated into Russian. On this particular trip John Peterson, an Olympic champion and AIA member, was part of our team at eighty-two kilograms while I was in the seventy-four-kilogram weight class.

Following a night in Moscow, the team flew to Tbilisi on Aeroflot. The next day, after our morning practice, we returned to our hotel. Shortly afterwards two KGB agents—a euphemism for thugs—grabbed my arms and guided me to a private room. The setting was surreal. Like a scene in a spy novel, the lights glared in my face as they began to interrogate me. Meanwhile, on the desk behind them was a small black-and-white TV showing *Midnight Cowboy* with Jon Voight and Dustin Hoffman, dubbed into Russian.

It might sound more captivating if I could say that the sweat poured down my forehead and my heart raced as my emotionless interrogators glared at me. But in reality it took all of my restraint not to laugh. As the agents questioned me regarding the dispensing of Bibles, I realized they had mistaken me for John Peterson. Irritated but not afraid, I did not try to reason with the interrogators. Instead, without divulging who may have passed out the Bibles, I told them, "Check my room. I assure you, you won't find any Bibles." As I suspected they might, they soon released me, warning, "You will remain under scrutiny." No kidding!

That they would risk the negative international press by detaining a member of a visiting sports team, was highly improbable. So, no one was allowed into my room for the remainder of my stay in the USSR. As if I would be naive enough to trade anything in my room. We were, of course, aware that our rooms were most likely bugged. When we arrived, the first item of business was to keep Big Brother busy. It was common practice to designate someone on the team to mention to his roommate that the radio, a lamp, or, if there were one, the TV was not working. Of course we would not report it to any of the hotel employees, including the security women parked at the elevator twenty-four/seven. If a repairman responded unannounced to fix the supposedly broken item, we knew our rooms were bugged. This game was something to amuse us over dinner.

This night at dinner the team had plenty of amusement. Our team leader, who had no prior experience traveling within the Soviet Union and was unaware that a few team members had smuggled in a few boxes of Bibles, was still in a state of shock. I think he may have feared the Russians would banish me to a Siberian prison camp on his watch. Of course, I could not let the opportunity pass. First thing at dinner that evening, in comments meant to be overheard by our team leader, I reminded John Peterson that he owed me since "one more cigarette burn and I was giving you up." At that moment, we all laughed, even the team leader.

Most similar anecdotes were amusing as well, but the next sequence of events was more real and seemed to menace, if not haunt me. On this particular trip, our first dual meet was scheduled in Makhachkala, the capital of the Republic of Dagestan, followed by a dual in Grozny, Chechnya, and finishing with a match in Yerevan, Armenia. Sagalov Abdulbekov, one of their national coaches and Olympic champion in Munich, was from Makhachkala, a dreary city on the Caspian Sea.

In Tbilisi, Abdulbekov invited our team leader, our referee, and me for dinner and drinks when we arrived in Makhachkala. I had come to know and like Abdulbekov from previous trips. Despite the degradation of living under an authoritarian regime he despised, Abdulbekov was surprisingly optimistic. Yet as one would expect, he was naturally cautious in establishing friendships. On the mat we expected nothing but the fiercest competition. Off the mat we shared a common respect and had become comfortable discussing even the sensitive issues between our countries. After all, we shared a common enemy, the authoritarian Soviet regime.

Criticisms of communism and its repressive elite were welcome, but on the other hand, slights toward their great country, which was not always Russian although it was in the Soviet Union, might elicit a visceral reaction. As Westerners our understanding of the peculiarities of Soviet cultural, economic, and ethnic dynamics was decidedly lacking. The competition among the Soviet republics at the Tbilisi tournament, though, gave us strong clues.

A particular fierceness revealed some of the disdain the Armenians harbored for the Azeri, but it appeared more like a rivalry than deep-seated hatred webbed in history. The thought of them laying siege to one another over ancient disputed territory following the collapse of communism was unimaginable. Only afterwards was it evident that being a member of the Soviet Union had done little to heal generations of hatred. Azerbaijan's close ties with Turkey, dating back to the Ottoman Empire, had withstood the test of time better than had the USSR's.

Fear of reprisal restricted most of the Soviet athletes and coaches from vocalizing their thoughts, but the wrestlers from the Caucasus region, where individualism was noticeable, seemed particularly resentful of the USSR and its attendant forces of repression. That may be a bit of a generalization, but from my vantage point it is fairly accurate. And it was always amusing to capitalize on this defining trait. Aside from the influx of Western wrestlers for the annual Tbilisi tournament, most of Soviet athletes had little contact with the West.

As the free-world competitors descended upon Tbilisi, the few days leading to the tournament transformed the practice facility into an ancient marketplace. There were no Ottoman lamps lining the passageway or distant chants calling the faithful to prayer at the Blue Mosque, but the aura of Istanbul's Grand Bazaar was everywhere. The Georgian wrestlers were eager to test their skills as merchants. Jeans, or "Levees," as they would say were the preferred item—a sort of a status symbol. Nothing seemed to say that you had "made it" more than wearing a pair of Levis while chewing gum.

Recognizing a Georgian from a Russian was almost as easy as distinguishing a Swede from a Spaniard. So when one approached with the look of an Oriental rug salesman in a Turkish bazaar, I customarily would greet them, "Rusky change Levis."

As I expected, his response was, "No Rusky, Georgian member of the Soviet Union."

Continuing my game, I would respond, "Same thing."

"No... Same t'ing, no same t'ing,", he would vehemently retort.

"Okay"—and we would commence bartering until we agreed upon a price we both knew at the outset we would reach. Nonetheless, the ritual was always entertaining.

Early on the day after the tournament we traveled from Tbilisi to Makhachkala. When we arrived, Abdulbekov was obviously annoyed and indicated that he had not yet received permission from the authorities (what he referred to as "protocol") for us to dine with him. Without the authorities' permission, of course, our plans would have to be canceled. Eventually we received the okay.

The dining experience was full of surprises. As custom calls for in the region, Abdulbekov started by pouring a hefty glass of vodka and offered a toast. As we raised our glasses, he fittingly said, "Protocall, protocall, sons of beeches." We all laughed and toasted to the perils of living under the capricious thumb of communism.

The first course was the finest Beluga caviar from the nearby Caspian Sea. Following the caviar was a tabbouleh-like salad and the main course was lamb kebob with a unique tangy sauce. Yet I could not ignore the fact that as we dined like aristocrats, the restaurant was as deserted as the ruddy cobblestone streets outside. As interesting as I found the evening, as a young man inculcated in American values, the restrictions on the people's freedom troubled me.

A brief review of Russia's past reveals that its citizens never had the right to elect their own leaders. Perhaps over time in such circumstances one becomes desensitized? My sense was that most Russians had come to prefer order to freedom. Yet, for those like Abdulbekov, whose life's experiences and inquisitive nature influenced his thinking, life under communism appeared discouraging. His scorn toward the authorities and the attendant hypocrisy was clear.

As the dinner progressed, the waiter placed a bowl of apples on the table. Small and worm-filled, they appeared inedible by American standards— something you would find on a neglected tree in an abandoned orchard. My first thought was, "Who does he think will eat them?" Soon I would find out. Abdulbekov proceeded to carve the apple until a tiny portion of edible apple remained. "Please, my friend, no preservatives," he beamed as he placed the piece on the end of his knife and offered it to me. Then it occurred to me, Abdulbekov detected the shortcomings of a repressive regime but failed to recognize its cultural indoctrination.

The next day the bus ride between the Caspian seaport city of Makhachkala and the Caucus mountain town of Grozny, Chechnya, seemed particularly long and not because of the excess vodka I had drunk the night before. By now I understood well that communism did not work. The lack of opportunity and restrictions on both political and economic freedom stifled its countrymen. In the Soviet Union, unless you were an accomplished scientist, artist, or athlete, you were confined to a restricted everyday life. The hopelessness of living as a worker in a degenerate state where nepotism and bribes were prevalent was a depressing thought.

I had pondered the issue in several instances previously during my travels to the USSR, but somehow this time it was more real. Even those in the privileged aristocracy of sports had to wrestle (pun intended) with restrictions. I realized that being able to control one's destiny was a privilege. If I failed to take advantage of the opportunities offered as an American, shame on me. One may think that Wall Street must have seemed far away from a bus ride to Chechnya, but working in the meritocracy of Wall Street, the citadel of capitalism, suddenly became appealing.

These life experiences help explain why I wanted to work on Wall Street but not why Salomon chose me over the countless other applicants with superior academic credentials. Within a few weeks the reason began to emerge. During lunch in Salomon's cafeteria, John Russell, a fellow trainee and friend, asked why I had missed the first two weeks of the training program. I explained, "I'd been the United States national wrestling coach and was the manager of our Olympic freestyle wrestling team in Los Angeles."

"Were you a world champion?" he suddenly asked.

"Yes," I answered. "Why?"

"The first question in my last interview was 'We just offered a position to a world champion wrestler. What have you done?' They must have meant you," he said.

Not that there was any doubt but my route to Wall Street was uncommon. Besides, by then I had heard countless times, "It doesn't take a rocket scientist to do this job." And they were right. Also my unusual route to Wall Street served as great party conversation. As I would say, "I was Salomon's Eddie Murphy. Like Randolph and Mortimer Duke in *Trading Places*, John Gutfreund and John Meriwether had a wager on whether anybody, regardless of background, could, if given a chance, become a successful bond salesman."

Salomon Brothers understood more than any other Wall Street firm that it didn't take a rocket scientist for every seat in fixed-income markets. They concluded that an Ivy League pedigree often said a great deal about a person. Yet they also understood it might say more about college-level potential than about a person's will to succeed, problem-solving capabilities, or wisdom. For instance, Lew Ranieri, a college dropout, revolutionized the securitization of mortgages and was head of Salomon's fixed income department. Sufficient intelligence, combined with creative thinking and drive, was a valuable skill set and added needed diversity to any undertaking. Salomon's training class was replete with others of atypical backgrounds. One, whom I remember particularly well, perhaps because of my many trips to the USSR, was Yury Fridman.

Yury was a Jewish émigré from the Soviet Union who earned an MBA from UCLA—probably the only one without an undergraduate degree. While discussing his desire to enter UCLA's MBA program, an admissions officer of the business school discovered that Yury did not have an undergraduate degree. The officer quickly pointed out, "To enter the MBA program, an undergraduate degree is a prerequisite." Yury asked, "Why?" Without any good reason and perhaps as an easy way to dismiss Yury, the admission officer proposed a high bench mark. "Okay, take the GMAT and if you score above 700, call me." Yury scored 740 and soon after earned his MBA—without an undergraduate degree. He dispelled the image of the buffoonish vodka-drinking Russian. He was soft-spoken but confident, with a strong sense of character. Think Aleksandr Solzhenitsyn not Nikita Khrushchev!

Although I did not know it at the time, entering Salomon Brothers' training class in 1984 was opportune timing, especially if you ended up as a mortgage-bond salesman covering the savings and loan industry. Arguably more than any other firm on Wall Street, Salomon's training program taught us about the fixed-income market—except for junk bonds. At the time the initial public offering (IPO) and mergers and acquisitions (M&A) markets were more prestigious and profitable. Most of Wall Street was content with the Salomon renegades' dominant position in the fixed-income markets, though that would quickly change and the competition would stiffen.

For five months Salomon would parade a host of experts conveying arcane bond math and other related topics to educate Salomon's next generation. Trading desk managers, heads of departments, research specialists, corporate and investment bankers, and even Chairman John Gutfreund all spent time imparting information to us. Interest swap market valuation, collateralized mortgage obligation(CMO), cash flow analysis, negative convexity of mortgage securities, and the evolution of the mortgage pass-through programs at the Government National Mortgage Association (Ginnie Mae/ GNMA), the Federal Home Loan Mortgage Corporation (FHLMC), and the Federal National Mortgage Association (FNMA) were just a few of the many topics examined. Salomon's investment in our proficiency was extensive.

As a trainee, you quickly became aware that the mortgage department held particular sway within both the firm and the capital markets at large. The sheer size of the mortgage market, the backing of the government— explicitly in the case of Ginnie Mae and implicitly in the case of FNMA and FHLMC—and the contribution to Salomon's profits from the mortgage trading desk commanded your attention. The rumors of the numbers discussed in the training class were difficult for me or any trainee to imagine.

Yet with even a brief reflection, it was easy to calculate that the potential of the U.S. mortgage market was gigantic. Just a back-of-the-envelope estimate of the number of homes, the average cost and the loan-to-value (LTV) ratio* gives one an idea of the scope, even if just ten to twenty percent were securitized. The Salomon training manual estimated that in 1984 roughly $180 billion new one to four family household conventional loans would be originated—a huge number at the time.

If you were not smart enough to figure this out yourself, the 1984 Mortgage Securities Department's manual spelled it out:

> Historically we have been recognized for our innovation and performance under all market conditions. One market that vividly exemplifies these qualities is mortgage securities. The Mortgage Securities Department was created in 1978, and was the first department of its kind on Wall Street. From a modest beginning, this vertically integrated department grew to over 250 specialists and support personnel originating, trading and clearing over 25 different mortgage related products. Our total commitment to this area can best be defined by our trade volume. During 1983, the Mortgage Securities Department traded over $200 billion in mortgages and mortgage related securities, $2 billion of which were traded in only one day.

> Some of the accomplishments which support our leadership position are:

>> Investment banker for the FHLMC and largest distributor of their PC securities; Co-Managed their initial $1billion offering of their CMO [...][2];
>> Created the first single-family conventional pass-through, as well as first commercial mortgage pass-through;
>> Managed the first FNMA conventional mortgage-backed security offering and also largest distributor of their securities; structured their first zero coupon issue;
>> Created the concept of FHA-insured project pools [...] [2]

The list of firsts would go on for another page, but I think you get the message: Salomon prided itself on its mortgage securities department, and justifiably so.

Salomon's training class, in my imagination at least, seemed similar to pledging a fraternity. (Since athletic training occupied an inordinate amount of my time, I had never joined a fraternity.) Most of us trainees would mingle in off-hours around various desks in an attempt to ascertain where the best fit was or maybe even catch the attention of the head trader. What captured your imagination: trading or selling bonds? The hiring process had already distinguished banking as separate from selling and trading.

Those aspiring to trading flocked each evening to the trading desks to recap the day's adventures. They quickly learned the vernacular and incorporated it into their daily routine; everything was making markets. Like Little Leaguers chewing a wad of bubble gum to imitate a professional pitcher grinding a plug of tobacco, they made markets in anything quantifiable.

The women quickly understood that a path to trading was unusual. Not that is was a prohibition or a burqa-style occupational restriction. In fact, there was a conscious effort to increase the number of female traders ("chicks with dicks" as they called themselves). Few female trainees, however, found the thought of gaining twenty pounds while sitting on a trading desk appealing. The tales of intrigue and riches depicted in the press seemed embellished. Unless, of course, one were Peiti Tung!

Just as Helen Thomas, the Voice of America, was to the press corps, Peiti Tung was to trading: a groundbreaker, a pioneer. Small in stature but with looming intelligence, discipline, and focus, she did not attempt to win any popularity contests nor did she partake in the daily shenanigans—a refreshing departure from many of the traders who took themselves too seriously. Eventually Tung would rise to the position of chief operating officer of Greenwich Capital.

Early each morning Tung arrived wearing her white ankle socks and sneakers. Quickly she switched to her patent-leather shoes, looking more like a freshman ready for the first day at the prestigious First Girls' High School in Taiwan (from which she had graduated) than Wonder Woman. Just a short conversation, which was all one would ever have with Tung, dispelled any misperception one might have regarding her stature or appearance. Though somewhat distant, she was the consummate professional. Tung depended on her superior understanding of the collateralized mortgage obligation (CMO) market in her unbridled pursuit of profits. She had no tolerance for traders who attempted to pick-off less informed customers.

As we approached the end of our training, other issues became important. Despite any allure trading or selling in New York may have had, my choices were narrow. With four children, the cost of adequate housing, and the burden of the long commute, positions in New York, San Francisco, or London were more than I could imagine my family enduring. Salomon office managers in Boston and Chicago had hired more trainees than positions available in their respective branches. Many of these trainees also had equally pressing reasons to return to either the Boston or Chicago offices. If at all possible, Salomon's management intended to fill those positions with a trainee hired out of that office. For me, therefore, Atlanta and Dallas were the most viable and practical options.

At least in the financial sector, the Atlanta office was growing; another advantage was that it was run by Bruce Koepfgen, a highly regarded and progressive manager. Besides, the sole position dreaded among the trainees was selling equities in Dallas. Not to insinuate that the equity department was inept, but within Salomon, equities generally were less profitable. Mortgages, on the other hand, were the most profitable and favored the mathematically inclined.

The cozy world of memorizing corporate bond history and relative credit spreads seemed less interesting to me than dissecting the complex aspects of securitization and the attendant effect on value. The mortgage market was on the frontier of a sweeping transformation of the global financial landscape. Salomon's leadership in innovative financial structures and enterprising moves in underwriting these securities set it apart from its rivals and positioned it to take advantage of this transformation. No other market seemed to personify Salomon as distinctly as mortgages. My mission was to secure a seat in the Atlanta office selling mortgages.

As the training class approached its conclusion, there was a heightened sense of anxiety. On everyone's mind, of course, was who would be the unlucky soul sent to Dallas to sell equities. Most had a firm sense of where they would be going but less certainty about exactly what they would be doing. As expected, the night before we were to learn our destiny was a sleepless one. Years of education, months of interviewing, and nearly five months of training and preparation were coming to a close.

In short order, the vital beginning of our professional lives would be decided, a decision which would affect each trainee's career. We were scheduled to receive the news on or around Thursday, December 20. Because of my background, perhaps I was somewhat more apprehensive than most;

I was more accustomed to the decisive world of wrestling with its one clear objective. Two wrestlers go on the mat, armed only with their will to win, and the one who scores the most points wins. Easy enough!

For most of the single trainees and those returning to their home area, when they got the news did not matter. On the other hand, time was critical for me because I had a tight schedule. I had to return to Lincoln, Nebraska, that afternoon and tell the moving company where to deliver and temporarily store our furniture. The following day my wife and our two youngest children would board a flight to the in-laws in Pittsburgh while I drove the distance with our two oldest children.

On Wednesday, December 26, my wife and I would have to fly, we hoped to Atlanta, to locate housing. Since trainees were scheduled to report to their respective offices on January 2, we did not have much time to make decisions. Knowing my circumstances, management mercifully put me at the top of the list to tell me we were moving to Atlanta. As I embarked on a more than twenty-year career on Wall Street, I never imagined the future would be entwined with so many crises. Little did I know what was in store?

* LTV ratio: a mortgage loan as a percentage of the home's value.

2

SALOMON BROTHERS' EARLY ROLE IN THE MORTGAGE-BACKED SECURITIES MARKET AND EVOLUTION OF SECURITIZATION

"Innovation—the heart of a knowledge economy—is fundamentally social." Malcolm Gladwell

Salomon Brothers was not the originator of securitization. Nevertheless, it played a vital role in its expansion. Securitization is a process that pools non-marketable debt assets and packages them into exchangeable securities, thereby transforming the fundamental characteristic of debt. Loans once stuck on banks' balance sheets are now in marketable form.

One of its earliest forms, the securitization of commercial paper, dates back to the 1950s. Yet not until the late 1970s, when residential mortgages were secured into a pass-through*, did securitization gain enough traction to entice Wall Street to support its growth. Salomon Brothers was at the forefront of this evolution.[1]

In the early development of mortgage securitization, government sponsorship was explicit or implicit for most of the mortgage market; therefore credit was not an issue. However, the right of homeowners to prepay the mortgage at their discretion, either by selling their home or refinancing, was an issue. In addition, borrowers could partially prepay their loan for any reason, by paying more than the required monthly mortgage payment—curtailment, in mortgage parlance.

Though some corporate and municipal bonds also have call provisions**, exercising of these options is efficient and measurable. For residential mortgages, however, prepayments or curtailments are neither precise nor predictable. It is impossible to know for certain the average life or the cash flows of a mortgage-backed security. No one can predict with any comfort when prepayments will occur. Most likely, when it is beneficial to the investor for the average life of the mortgage to shorten, it will lengthen, and when the lender benefits from a prepayment, it will most likely not occur. If mortgage securitization were to become viable, the unpredictability and uncertainty was a risk the market had to accept.

Though Robert Dall established Salomon's mortgage securities department in 1978, Lewis S. "Lewie" Ranieri is generally accepted as the father or "godfather," as Salomon employees would say, of the mortgage market. Ranieri originally thought the easiest solution was for lenders to originate mortgages with prepayment penalties attached. Of course, a mortgage with a prepayment penalty would have a lower interest rate. The borrower would not be precluded from paying off his loan at the closing of a sale but in the event of refinancing, he would incur a penalty. Despite Lewie's tenacious efforts, Congress was not willing to allow the homeowner to forego the right to refinance.[2]

Thus, homeowners maintained their rights to either partially or fully prepay the mortgage, and Ranieri was left to find another solution. Salomon would amass the brightest research department on Wall Street to educate investors and identify value in the mortgage market and, of course, a trained sales force to disseminate the information and create trading flows for its trading desk to expand the market. Salomon was confident that mortgage-backed securities had value and placed a great deal of capital at risk to prove it. As Ranieri preached, "The challenge is to now convince the world that as investors they are being generously compensated for assuming prepayment risk."

Salomon's Bond Market Research Department, under the auspices of Henry Kaufman, was best positioned to undertake such a challenge. It had a developed a research division called Bond Portfolio Analysis, led by Martin Leibowitz, PhD-a mathematician turned Wall Street wizard, whose quantitative methodology of analyzing fixed-income markets seemed uniquely suited to tackle the complex valuation problems facing the mortgage markets. Kaufman and Leibowitz realized that research must fulfill its duty to uncover and reveal the intricate nature and obscure risks that accompany these securities.

As a pattern, when Salomon expanded into new markets, research grew to support the effort. The expansion into the mortgage market was no exception. Salomon's management wisely realized the vital role research would play in the development of the mortgage market. Soon cadres of "quants," as we called them—many with PhDs—were assigned solely to research the mortgage market.[3]

The pooling of residential mortgages was not a totally new concept. In 1938 Congress authorized the establishment of the Federal National Mortgage Association (Fannie Mae/FNMA). It was originally formed to lay the foundation for a secondary market for Federal Housing Administration (FHA) insured mortgages. In the late 1960s, Congress then divided the original Fannie Mae into Ginnie Mae and the current Fannie Mae.

In the early 1970s, the Government National Mortgage Association (Ginnie Mae/GNMA) guaranteed the first mortgage pass-through. Around the same time, the Emergency Home Finance Act of 1970 authorized the formation of the Federal Home Loan Mortgage Corporation (Freddie Mac/FHLMC) in order to create a more competitive marketplace. That year, Freddie Mac issued its first participation certificate (PC). Technically speaking, PCs were undivided interests in pools of Federal Housing Authority/Veteran's Administration (FHA/VA) conventional mortgages. Collectively, the three agencies were designed to be the cornerstones to build a secondary market for residential mortgages and facilitate the availability of funding for residential housing.

In order to slash mounting debt obligations when confronted with the rising costs of the Vietnam War, President Lyndon B. Johnson decided to privatize FNMA—a sort of camouflage to understate the government's involvement as well as its cost in the U.S. housing market. In 1968, FNMA became a shareholder-owned company. It could now buy any residential mortgage and was no longer limited to only those insured by a government agency.

In late 1981, FNMA initiated its Mortgage-Backed Security (MBS) and FHLMC started its Guarantor Program. The purposes of the programs were to improve the marketability and liquidity of mortgage loans and aid in the restructuring of savings and loan companies (S&Ls). Following the introduction of these programs, initially S&Ls and mutual savings banks (to a lesser extent) delivered lower coupon, seasoned—as opposed to newly originated—mortgage loans for FHLMC and FNMA guaranteed mortgage pass-through. This gave the S&Ls a more fungible or exchangeable asset, in layman's terms.

As the agencies competed for business, both expanded their programs to include newly originated loans, commercial and multifamily mortgages, and overseas markets.[4] In 1985, FHLMC added a global entree to the menu by issuing the first foreign-targeted mortgage pass-through. It was at least partially prompted by the long-awaited withdrawing of a 30 percent withholding tax on foreign investors. In the same year, Standard & Poor's (S&P) for the first time rated a nonrecourse security backed entirely by commercial real estate. A nonrecourse security is one based on an agreement in which the lender has no right of recourse to the borrower's assets beyond stated limits.

Then, in short order FHLMC came to the market with the first two publicly offered pass-throughs ever backed by multifamily loans; one for the U.S. markets, the other designed for the Euromarkets. The only hurdles remaining to global acceptance were the lack of understanding and trepidation of foreign investors. And no one was better equipped to handle the task of educating these nascent investors than Salomon.

Salomon Brothers' investments in the mortgage market proved to be prescient ones. With the assistance of the three established government-sponsored entities (GSEs), the investor base for mortgage securities expanded exponentially. The market's acceptance of mortgage-backed bonds unleashed Wall Street's creativity and a wave of new structures. Adjustable rate mortgages (ARMS), graduated-payment mortgages (GPMs), collateralized mortgage obligations (CMOs), real estate mortgage investment conduits (REMICs), and interest only and principal only (IO/PO) strips were but a few of the early innovations. This "alchemy," as Ranieri sometimes referred to it, removed financial barriers from the American dream of home ownership and created a model for allocating funds globally.[5]

Wall Street's innovative designs repackaged mortgage cash flows for the entire spectrum of investors. The innovations also expanded borrowers' options, in both the type of loans, and the financial institutions that offered financing. The assets that at one time remained primarily on the books of the original lender were now securitized, sold into the capital markets, and widely traded. As Ranieri professed, "Funding for housing, which before was in large part a function of mortgage availability in the banking industry, now has access to broader credit markets. Homeowners in Omaha, Tulsa, or Spokane receive funding from London, Tokyo, or Hong Kong."

For the first time, broader capital market funding was available to residential and commercial mortgage borrowers. What's more, the ultimate result was a more efficient pricing of this inherent prepayment option. In the end, Ranieri was correct: the marketability of mortgages would increase, spreads would narrow, and the homeowner would reap some of the reward through lower mortgage rates. And of course Salomon extracted due return for the role it played in expanding market efficiency.

Unfortunately, the eventual consequence of this evolution was a combination of mortgage choices that even savvy borrowers found confusing. Combine increasingly greater numbers and types of financial entities offering mortgage loans with a complicated assortment of selections and one exposes the vulnerable to the unscrupulous. These complex loans helped mask the moral failures of lenders, borrowers, and underwriters. Financial innovation outpaced common sense!

The foibles and, in some cases, fraudulent deception by many loan originators and appraisers have been widely documented. The misdeeds of borrowers and underwriters, however, have received less attention. But all perpetrators of financial misdeeds should be held accountable. A duped ex-trader argued that the predatory lenders who, without regard for the financial position of the borrower, pressed or deceived borrowers into loans they were ill-equipped to understand; the lax underwriters or trustees whose financial relationship with the lending institution made their role appear more like a joint venture than as an independent trustee; and the deceptive borrowers who inflated or falsified information on loan applications, were all complicit.[6]

Even for those who abide by the notion that average consumers fail to understand what is in their best interest, it is difficult to argue that the borrowers, with no or little down payment and no documentation (the applicant discloses a minimum of information and employment is not verified), misunderstood this concept. Any person borrowing money knows well that the predominant risk remains with the lender or, as the case may be, the eventual investor.

Borrowers with little or no down payment are not homeowners, but really only renters with an option to buy. As long as they make their timely monthly payments, they should retain their eventual right to buy and reap any upside in appreciation. Should they fail to meet their monthly payments on time, or the value of the property falls, they walk away with little consequence to themselves, and the lender is left holding the property. Low or zero down payment borrowers deserve the consumer protections afforded any renter, nothing more and nothing less.

Retroactively granting bankruptcy courts the prerogative to force a loan modification—a suggestion that fortunately seems to have failed to gather support—would most likely add more costs than benefits. Aside from the FHA or other government sponsored lenders, few if any private lenders would be willing to risk capital without an assurance that lending agreements would not be altered at the discretion of the courts. Also, if or when market participants offer funding, a risk premium would be required as compensation for this risk. The greatest cost would be borne by the largest percentage of the U.S. housing market: the responsible homeowners who make timely mortgage payments.

Market participants remain leery. The difference between the sales of low or moderately priced homes compared to higher-priced homes makes this evident. As I write, only conforming loans ($417,000 or less in most areas but as high as $729,750 in a few select high priced places) packaged as FNMAs, FHLMCs or GNMAs have adequate sponsorship. A review of the mortgage related government-sponsored enterprises' (GSEs) records reveals that nearly 88 percent of all the mortgage-backed securities issued in 2009 were approved by a government sponsored agency. This in large part reflects newly instituted rescue plans sponsored by the government.

Offering first-time buyers a federal tax credit of up to $8,000, expanding the directive of the FHA, which guarantees loans with down payments as low as 3.5 percent, and purchasing FNMA and FHMLC securities in the open market has pushed mortgage interest for conforming loans to a near fifty-year low. The combination spurred the sales of low and moderately priced homes—government subsidized funding disguised as credit-enhanced lending.

Some of the more exaggerated slowdown in the sales of higher-end homes should be expected and be temporary, while others may be more secular in nature. The evaporation of wealth caused by a trade-off in the equity markets put a significant dent in the funds available for expensive homes. This may be temporary. As stock markets recover, more wealth will be available to build or buy higher-priced homes.

What may not return is America's perception of "how much house is enough." The idea that one can no longer count on home appreciation and the increased comfort from a larger cash cushion may discourage home buyers from buying the most expensive home they can afford. Most high-end home buyers, drawn to their communities for the lavish lifestyle and proximity to top schools, never contemplated a significant decline in home prices. For the first time since the Depression, downsizing in lieu of moving up is the theme. "How much do I need?" may be the new reality.[7]

The veracity of the underwriting by the rating agencies for nonconforming mortgages remains suspect. It is incumbent upon underwriters, issuers, and regulators to restore confidence in the underwriting process. The technology is available to help investors extract the requisite data on the underlying loans. Diligent investors will most likely demand all of the data in addition to more equity. Larger down payments or even a progressively higher percentage of the purchase price as the monthly payments grow relative to comparable rents or disposable income, may become the norm.

Disclosure guidelines to protect the consumer may be necessary but may also prove to be insufficient. Regulators' and rating agencies' ability to remain abreast of market innovations and offer adequate oversight is suspect. A higher standard of suitability requirements, similar to those required for certain investment products, may be necessary to produce adequate comfort for lenders. On the other hand, legislation that restricts the flexibility to offer exotic loans to suitable consumers would unduly penalize this market segment.[8]

The goal is to remake the regulatory landscape to protect less sophisticated consumers from exploitation without stifling innovation. Painting everyone with the same brush may be a mistake, and will not restore confidence in the process. Qualified borrowers' access to complicated financial instruments that better match their time horizons and risk profiles will expand the housing market, as it has done in the past.

Competitive capital markets, when translucent, generate sufficient profits to induce a steady flow of innovative financial instruments for those willing to risk capital. These innovations revolutionize the way credit is allocated and supply profits for the innovators. The speed at which financial instruments go from concept to market acceptance has accelerated, yet Wall Street continues to be handsomely rewarded for innovation. Despite a desire to covet "proprietary information," opacity restricts market efficiencies. Transparency is a prerequisite to properly functioning markets.

Today, market participants are global and, more importantly, mobile. Without confidence in the underwriting standards, investors will not return. Most likely many past market innovations will never again receive significant sponsorship in the capital markets. The structures that do find support should require issuers to provide detailed information regarding the composition of the securities, as well as ongoing performance evaluations, before investing in these types of securities again. And any market participants who fail to demand such transparency should be considered delinquent.[9]

An apt example of the effects that escalate when complicating and expanding the possibilities available through a security is a collateralized debt obligation (CDO)–the first in a sequence of increasingly more convoluted securities (followed by synthetic CDOs and CDOs-squared). CDOs are a type of structured security created by establishing a "special-purpose vehicle" to hold an interest in a grouped pool of assets. The assets packaged in CDOs vary and in many cases include riskier, lower-rated, thinly traded classes of other securities. Subprime mortgage classes were often the primary ingredient.

The magic was supposed to lie in prioritizing cash flows and redistributing the risk. A large batch of subprime mortgages often rated triple B or lower, for example, were packaged, carved into classes, and then sold to investors around the world. The senior class and first-in-line to receive the cash flows collected from these bonds was anointed a triple A rating, the highest credit rating. At the height of the delusion, triple A-rated classes of CDOs were judged so safe they traded at interest rates only slightly above the comparable maturity U.S. Treasury notes.[10]

The "alchemy" lay in the fact that the ratings for the package as a whole exceeded the sum of its individual parts. This mistake was rooted in the rating agencies' erroneous belief in the power of diversification. Wall Street convinced the rating agencies that the sum of a diversified pool was inherently less risky when bundled and sliced into pieces. Statistically this could be defended. However, had the rating agencies better understood the inner workings of Wall Street's models when reviewing the collateral, they would have recognized that diversification within a pool of similar assets fell short of its espoused potential.

Wall Street touted its superior ability to identify, package, and slice the pool in such a way as to create a perceived "added value." Like an expert vintner of their favorite French tipple, Wall Street pundits claimed a talent to identify choice Cabernet Sauvignon, Merlot, and Cabernet Franc grapes and blend them through fermentation to produce eloquent Bordeaux wine worthy of a premium price. Unfortunately, Wall Street was neither the expert winemaker it professed to be, nor was it capable of selecting superior grapes. As it turned out, diversification was not the alchemy once promised and the wine produced more closely resembled Trader Joe's "Two Buck Chuck" than first-growth Bordeaux.

The buyers of rarified, triple A-rated CDOs were often global investors such as Scandinavian school districts, international sports federations, Japanese pension funds, and other investors, required by their covenants to invest primarily in bonds worthy of only the highest rating by the rating agencies—the so-called safest bonds. It was this AAA rating that sold them on the illusion.[11]

Unfortunately, like a cult wine, the appetite for CDOs was greater than the supply. So Wall Street, under the guise of expanding liquidity, created "synthetic" CDOs as regulators idly stood by. A synthetic CDO is a financial security whose value is derived from a defined pool of reference as opposed to owned securities. As one ex-money manager summed it up, "Synthetic CDOs are Wall Street quants' form of fantasy football and the AAA ratings were simply wishful thinking. I cannot think of a good reason to construct a synthetic CDO other than to mask, or at least to alter the perception of risk. If ever there were a device to exploit irrationality, it's the synthetic CDO."[12] Complexity camouflaged chicanery!

Eventually, the government blessed rating agencies recognized their mistake and began to adjust the criteria used in rating models. Yet curiously, these arbiters of risk did not immediately re-rate existing CDOs. In conversation, an observant senior Wall Street manager phrased it perfectly; "I'm amazed. Rating agencies live a charmed life. The press and SEC seem oblivious to the fact that they were at the core of the problem. How can rating agencies justify changing the models used to rate new deals, yet not re-rate past deals using the same models? I pity the investors who took the ratings at face value." [13] At a time when the expertise of rating agencies was needed most, they failed to deliver.

In a financial crisis commission's probe of the role the issuer-pays model played in the meltdown, several investors testified, oddly enough, that they did not want to pay—as if to insinuate they were not incurring the cost. If one follows the money, whether the payment is directed via the issuer or the investor, it is borne by the investor and ends up in the coffers of the rating agencies. The incentive of the rating agencies, however, is smartly different when buyers control the payment. Market participants should be demanding that rating agencies provide the transparency they need and want, not the rating they are forced to use.

Today's global financial markets are vastly different from those of the past. Up until the early to mid-1980s, banks were primarily structured to gather deposits and originate loans such as commercial mortgages, credit cards, and auto loans. Today the technology of pooling mortgage loans has been exported to other asset classes. Credit card receivables, home-equity loans, auto loans, aircraft leases, commercial mortgages, and even sovereign debt—all are repackaged to form securities. Such securitization inextricably links the world's capital markets. Financial assets previously confined to balance sheets of banks are now packaged into marketable—and let me emphasize, exchangeable, not necessarily, liquid—securities.

Although the securitization process was maligned, those who call for restrictions and burdensome regulations should be careful. Allowing underwriting, securitizing, and distributing duties to reside within one entity has increased the risk of manipulation and introduced some conflicts of interest. Yet the benefit of providing borrowers access to global funding that was previously unavailable still plays a vital role. Innovative structures have enabled those who need funding to match the investment preferences of global capital market investors. As a result, the amount of global money available to fund viable projects is greater, and the cost is lower than it would be otherwise.

Consumer choice, innovation, and honest competition are the cornerstones of a successful global financial system. Stymieing the securitization process with stiff regulations will make our financial system less efficient and reduce the choices available to consumers. When the music is lousy you do not smash the instruments; you find better composers and musicians. Remember Shanen's adage: "It's a poor craftsman who blames his tools."

Now the challenge is to harness the potential of securitization without stifling innovation. The quest should be to devise alternative structures within the banking system that assure transparency and segregate functions rather than introduce regulations that fail to govern as intended. Market participants must demand the detailed loan data that underlies each security. The primary purpose of securitization is to provide a vehicle that allocates capital more efficiently, not to supply, cover, and mask the risk from market participants.

* A **pass-through** is the most common mortgage-backed security. As the name suggests, the servicer collects the mortgage payments from the borrowers and passes them to the certificate holders.

** A **call** permits the issuer to retire the bond, typically within a specific time window and at a stated price.

3

DERIVATIVES MARKET

"Beware of Greeks bearing gifts" Virgil, The Aeneid

P erhaps it is better said: Beware of finance geeks bearing gifts. Salomon Brothers' growth continued through the 1980s and into the early 1990s. Its leading role in trading as well as its research machinery were easily exported into the derivatives* market. Salomon's mature research department and early experience in the development of the mortgage market positioned it well. It did not take long for Salomon to establish itself among the innovators in the derivative market evolution.

During Salomon's training class, the derivative department was as proud as the mortgage unit of its accomplishments. Repeatedly, Salomon's derivative specialists touted the 1981 Salomon-designed currency swap between IBM and the World Bank as the start of a new era in global financial derivatives. In painstaking detail, instructors described the creativity, negotiations, and subsequent efficiencies realized by both IBM and the World Bank. Salomon's claim to the trainees was that this innovative design was the model for the globalization of the financial service industry. Worldwide financial markets were suddenly evolving to keep pace with the globalization of the world's major economies.

The modern fixed-income derivative market evolved from the fixed-for-floating interest swap: an over-the-counter (OTC) agreement between two entities where each is responsible to make periodic payments to the other. Succinctly, the training manual described: "One side of the agreement

41

paid an agreed upon fixed coupon based upon a time horizon and notional amount. The other, for the identical time horizon and notional amount, agreed to pay a coupon based on a floating money market index, usually the London interbank offered rate (LIBOR)."

To dumb it down for the sales force, the derivative geeks described an interest swap as follows:

The easiest way to look at a generic or "plain vanilla" (as it is known on Wall Street) swap is to view it as a simultaneous exchange of two hypothetical bonds with identical maturities and equal par amounts. For example, let's say the fixed-rate payer issues a fixed-rate bond to the floating-rate payer maturing 3/1/2020 with a 3.80% coupon and $100 million par amount. At the same time the floating-rate payer issues a $100 million floating-rate note with the same 3/1/2020 maturity and a six month LIBOR floating-rate coupon, currently .40%. Both the bond and the note have the same maturities and notional amounts so no cash exchanges hands at either origination or at maturity. The only cash flows result from the differences every six months of the respective interest payments. Either viewing it as an agreement to periodically exchange interest payments or a swap of securities, the net cash flows are identical.[1]

The OTC interest swap was one of Wall Street's earliest innovations to bring global markets together in order to close their inherent funding gaps. The swift growth of the global OTC swap market mainly resulted from its ability to address funding and currency mismatches on the balance sheets of the worldwide financial community. At inception, interest rate swaps were used primarily by international banks and savings and loans. For instance, the S&L's deposits were generally short term while their assets were mostly thirty-year mortgages, exposing them (and by the nature of deposit insurance, the FSLIC/taxpayer) to any increase in short-term interest rates, especially in a flattening yield curve. In contrast, the European banks' deposits were longer and their housing loans floated periodically off of LIBOR, putting them at risk to falling short-term rate.

An essential contributor to the growth of the OTC swap market was the readiness and flexibility of market makers to structure swaps to satisfy specific individual requirements. An example often used by Salomon's Bond Portfolio Analysis Group:

Let's say a national airline finances its aircraft with a twenty-year fixed-rate bond. There was a well established market for twenty-year fixed-rate bonds backed by aircraft called Equipment Trust Certificates (ETCs) but little or no market for floating rate ETCs. The airline, however, might have preferred floating rate debt so that in a weak economy, when its revenues fell, its interest rate costs would also likely go down. Likewise in a strong economy when revenues were increasing, rates would likely go up. The airline's management may not have had a view on interest rates but simply wanted its interest cost to mirror what it views as its ability to generate revenues. The interest rate swap accomplishes the change and turns the fixed-rate payment into a floating rate payment.

The early evolution of the OTC derivative market typically involved variations using the "plain vanilla" swap as the base. Adding option features to interest rate swaps, two avant-garde sectors of financial innovation in the late 1980s, broadened the scope of swap applications.[2]

One such innovative structure, devised by Eric Rosenfeld, later of Long Term Capital notoriety, combined a generic swap with options attached to the floating-rate payment side of the agreement. The term sheet described it as follows: In contrast to a plain vanilla swap, the fixed-rate payer (Salomon's desk) has the option—the right but not obligation—to choose the three-month LIBOR rate on either the first or last day of the quarter. For that right, Salomon's derivative desk agrees to pay a higher fixed-rate coupon. The amount higher is a function of volatility in the LIBOR market—generally, the greater the volatility and the longer the time horizon, the more valuable the option.

Rosenfeld and I were in the same Salomon training class. He was a scholarly, mild-mannered, wire-rimmed former Harvard professor with a PhD from MIT—not your typical tightly wound Wall Street trader. Needless to say, Rosenfeld spent most of his time devising quantitative computer programs for the derivatives desk and little time in the training class, except for Friday's football pool. Physically he was diminutive, but intellectually he was commanding. His appearance of a meek Ivy League professor overshadowed his perpetual drive to craft the next tool to bounce on market inefficiencies. Rosenfeld had a unique talent that allowed him to break the most complex financial concepts into easily understandable components. This attribute made him perfectly suited for the nascent derivatives trading desk.

Most of the thrift industry's management at the time was ill-prepared to grasp option pricing theory. Option pricing as a function of volatility was not in the realm of the everyday thrift business. Most of the thrift industry's managers had not yet recognized that the banking business was entering a global era. For expedience, the best strategy was to start with the most sophisticated thrift account and work backwards from there.

At the time, a Florida savings bank called American Pioneer was the perfect place to start. It was managed by a pair of PhDs who fully understood that deposits were far less volatile than LIBOR, as well as the role volatility played in the pricing of options. Volatility was particularly high; hence, over the life of the swap it was probable that the floating rate payer would capture the current inefficiency and realize much of the additional coupon offered by the fixed-rate payer. The strategy to work backwards from the most sophisticated was successful and before long Salomon had negotiated its first interest-rate swap with an option attached.

Following the transaction, Rosenfeld called to congratulate me. Since I beat everyone else to the punch, he said that "naming the structure" was up to me. But, before I had time to contemplate a name, he offered a suggestion. "Because the floating rate payment has an option at reset, how about optional reset swaps?" "Sounds great," I agreed.

On Monday's intra-firm call, Rosenfeld announced: "The first ever interest swap with a floating rate reset option attached was transacted in Atlanta last week." He went on to suggest that I had chosen to call the structure "optional reset swaps" and that it would trade under the acronym ORS.

Following the call, I received a call from an associate in Salomon's New York office. "How did you come up with ORS?" he asked.

I replied, "I didn't—Eric did."

"That makes more sense, I didn't think you were that creative," he said, and hung up.

As everyone on Wall Street knew, windows of opportunity closed quickly and there was little time to waste. Among the Salomon sales force there was sense of urgency to canvass the accounts and capture the attendant value. In short order, competitors would re-engineer the investment characteristics and mimic the transaction. This, of course, would increase demand. Markets soon would force prices into equilibrium and the early users would extract the lion's share of the benefit from the inefficiency.

No matter how novel or useful the innovation, there was little inclination to pursue financial patents. The cost, time, and potential reward of enforcing any infringements were of dubious value. It was far more valuable for the desks to keep competitors in the dark for as long as possible, allowing the firm and its customers to reap the rewards.

So far so good: these innovative advancements enabled asset managers to tailor the performance of their portfolios and created an active market to transfer risk among worldwide market participants. Derivatives have been invaluable instruments used by countless Main Street firms to manage the risk associated with their day-to-day business.

Now the bad news: the proliferation of complicated and increasingly sophisticated derivatives eclipsed the capacity of the supervisors, market participants, and risk managers to adequately monitor the leverage and allowed risk to accumulate. This aggressive posture is partially to blame for the severity of the current crisis.

The initial goal of devising innovative structures to encourage the broader use of this valuable asset-liability management tool to reduce risk would eventually give way to a perplexing assortment of structures in which more value was crafted than created. The variations became increasingly more complex, mechanically as well as conceptually. Virtually any asset characteristics could be replicated using derivatives, which mutated into a deceptive array of exotic instruments. The seamy side of derivatives reared its ugly head. In many cases, convoluted structures provided no meaningful purpose other than to obfuscate the true intention or time-horizon. An ex-derivative trader suggested that in many cases, it was just trying to make a silk purse out of a sow's ear.

The efforts of Wall Street's finest to disclose risk eventually became less fervent than their zeal to promote the benefits. There was less of a search for market inefficiencies and more time crafting persuasive sales pitches. When quizzed as to the consequences of failure, the standard reply was, "If that happens, we have much bigger problems to worry about." Oops! Eventually even senior management, especially those unschooled in the derivative market, did not understand the convoluted structures. Puffery trumped substance!

Wall Street's risk managers have long realized OTC contracts were never foolproof and posed a potential disaster. They knew no one was prescient enough to anticipate every contingency. And when the unexpected arose, the counterparties would act to their benefit within the gray areas of the contract. Derivative contracts were no exception. The uncertainty of market pricing and early termination disputes are inherently destabilizing.

To many in the business, it was becoming apparent that as long as the derivative market proceeded as an OTC-negotiated market, structures would be as varied as the individual assets. There were early calls for creating a central clearinghouse** to standardize structures, guarantee trades, improve liquidity, and lessen the risk of default. Underwriting counterparties' risk, calculating daily marks, and managing margin accounts are cumbersome and more efficiently administered by a clearinghouse.

Clearinghouses ensure payment and ease the execution of transacting business. As opposed to bilateral trading, a clearinghouse acts as counterparty to all market participants. A central clearing body for standardized derivatives that lessens counterparty risk and prevents markets from seizing up as they did when Lehman collapsed would have been welcomed. Like a bookie, it stands in the middle and manages the bets.[3]

The issue as to which firms would have a stake in the ownership of the clearinghouse and a quest for outsized profits from an institutional knowledge gap, however, impeded the concept from gaining sufficient sponsorship and becoming a reality. Innovation was rampant and the bid–ask spread accompanying new innovations made short-term profits trump the desire to create a framework for orderly markets. After all, when opacity is the norm, profits abound. The common sentiment was that traders were diligent enough to manage counterparty risk and prescient enough to head for the exit before everyone else.

Today, market participants continue to complain about the dominant role a few major banks play as owners in the credit-default swap pricing service, such as Markit Group Holdings Ltd., an entity founded to collect and collate daily pricing information on credit derivatives. Though theoretically created to provide price transparency and an infrastructure to reduce risk, some find it problematic and oligopolistic that the larger dealers who make markets also have ownership and provide the market pricing service with market valuations. The calls for trading derivatives on an exchange are becoming louder.[4]

The turmoil in the aftermath of Lehman's failure has focused attention on the risk of contagion and on just how much global finance has changed. The potential catastrophic consequence of a financial meltdown when counterparties of privately-traded derivative contracts go under and initiate a cascade of related failures was averted this time, but not without significant costs. Immediately after allowing Lehman to fail, the United States government had to decouple the viral web of OTC derivatives and bail out American International Group (AIG) to stave off a financial collapse.

The loudest cries come from non-financial companies not wanting to meet or readjust collateral requirements. Warren Buffett, who described derivatives as, "financial weapons of mass destruction," curiously contends that "our existing derivatives should be exempt from posting margins to cover potential losses." For Buffett, whose substantial cash on hand provides an adequate cushion against falling prices, this may be true. But most non-financial companies have not set aside sufficient cash or collateral to absorb the risk of potential collapse. Any substantial movement in derivative valuations puts the taxpayer at risk.

These market participants prefer, of course, for the tab to go on the taxpayer's MasterCard. They privately like the "too-important-or-interconnected-to-fail" policy. When the government rescued AIG, making derivative counterparties whole, they reaped the windfall of having the government as the counterparty in lieu of AIG. Acquiescing to the wishes of those willing to potentially disrupt the global financial system is irresponsible. Sufficient margins serve as the buffer against a chain of interconnected worldwide failures.[5]

Providing more information regarding trading exposures and requiring larger margins are improvements, but do not go far enough. In the long run, clearing the lion's share of derivatives through a clearinghouse is in the dealers', if not the trading desks', own best interest. Also trading them on an exchange serves a valuable function in a world of erupting volume. It increases the pre-trade transparency, which levels the playing field and improves price discovery. Both should be the rule, not the exception. Each exception to trading through a clearinghouse adds a potential taxpayer bailout when counterparties fail and it spreads like a virus throughout the economy. Greater variety of contracts traded on an exchange with its transparent pricing provides market participants with a larger number of inexpensive avenues to manage risk.

Trading derivatives on exchanges is not a new concept. It dates back centuries. The world's oldest continually operating exchange, the Chicago Board of Trade (CBOT) was established in 1848. It is now part of the Chicago Mercantile Exchange (CME). Primarily formed to address the concerns of the agricultural community, it was the first to list an exchange-traded futures contract. Options and futures exchanges have flourished as the primary trading, settlement, and clearing vehicle since I first started in 1984.[6]

Most would agree that derivatives have played a vital role in the efficient allocation of funding. Absent new derivative innovation, our financial system runs the risk of restricting access to capital in the global public markets. Yet it is naïve for Wall Street risk managers to think self-interest does not cross the line to unfettered greed. As a risk manager once told me, "innovators strive to limit price discovery and maintain a profit advantage for as long as possible. The challenge for us risk managers is to move customized contracts onto listed markets as quickly as possible."[7] The benefits of minimizing market dislocations in the wake of unforeseen crises simply outweigh any costs. OTC derivative contracts should be required to maintain onerous capital levels as a cushion in order to push as many onto an exchange as possible.

The essential reason for financial innovation remains: to find solutions for complex business problems and expose inefficiencies in the allocation of capital. There is no excuse for flouting the rules or concealing risk. Financial institutions that originate and customize derivative contracts may be wise to see the advantage and to institute a disclosure process to assure full transparency. Otherwise, regulators may introduce controls that stifle the ability to customize derivatives. Letting lawmakers take over the process risks introducing new legislation with a negative consequence of restricting innovation.

* As the name suggests, **derivatives** derive their value from the price movement of some other asset. It may be a currency such as the Euro, a commodity such as corn, or even a debt instrument such as a Lehman indenture.

** A **clearinghouse** serves as a middleman guaranteeing the obligations of the buyer and seller. It marks-to-market or values positions daily, then calls or requires counterparties to post collateral as needed to ensure sufficient cushion against default.

4

GAMING RISK-ADJUSTED CAPITAL

"Oh! What a tangled web we weave, when first we practice to deceive!" Sir Walter Scott

nother lesson that seems to have faded along with financial crises: Requiring big banks to hold larger risked-adjusted capital cushions at the holding-company level has not worked. Worldwide central bankers have duly noted that the financial industry is far too creative and imaginative in finding ways to mask leverage and thus risk. The evolution of increasingly complex securities, the structured investment vehicles (SIVs) off-balance sheet fiascos, and creative capital structures that disguise leverage, illustrate this concept quite well.[1]

Since the inception of the collateralized mortgage obligation (CMO) market in 1983, Wall Street has crafted countless structures. As the reader may recall, a CMO bundles a group of mortgage loans and issues a multiclass security in which cash flows are directed to individual classes of varying coupons and maturities. The servicer of a CMO collects the principal and interest payments (P&I) from the borrowers and then allocates the cash flows to create different classes of securities. By prioritizing the cash flows, a CMO creates a staggered series of short-, mid- and long-term classes, with various coupons and risk profiles. By carving up cash flows to match the investment characteristics preferred by global investors, innovative issuers have efficiently attracted funding. That is the good part.

Though the worthy goal may be to arbitrage mortgage cash flows against the risk premium, investors are willing to pay for cash flows that match their risk and duration preference; sometimes these innovations become vehicles with less noble purposes. One of these inventive structures is an inverse floater. The hidden leverage in the CMO inverse-floater market was not easily recognized at the outset. Sort of like a new designer steroid that is not yet detectable by current drug tests.

In its simplest form, an inverse-floater is created by dividing one of the fixed rate classes of a CMO into a capped floater and an inverse-floater. The floater is capped to ensure that in the event of large interest rate increases, the floating rate coupon does not exceed the coupon of the underlying fixed rate tranche. Yet the purpose is not to understand the details or nuances of the security; rather it is to illustrate the potential to mask leverage.

If you think about it, a distinct relationship emerges. This is the key point in understanding the concept:

Inverse-floater = Receiving the fixed rate coupon minus paying the capped floater[2]

One Salomon innovator explained to the sales force that owning an inverse-floater is equivalent to purchasing the underlying fixed rate tranche and funding the purchase with capped floating rate debt. The punch line: When a financial institution purchases a fixed-rate security, the balance sheet would fully reflect the asset and liability; while in the case of owning an inverse-floater—possibly with no principal—the asset is only a tiny fraction of the size, potentially concealing the true leverage.

At the time, Japanese banks were particularly fond of leverage and were active participants in the inverse-floater market. Each morning after reviewing the overnight changes in the trading desk's positions, I would commonly jest, "If LIBOR ever spikes upward, the Tokyo office may singlehandedly balance the U.S. trade deficit with Japan. We may even be able to buy back Pebble Beach and Rockefeller Center." Little did I know that Peter Uberoth and company would repurchase the Pebble Beach golf course from Isutani and that Mitsubishi would pass ownership of Rockefeller Center to the Real Estate Investment Trust (REIT) that held the mortgage. There may be something to the proverb, "Many a truth is said in jest."

History provides ample examples of expanded leverage attributable to creative masking and an influx of product innovation. But none furnishes a better case study than Japan's fondness for excessive leverage and its episode of massive deleveraging. Although Japan's meltdown had a relatively small impact outside of Japan, the lessons of masking excessive leverage and the cost of subsequent deleveraging are nonetheless instructive.

In 1988, the leading industrial nations, referred to as the International Monetary Fund's Group of 20, met in Basel, Switzerland. The group agreed to a set of rules for global bank regulators. The accord, called Basel I, set risk-based standards to instill confidence in the solidarity and soundness of the global financial system. The group devised complex formulas that assigned measures of risk for what it believed were the gamut of bank investments. In spite of the noble efforts of these international regulators, the accord did little to ensure prudent capital levels among global banks.[3]

Japan's tango with perpetual preferred securities may prove insightful as a creative disguise to camouflage the true amount of capital protecting the financial system. Japan's perpetual preferred stock was subordinated to debt but displayed characteristics of both debt and equity. Generally, it had no voting rights like debt. Yet the floating rate dividend reset quarterly at a spread to an index (LIBOR), giving it price performance similar to a debt instrument. The rating agencies saw it as equity because all interest obligations to debt holders had to be satisfied before preferred dividends could be paid. Likewise, for regulatory purposes, Japanese supervisors treated perpetual preferred stock as equity.

Japanese authorities restricted banks from owning each other's perpetual preferred stock (reciprocal ownership) but did curiously little to prohibit banks in general from owning perpetual preferred stocks. From the point of view of the isolated transaction, it looked as if capital was raised, but from the system's point of view, it was a mirage. In reality, insured deposits or other debt funding sources were being miscast as equity.

All you have to do is follow the money: Insured deposits from bank A fund the purchase of bank B's perpetual preferred stock; at the same time, bank B's insured deposits fund the perpetual preferred stock purchase of bank C; meanwhile bank C uses insured deposits to purchase bank X's perpetual preferred stock, and so on. There are no reciprocal ownerships, so the purchases qualify as capital. Yet, from the financial system's point of view, the net effect is simply to recast insured deposits as equity. What is more, the perpetual preferred stock dividends are tax-exempt to corporate investors, which include banks. Performance-enhanced capital!

At the time, several Japanese banks sought to enter the U.S. and U.K. markets. British and American regulators, concerned that the propitious supervisory provisions provided the Japanese with a competitive advantage, dragged their feet in approving banking licenses for Japanese banks. Soon the Japanese regulators began to recognize that their lenient definition of capital hindered their banks' ability to enter other markets, and tightened capital standards.[4]

Although Japanese banks continued to be allowed to own stocks, the regulators eventually cracked down on the perpetual preferred stock scheme. As the Japanese banks began to unload perpetual preferred stock portfolios, spreads widened significantly and perpetual stock prices tumbled precipitously. For the astute investor, this provided an investment opportunity. Realizing the Japanese banks would be compelled to buy back their perpetual preferred stock at a price much higher than the current crisis price rather than continue paying a premium preferred coupon, many shrewd investors gathered diversified portfolios of perpetual preferred stock. While clipping attractive coupons, these investors patiently waited for the Japanese to deleverage and repurchase their perpetual preferred stock. Much to its chagrin, the Japanese financial system mastered leverage.

I recall a visit to Salomon's Tokyo office in 1990, near the peak of Japan's stock and property bubble. The World Wrestling Championships were in Tokyo and my wife and I were on vacation watching the competition. While there, I thought it would be instructive to visit Salomon's office. At long last I would meet the salesmen that I occasionally joked might someday recapture our budget deficit by piling up inverse-floaters in Japanese banks' portfolios.

A brief conversation with one of Salomon's mortgage-backed traders confirmed my suspicions of Japan's grossly inflated property valuations. He described his weekend golf ritual: "I wake up before dawn, trudge my golf clubs onto a series of cramped trains, only to spend hours behind inexperienced golfers hacking around a confined course." But when he divulged the green fees, the inflated price the Japanese paid for Pebble Beach Golf Resort began to make more sense. As the Salomon trader complained, "The Japanese can hop on a flight to the west coast, stay at a luxury resort, play a few rounds of golf each day for a couple weeks on a course overlooking the Pacific Ocean and nearly fund the trip with what they save in green fees. Under those circumstances Pebble Beach Resort must have looked like a bargain."

At the time, Japanese banks consistently boasted about excess risk-based capital. Unfortunately, Japanese banks' extravagant leverage fueled easy credit and contributed to a significant overvaluation of stocks and real estate in Japan's market. Increasingly, the Japanese made riskier loans to speculative buyers and pushed prices to illogical levels that could only be justified by assuming indefinite growth rather than cash flow fundamentals. Sound familiar?

At the height of Japan's twin bubble, the Tokyo Stock Exchange was the world's largest and accounted for an astounding estimate of roughly 60 percent of the entire world's stock market capitalization. Records show that prime properties in Tokyo's Ginza district sold for astronomical prices, reportedly reaching as high as $1.5 million per square meter. But the music stopped when the Bank of Japan decided to rein in the leverage and pricked the twin bubbles.

First stocks faltered, then real estate, and finally a destructive mood of deflation settled into place. The overly leveraged banks, strapped with non-performing loans and steadily falling property values, lacked the capital to absorb the losses. A chronically flat yield curve compounded the problem by making it more difficult for banks to make money and rebuild their capital base. Nearly twenty years later, the Japanese continue to pay for the mistake. The Nikkei 225 index traded at close to 39,000 in December 1989. Today, the Nikkei 225 remains nearly 75 percent below its peak and some luxury vacation properties are worth only a fraction of what they sold for in 1990. The exorbitant prices the Japanese paid for trophy properties and excessively leveraged balance sheets of their financial entities are still etched in their memory.[5]

Japan's adventure shows that relying on risk-adjusted capital opens the system to potential gaming, especially during prosperous times. It would be unwise to ignore Japan's struggles. Remember, at quarter-end on August 31, 2008, Lehman reported nearly three times the required core capital and a Tier 1 capital ratio of 11 percent. Just two weeks before filing for bankruptcy, Lehman's capital still looked good.

Yet the gaming continues. The October 1, 2009 *Wall Street Journal* had an interesting and easy to understand illustration of capital gaming entitled, "Wall Street Wizardry Reworks Mortgage." The article is about a reintroduction of an older security called a re-remic, which stands for re-securitization of a real estate mortgage investment conduit (REMIC). REMICs were created as part of the Tax Reform Act of 1986 to assist the process of issuing collateralized mortgage obligations (CMOs).

A re-remic simply takes the process another step. Similar to a collateralized debt obligation (CDO), an issuer gathers several REMICs and reprioritizes the cash flows into a new security. A privileged class referred to as the senior class and first in-line receives these favored cash flows. The astonishing part is that the rating agencies anoint the senior class with a triple A rating. Prior to the re-securitization, the underlying remics may have been rated triple B.

The reader may ask, for what purpose? The first argument: Unleash securities that otherwise would have remained orphaned on banks' balance sheets by restructuring them to meet buyer's criteria—a triple A rating. The second or less noble reason: To game the system by carving securities in a way that ends up requiring less capital.

The *WSJ* explains it more precisely:
A hypothetical example cited in research by Barclays capital said that a $100 million asset that required $2 million in capital at a triple-A rating may require $35 million if downgraded to double-B-minus. At triple-C, the capital requirement might rise to 100%, or $100 million. In a re-remic, three-fourths of the same assets may regain a triple-A rating, requiring just $1.5 million in capital, Barclays said. The remaining one-quarter may require 100% capital, but the total capital requirement would fall to $26.5 million.[6]

More bluntly, I would say, the same securities repackaged now require less capital. A sleight of the hand—or should I say dubious structuring—and the taxpayers have less of a cushion. And let's not forget the fees. The *Wall Street Journal* reported, "The cost in fees to the rating agencies, investment bankers, and law firms at roughly .35%—money that should have been retained in capital."[7]

As one might imagine, the potential to miscast the investment characteristics and to shroud risk are magnified as securities become more complicated. One cannot expect even the most talented and diligent supervisor to remain abreast nor possess the capacity to dissect all of the innovations devised by Wall Street's rocket scientists. It requires supervisors to be more specialized and fully conversant with the latest financial instruments and to have the authority to impel trading desks to comply.

The training level and supervisory structure are not currently advanced to keep abreast of the evolving markets and complex financial instruments. Training capable supervisors raises a serious challenge, the antiquated infrastructure needs updating and the capital structure needs to be simplified. Unless regulators and Wall Street risk managers are sufficiently trained and equipped, no regulation, regardless of how wisely it is constructed, will prevent the next crisis from spilling over into the broader economy. The lesson is straightforward: It is far too easy for Wall Street to game the current risk-adjusted capital requirements.

5

THE THRIFT INDUSTRY'S REGULATORY DEBACLE

"In the land of the blind, the one-eyed man is king." Erasmus, 1510

U ntil the late 1970s, the U.S. housing market was something of a free-market anomaly. Supply, not demand, often influenced the amount of new residential housing construction; not the supply of land, developers, or physical material, but rather of mortgage capital. The main cause of the lack in funds was that the Federal Reserve's Regulation Q (Reg. Q) capped the interest rate that deposit-gathering institutions could pay. Whenever the prevailing level of rates exceeded the Reg. Q caps, depositors sought higher returns outside of the banking system. Disintermediation—the withdrawing of deposits within the system to invest elsewhere—was not the most significant part of the problem. It was new money, especially from large depositors, that proved to be most sensitive to the difference. When faced with the choice of lesser yield, these depositors opted out of the banking system. The result in many cases was insufficient funds to meet the demand for qualified housing loans.[1]

During the same period, S&Ls and savings banks were forced to respond to more intense competition from banking industry outsiders. Dramatic changes were taking place in both the demand and the method of delivering financial services. In reaction to both the problem and increased competition, policymakers introduced a series of deregulations freeing thrifts to compete. By the mid-1980s, virtually all interest rate ceilings on deposits were removed, usury rate laws were rescinded, and thrifts were granted more expansive lending and investment authority.

As a senior research managing director told Salomon's sales force; deregulation of deposit rate restrictions, removing usury ceilings, rapid development of derivative securities, and perhaps most importantly, the federalization of the mortgage market (FNMA and FHLMC) assured that capital supply constraints would no longer rule the demand for residential housing. Demand as a factor of residential construction was never absent, but in the 1980s it would become more critical. The thrift industry was now operating in a largely deregulated environment and exposed to a market cost of capital. As a result, the industry's ability to collect deposits was significantly enhanced but the basic structural problems remained, and in many cases worsened.[1]

Operating under the new deregulated conditions intensified the thrift industry's maturity gap, the difference in maturity between assets and liabilities. The new savings flows were predominantly short maturity deposits. The long-term structure of their assets and the contrasting short-term nature of the liabilities became particularly troublesome as interest rate volatility increased. These shorter liabilities were more sensitive to rate changes since they were reset more often. The prices of the longer-duration mortgages currently held by the thrift industry had greater price fluctuation than short-dated securities. Hence any increase in interest rates had the twin adverse effects of increasing the thrift's cost of funding and magnifying the loss of market value in their assets. Given the scant capital requirements, this asset/liability mismatch created substantial risk for the taxpayers via the government-administered deposit insurance fund (FSLIC).

At a Salomon-sponsored thrift conference a researcher observed, the unexpectedly high interest rates of the late seventies proved to the thrift industry that the tranquil days of stable interest rates and a positively sloped yield curve had passed. And with it, went retaining thirty-year fixed-rate mortgages in portfolio and funding them with short-term deposits as a sustainable business model.[2]

Thrifts began to recognize an urgent need to more closely balance the maturity of their assets structure with the maturity of their liability structure. Thrifts were pressured to either shorten their assets and/or to lengthen their liabilities. As a rule, most thirty-year fixed-rate mortgages were increasingly issued into a pass-through for sale directly into the market or mortgage-backed debt instruments. The same researcher emphasized that the pace of residential mortgage securitization accelerated to levels previously thought unsustainable. Except in a brief 'warehousing' period–the time from underwriting to delivery to the housing quasi-agencies—FNMA or FHLMC—there is little or no interest rate risk. The practice of originating loans for the relatively stable fee income and not as a portfolio investment set a new mortgage paradigm.[3]

Separately, market forces propelled Wall Street modelers to creatively slice mortgage cash flows to appeal to a broader swath of the capital markets. These new instruments bolstered both the demand and supply for mortgage loans. On the asset side of the balance sheet, several straightforward shorter maturity mortgages were designed and offered. Shorter-maturity mortgages such as fifteen-year and various graduated payment mortgages (gradual annual mortgage payment increases) were introduced. Also adjustable rate mortgages (ARMs) became increasingly more popular as an asset class among thrifts. Despite their long maturities, ARM's annual reset made them partially interest-rate sensitive within their periodic and lifetime caps.

In an attempt to better match their assets and liabilities, thrifts introduced several adjustable-rate mortgages tied to components of their funding. The most popular—devised by West Coast thrifts—was the cost-of-funds indexed (COFI) ARMS. COFI represented the weighted-average source of funds—savings, checking accounts, advances, and such, paid by thrifts. Though approved by thrift supervisors, borrowers quickly realized the index was less responsive and lagged behind the other indices, such as the London interbank offered rate (LIBOR) and one-year Treasury rate, in both upward and downward trending movements. It did not take long before borrowers only opted for COFI ARMS when rates were particularly low.

As competition for ARMs surged, thrifts began to offer attractive features to prospective adjustable rate borrowers. The most appealing of these features was the low initial interest rate, a "teaser rate" as it was called. In theory the initial "teaser rate" concession was to entice the homebuyer to assume some of the interest rate risk now being borne by the thrifts. Mortgage insurance companies, regulators, and FNMA/FHLMC fortunately recognized the potential hazard of "payment shock" at reset and required higher insurance fees as a sort of moral suasion.

In due time, thrifts realized the inherent quandary in the structure of ARMs. On the one hand, periodic and lifetime caps were necessary to mitigate the potential for payment shock to the borrower and the attendant high incidence of loan default this might cause. On the other hand, those same caps precluded ARMs from becoming truly interest-rate sensitive and hence less appropriate as a portfolio asset class. By the same token, the borrower now had more selections to optimize his mortgage cost against his expected time horizon. Rarely would there be a scenario where ARMs would match the performance of fixed-rate mortgages (FRMs).

Eventually the prudent thrifts concluded that originating ARMs as a portfolio investment was not the panacea it was once considered. Originally designed in response to investors' demands for shorter assets, the shorter maturity and adjustable rate mortgages became a more appealing alternative to borrowers than thrifts, especially in a steep upward-sloping interest rate curve.

During this time, Salomon Brothers offered a unique platform to support the thrift industry's transformation and the accelerated pace of mortgage innovation and securitization. Salomon was positioned well to capitalize on the institutionalization of residential lending and engineering of new financial instruments. Yet this was not just because Lew Ranieri was (as legend had it) held in esteem by many of the thrifts' CEOs. After all, Salomon had made an extensive research effort, abundant capital allocated to the mortgage trading desk and had both a thrift and derivative specialist group with a proprietary asset/liability model, and—lest we forget—a well-trained sales force. This is not to suggest that Lew Ranieri's reputation did not matter, but there were other important factors.

As Salomon trainees we heard incessantly the folk tales of Lew Ranieri's renowned influence over the thrift industry; but I was suspicious. His blue-collar demeanor and fashion selections supposedly made a certain statement: "I am not an Ivy League-educated schmuck; I am more like the typical thrift CEO." Perhaps because I did not have an Ivy League pedigree, I failed at first to grasp the difference. Also, the polyester suits were a bit of an embellishment. Disheveled yes, but at Ranieri's weight and shape, one could hardly help being unkempt.

Ranieri's appearance may have made the statement that he arose from the depths of the back office to lead the most advanced mortgage trading desk in the world; but that did not, in and of itself, align him with the thrifts. A better explanation was that Ranieri knew more about mortgages than anyone else. He knew when the premium for the inherent prepayment risk was misaligned. And he knew how the dispersion of coupons or average remaining loan balances within a pool of mortgages affected its performance. Lew Ranieri may have touted his blue-collar background to shape his persona for the benefit of the thrifts, but mortgages were his passion and at the time he knew more about them than anyone else.

Shortly after arriving in Atlanta I experienced firsthand an incident that may demonstrate Lew Ranieri's unique position and sway over some thrift CEOs. Sitting at my desk, I heard someone call over to the salesman at the desk across from me: "Herron, Lew Ranieri's office for you." Herron picked up the line and after a brief discussion began writing a sales ticket.

I asked, "What are you doing?"

"Lewie just sold a package of whole loans to David Paul," Herron replied.

David L. Paul was real estate developer turned CEO of the Cen Trust Savings Bank of Miami, and Lew Ranieri was rumored to be the godfather of Paul's son (which Herron cleverly avoided discussing). Well-known as the poster child for the S&L debacle, Cen Trust was the infamous Savings Bank that permitted Paul to spend lavishly on extravagant yachts, famous artwork, and gold-plated bathroom sinks. Paul would serve nearly a decade in prison for his role and Cen Trust would ultimately fail—but more so because of its ill-advised junk bond investments and extravagant spending than because of its mortgage loans.[4] From that time on, I could not help but pay more attention to how thrift CEOs dressed. I remember the first time a thrift executive arrived at a meeting wearing a polyester jacket, gold chain necklace, and diamond pinky ring—right out of a scene from *The Sopranos*.

More important than Ranieri's mystique, Salomon's research effort had strong and capable leadership in Henry Kaufman and Marty Liebowitz that safeguarded its objectivity, even if near-term profits were at risk. The research department's recommendations were widely distributed and were never compromised as to either content or allotment. Market participants and salesmen alike knew the head of research held one of the highest managerial positions within Salomon Brothers, and all trusted the veracity of its research.

Over time, Salomon's research effort gained worldwide recognition. While authorities relaxed restrictions on the investments thrifts could make, Salomon diversified its research effort. Market experts and recognized authorities from academia were recruited into every facet of real estate. These experts introduced quantitative methods that analyzed the complexities of mortgage prepayments, established value, and identified opportunities and risks within the mortgage market. Salomon's investment in research was never limited. Senior management recognized the vital role research plays in the dynamics of new market development. Moreover, Salomon knew that compromising research jeopardized its franchise and installed safeguards to avoid compromising the opinions of research or providing an overly optimistic report to take advantage of a trading position.

Research's compensation was dependent upon feedback from clients and sales, not trading—a vital point often lost today. Nevertheless, one area where Salomon was noticeably absent and failed to sponsor a research effort was in junk bonds. Henry Kaufman's resistance to the high-yield market was widely known within the firm. At the time, as Drexel Burnham Lambert's junk bond machinery was capturing increasingly more business, many (myself included) questioned the logic of the decision. In retrospect, at least for deposit-insured institutions, Kaufman's wariness was most perceptive.

The timely and accurate dissemination of information produced by research rested in large part on the shoulders of the sales-force. Early each morning sales, research, and trading would huddle to discuss opportunities and their potential risks. The process was simple: the more cogent the argument or compelling the reasoning, the greater focus from the sales force. More often than not, traders discussed ephemeral issues that affected only the near-term pricing of their positions. Researchers generally were more interested in long-term forecasts and fundamentals. They were more concerned about asset allocation and broad market strategies than daily trading anomalies.

Naturally, research and trading often disagreed. Traders' short-term tactical views often differed from researchers' longer-term strategic perspectives. Nonetheless, interaction and debate seemed to benefit all parties. The composition of the market participants and their time horizon trends were best spotted by sales and trading, for example, but had long-term potential consequences for research. All participants seemed to view the daily dialogue as indispensable. It provided the necessary information to prioritize daily sales calls, even if the trader disagreed with the data's conclusions.

First on the list of calls was the near-term market color—Wall Street-speak for the economist's and strategist's view of key issues. These tactical concerns were directed to clients whose time horizon made them most concerned with information affecting particular trades. Rarely were the calls specific "buy" or "sell" recommendations; rather the focus was on identifying the market forces that propelled the skewed conditions, such as the specific reasons and ways of exploiting the misalignment or inefficiencies of prices in certain segments or coupons. Formulating an opinion was important. Regurgitating the thoughts of the trading desk was insufficient, since other issues, aside from optimal execution, often drove the trade.

Customers expected the salesperson to understand and filter that information. The most sensitive discussions, however, were about divulging information regarding desk's positions. Entrusted salespeople had a moral responsibility to use this information judiciously. Violating the trust while placing the trading desk at risk would certainly curtail the client's-as well as the sales-person's-participation in such information going forward. Protocol would be for the client to reciprocate; something typical would be: "I agree, I am looking to add to my position. If your desk sees the market widening, give me a call"; or "If it fits your desk, I am a better seller." Daily market sharing with the most active and larger market participants was essential.

As one reviews the process it is evident that there was a natural selection. The timeliness, breadth, and scope of information were different depending upon the desires and the importance of the customer. Discerning value, digesting the key causes, and prioritizing the calls were the sales-person's primary responsibilities. The internet and email had not yet been commercialized, so the larger, more important customers with a short time horizon received the first calls. There were no vehicles to distribute ideas widely. This was an advantage to those receiving the first call. Today, blast emails and web posting enable a broader and more equitable distribution of trading ideas, leveling the playing field somewhat, but the basic aspects of trust remain in place.

Exchanging market color between market participants and trading desks through the lens of proficient salespeople was invaluable. The daily market-color sharing was essential for some but played only a very small role within the thrift industry. As a rule, only a few in the industry engaged in any meaningful portfolio trading. The attention of most thrift executives was devoted to long-term strategic issues. Broad asset-allocation and rebalancing strategies were more topical and far more germane as the thrift industry tried to solve its twin problems of an inefficient delivery system and the asset/liability mismatch.

Many of the long-term strategies emanated from Salomon's research, asset/liability, and/or derivatives specialist units. In concert, these groups designed innovative tools and strategies to assist the thrift industry in crucial asset/liability management decisions. Two of the most creative and popular innovations were the collateralized mortgage obligation (CMO) and the risk-controlled arbitrage. When first created, CMOs provided the thrift industry with a unique debt instrument to manage the uncertain cash flows generated from residential mortgages.

For several reasons the CMO, first introduced by FHLMC with substantial assistance from First Boston and Salomon, was a particularly attractive debt instrument for healthy, well-run thrifts. It provided thrifts with access to long-term funding at relatively attractive levels. For a short period, because it was first categorized as a debt instrument, it enabled them to utilize underwater mortgage without realizing an upfront loss. A CMO was a limited-purpose, legal entity completely separate from the institution that created it.[5]

The fundamental advantages of CMOs for the investors included more targeted maturities, semiannual or quarterly coupon payments, and a limited amount of call protection*. The limited form of call protection and the shorter tranches created in CMOs allowed the mortgage market to attract a larger mix of investors. Capital market participants not previously interested in the mortgage market were actively investing and supplying funds to the housing market. For the investor, the CMO proved to be a flexible tool to create bonds that satisfied specific needs.

As new investors entered the market, the pace of innovation accelerated. Increasingly, mortgage-backed securities would be repackaged and sliced into novel and sophisticated classes. CMOs started supplying an extensive chain of investment alternatives. For the viable thrifts, the CMO was a vehicle to exploit the yield differential between the series of CMO classes and the underlying mortgage loans, thus freeing funds for other purposes.

The supply of mortgage securities, though growing, was increasingly being carved into more and more creative CMOs. This increased demand for fixed-rate mortgages eventually led to narrower spreads. As Salomon's research department smartly explained: "Mortgage rates were lower than they would have been minus the additional demand generated from these new innovations."[6]

When Salomon's sales force and research staff canvassed the nation's thrifts and scoured portfolios to uncover fallow mortgage loans to repackage into CMOs, the resistance was baffling. The expected yield differential between the cost of funding the CMO and the cash flow yield of the collateral often approached 100 basis points (1 percent), an unheard of inefficiency that surely would be arbitraged away over time. Nonetheless, some in the thrift industry, under the guise that the spread was insufficient to cover their overhead costs, chose instead to forego rebalancing and gamble for recovery—with taxpayer-backed deposits.

Many of the thrifts were already technically insolvent or on the brink of failing. Only because of forbearance** by the regulators were they able to continue to operate. The industry's choices for survival were limited. Those on this sort of regulatory life-support could either continue funding their long-term fixed-rate mortgages with short-term deposits rolling the dice that interest rates would fall, or take advantage of the recent lifting of restrictions to invest in lesser-quality nontraditional assets. Either way, with no good choice, the troubled thrifts gambled with the FSLIC's and taxpayers' money.

Another attractive Salomon innovation, risk-controlled arbitrage, deployed interest rate swaps to manage the thrifts asset/liability mismatch inherent with funding long-term assets with short-term liabilities. As Salomon's research spelled out, "Generic interest rate swaps are negotiated devices whereby two parties, a fixed-rate payer and floating-rate payer, commit to exchange interest payments for an agreed upon period of time and notional amount[8]. Each party is responsible for making periodic payments to the other. The fixed-rate payer promises to make a predetermined fixed-rate payment. The floating-rate payer promises to pay based upon a floating-rate money market index, typically London Inter Bank Offered Rate (LIBOR)."[7]

The thrifts, with better designed business models, were extensive users of risk-controlled arbitrage, especially when the expected spread was in the 100 basis point (1 percent) range. Generally described in Salomon's research, a "risk-controlled arbitrage is a self-funding transaction that attempts to extract the excess spread offered from mortgage loans. A thrift entity purchases mortgage-backed securities and at the same time agrees to fund the securities with a reverse repurchase (repo) agreement. The term and rate of the repo agreement typically correlates with the floating rate side of the interest rate swap. To offset the inherent interest rate risk of the transaction, the thrift also agrees to pay fixed rates in a series of graduated maturity interest rate swaps designed to match the duration of the MBSs."[8]

In theory, Salomon's asset/liability group suggested, the risk-controlled arbitrage should realize the spread between the pool of MBSs and the accumulative cost of the interest rate swaps. Unfortunately, the expense of rebalancing the risk-controlled arbitrage during periods of high prepayments often absorbed much of the spread, and the appetite for risk-controlled arbitrage among thrifts consequently diminished. The concept of immunizing the weighted average maturity of assets against the weighted average maturity of the liabilities, however, remained an important and valuable financial management tool.[9]

New developments in the evolution of the mortgage market often produced opportunities for the innovator. Until other market participants re-engineered and evaluated the investment characteristics of the new instrument, the pathfinders had a substantial advantage or head start. One such novel contribution to the development of the mortgage market was stripped mortgage-backed securities (STRIPs). STRIPs segregate the monthly mortgage cash flows into two distinct complementary classes. One receives the principal-only (P/O) portion of the monthly mortgage payments and the other the interest-only (I/O) portion.

On the surface, one would assume that when combining the I/O and P/O in the proper portion, the prices should equal the price of the underlying mortgage. Otherwise market participants would either buy the I/O–P/O combination and reconstruct the MBS or buy the MBS and strip the cash flows, whichever was in disequilibrium. When STRIPs were first inaugurated, disequilibrium prevailed. The Salomon traders in the daily market reviews maintained that the sum of the I/O and P/O prices are chronically cheaper than the underlying mortgages.

Less liquidity and fees, of course, accounted for some of the difference. If one simply sold existing holdings of MBSs and then simultaneously acquired the comparable I/O and P/O, the change in form added liquidity risk. As a "buy and hold" investor, the reduced liquidity was less important for the thrift industry. The more important issue was that the structural change provided an opportunity for those who could identify among individual I/Os or P/Os which one offered outsized value in a "self-funding" arbitrage.

One such example involved a risk-controlled arbitrage structure that utilized a synthetic mortgage constructed from a combination of high-coupon GNMA I/Os (interest-only) and low-coupon FNMA P/Os (principal-only) as the asset. Research, utilizing Salomon's proprietary prepayment and mortgage option pricing models, noticed that the markets were mispricing both the current coupon FNMA P/Os and the GNMA higher coupon I/Os. Salomon's research argued convincingly that "combining a FNMA 9% P/O with a GNMA 11.5 % I/O to create a synthetic 9.5 % mortgage security offered the potential for superior returns.[10]

The unusual convexity[ββ] characteristics of these two particular I/Os and P/Os, when combined, indicated that the combination would outperform conventional mortgage securities and was less expensive to hedge. Constructing a risk-controlled arbitrage using a synthetic mortgage created from this combination offered the investor the potential for substantially superior returns. After carefully analyzing the data, Richard "Dick" Jaegel from Salomon's Asset/Liability Group and I began to prioritize, then schedule meetings with clients in the southeast to determine where the combination best fit.

Jaegel was jovial, genial, and most importantly, principled—a consummate professional. As an accountant he played an essential role. Any questions regarding the most likely accounting treatment were Jaegel's purview. My responsibilities were to describe how the investment features of this combination differed from other mortgage securities. This centered closely on more vigilant rebalancing of the combination.

One of our earliest calls was to the president of a mid-sized Southern Florida savings and loan. He was thoughtful and direct and had worked his way up through the organization. Originally the bank's accountant, the president understood the challenges facing the industry and his institution. Yet more importantly, unlike many of the industry's leaders at the time, he was reluctant to gamble in more risky nontraditional assets. After a lengthy discussion that included the investment characteristics, attendant accounting issues, potential pitfalls, and rebalancing mechanism, he was receptive to further investigation of the concept.

Since I/Os and P/Os were new asset classes, no accounting standards existed. The Financial Accounting Standards Board (FASB) had not yet offered an opinion regarding the appropriate accounting treatment for either the I/O or the P/O. It was reasonable to assume that the P/O would accrete into income using the original issue discount (OID) rules currently in place for zero coupon bonds, but how FASB would require the accounting for the I/O was less clear.

The president preferred a "most likely" as opposed to a "more likely than not" opinion for the accurate accounting of the accretion of the P/O and amortization of the I/O. Also he wanted to review the composition of the pool of mortgages in the GNMA. A conference call with a member of the FASB, a private, not-for-profit organization designated to establish accounting standards, did not furnish the "most likely" opinion he sought but gave him sufficient comfort in the proper accounting concept.

Next, a review of the underlying mortgages comprising the pool of collateral in both the GNMA and FNMA securities was required. It was the bank president's supposition that a recent behavioral change was not properly captured in Wall Street's prepayment models. He referred to it as the "USA Today effect." As mortgage rates moved lower, USA Today would publish tabular displays calculating the monthly payments of current mortgage loans offered by the largest residential lenders in the U.S.

Horizontally across the top of the table were loan amounts in increments of $50,000. Vertically in the left-hand column were the current posted mortgage rates. The columns under each increment calculated the respective monthly payments. Never before had market rates and the corresponding monthly payments been so widely disseminated! Even the mathematically challenged could calculate the monthly savings and the time required to recover their refinancing costs. He concluded that going forward, refinancing among the now more informed public would be more sensitive in rallying markets than models were predicting.

In addition, he contended that lower rates had a greater impact on the newer low rate FNMA P/Os than on the older, higher-coupon GNMA I/Os. His theory was that the higher-coupon GNMAs had older origination dates, and hence they most likely had small remaining balances—so small that no matter how low rates went, the cost of refinancing would not compensate for the fixed cost or inconvenience of refinancing. In contrast, the newer FNMA P/Os had larger loan balances and the "USA Today effect" would accelerate prepayments in any interest rate rally. The price-sensitivity characteristics of the combination were, in his view, even better than Salomon's researchers were proposing.

A review of the collateral revealed a large number of relatively low-balance loans in the GNMA 11.5 percent I/Os. Salomon completed the first FNMA 9 percent P/O-GNMA 11.5 percent I/O combination risk-controlled arbitrage transaction. As Salomon's arbitrage group and trading desks began to incorporate a more dynamic approach to prepayments, a more accurate pricing of I/Os and P/Os emerged. The GNMA 11.5 percent I/O-FNMA 9 percent P/O combination risk-controlled arbitrage spread would quickly be compressed.

Only a few more similar transactions were completed before the major mispricing was corrected. Researchers and traders would be left to ruminate as to how a mere savings and loan president—generally viewed with contempt—could recognize a secular behavioral change (overarching, long-term trend) that had escaped the notice of the Wall Street rocket scientists? It must have been a stressful week.

Despite the substantial increase in volume, mortgage pass-through returns continued to outpace similar duration government and corporate bonds. The quasi or implicit government backing with increasingly larger volume of trading was a unique combination that attracted a diverse group of potential buyers. Wider choices and narrower bid/ask spreads contributed to improved liquidity and healthier markets. The result: borrowers and investors both benefitted from unprecedented innovation and broader access to capital.

Yet, in spite of the initial appeal and the broader choice of shorter maturity securities, few if any of these innovations fulfilled the needs of the thrift industry. As the narrowing of mortgage-backed securities spreads unfolded, it was becoming clearer to many of us on Wall Street that the window of opportunity for the thrift industry was limited. This is not to suggest that at the time this was simple to predict; day-to-day fluctuations and dynamic market forces masked these trends and made the process quite complex. Yet it was more than a hunch; the evidence of a long-term trend toward tighter conforming mortgage spreads was compelling. There was urgency among Salomon's sales force to scour the balance sheets, uncover fallow assets, and rebalance the asset/liability mismatch. Unfortunately, it proved to be too little, too late for most of the industry.

In spite of the efforts to more closely match the interest-rate sensitivity of their assets and liabilities, the rates many S&Ls were paying on deposits—after accounting for the costs—still exceeded the income generated from their current mortgage portfolio. This caused the industry to face a serious earnings problem. Armed with government guaranteed deposits, a common strategy was to try to grow and diversify their way out of the problem. Under the promise of higher returns and shortening the maturity on the asset side of their balance sheet, these thrifts took advantage of their new-found regulatory freedom to invest in "nontraditional" assets, away from home mortgage lending.

Some ventured cautiously while others dashed into investing their portfolios in nontraditional assets, mostly junk bonds and lesser quality commercial real estate. Junk bond managers and commercial real-estate lending officers were hot commodities. Even those with dubious credentials commanded generous compensation. Misguided bonus structures rewarded volume over quality or long-term performance. Junk bonds and commercial real estate values soared because of the buying binge. Too many unqualified lenders with too much (taxpayer guaranteed) money were chasing too few quality assets.

In the aftermath of the Great Depression, policymakers instituted the Federal Deposit Insurance Corporation. They deemed, correctly or incorrectly, that many average depositors did not have the resources, time, inclination, or capacity to underwrite the financial institution in which they held their deposits. To forestall a recurrence of a systemic run on the bank, regulators concluded that it was necessary to assure depositors that their funds were secured by the full faith and credit of the U.S. government. Henceforth all small depositors' savings balances held in FDIC- or FSLIC-insured financial entities would be guaranteed by the federal government.[11]

At its inception, deposit insurance was limited to a relatively small dollar amount, but over time it increased substantially. Policymakers also chose not to differentiate among financial institutions. A flat fee for all federally insured deposit-gathering entities was instituted. The larger limits, account segregation, and institution allocation meant, for all practical purposes, that deposits held by individuals were federally insured in their totality.

As would have been expected, in lieu of due diligence, depositors relied (and continue to rely) solely on deposit insurance when deciding where to place their savings. Regrettably, the consequence of increasing the near-term stability in the banking system turned out to be costly. Despite ample warning signs, thrift regulators ignored the problem. Wall Street analysts continually harped that the method of pricing deposit insurance, meager capital requirements, forbearance, and relaxed asset restrictions together created a perverse incentive for risk-taking by teetering FSLIC-insured thrifts, but to no avail. The moral hazard of flat-fee deposit insurance proved to have an expensive price tag for the taxpayer.

High Yield/Junk Bonds—Wrestling with Common Sense

Just as Lew Ranieri and Salomon Brothers were widely recognized for their mortgage effort, so too were Michael Milken and Drexel Burnham Lambert (Drexel) known as the founders of modern high yield (junk) bonds. Before Milken, there were companies who for a variety of reasons stumbled and were downgraded by the rating agencies to less than investment grade, but there was not an active new issue junk bond market. For the first time, a whole new grade of companies could secure financing more readily through the capital markets. Some of these impaired corporate credits matured into profitable well-known entities.

Milken professed, to whoever would listen, that a well diversified portfolio of high-yield bonds would outperform a comparable investment-grade portfolio. While vying for the S&L investment dollars, Drexel's well-prepared sales force argued, convincingly in many cases, that junk bonds offered the benefits of generally shorter maturity and significantly higher yield. It was not long before Drexel became the dominant underwriter of junk bonds. Aggressive investors, including some in the thrift industry, were eager buyers. As is now known, that euphoric demand—performance-enhanced by taxpayer-guaranteed deposits—pushed asset prices to unsustainable levels.[12]

Again allow me to remind the reader that predicting overvalued markets is a complex undertaking. Anticipating when and to what magnitude markets will correct themselves is even more difficult. As pundits look back, some will cite reports warning of the impending dangers, but few suggest viable remedies. And when they do, the average annual returns from their recommendations often fail to match the long-term returns of the questioned assets.

In any case, the issue was not the relative value or the role of junk bonds as an investment vehicle, but rather the decision to risk federally-insured deposits by ill-prepared S&L portfolio managers who failed to grasp the inherent perils or provide a rational evaluation of risk. A well managed, diversified portfolio of high-yield bonds may even be expected to outperform a portfolio of similar maturity high-grade bonds.

Yet the thrifts' scant capital levels were inadequate to withstand the changing market conditions and attendant spread volatility of junk bonds or, for that matter, even lesser-quality real estate and commercial loans. Given the capital levels of the thrift industry at the time, the risk was for the FSLIC/taxpayer and somewhat less for the other stakeholders. Simply put: High yield bonds were ill-suited, given the lack of expertise and inadequate amount of capital in the thrift industry.

In the late 1980s the Security and Exchange Committee (SEC) accused Drexel of multiple violations of securities laws. Also, some suggested that for politically driven reasons Rudolph Giuliani, then U.S. Attorney, made a full court press and threatened an indictment under the powerful Racketeer Influenced and Corrupt Organizations Act (RICO). Unnerved, Drexel agreed not to contend the charges and paid a hefty fine. Part of the agreement included a separation from its junk-bond impresario Milken.[13]

At first Drexel seemed to have survived the ordeal, successfully placing several key high-yield deals including RJR Nabisco for Kohlberg Kravis & Roberts (KKR). Yet rumors on Wall Street swirled. Without Milken's loyal followers, the holes in Drexel's armor began to appear. First, Drexel had trouble rolling over several short-term high-yield funding programs. Soon a sense of fear began to emerge in the high-yield market.

Compounding the problem, Congress passed the Financial Institutional Reform, Recovery, and Enforcement Act (FIRREA). Signed into law in late 1989, FIRREA required thrifts to mark-to-market (record at a realistic appraisal or current market price rather than book value) their high-yield bonds, prohibited them from making additional purchases, and mandated that they rid themselves of their junk bond holdings by midyear 1994. FIRREA not only meant that a significant source of demand for high-yield bonds would be eliminated; it also meant a substantial supply of bonds would soon be flooding the market. FIRREA would both negatively impact the prices of bonds already issued and impede pending financing.[14]

As the industry began liquidating, junk bond spreads widened, and their failure rates escalated. The volatility and thinness of the market became evident as the foundation began to crumble. As prices fell, several thrifts with large portfolios were pushed into insolvency. FIRREA brought to a head the troubles facing the thrift industry. As it seized insolvent thrifts, the Resolution Trust Company (RTC) unloaded the portfolios into the market. Several state pension funds curtailed further investments, and some even sold off their holdings. Junk bond prices continued to sink, in many cases dragging under the good with the bad. Junk bond defaults escalated, and Drexel was allowed to fail. Drexel, a formidable competitor, was gone.

Not that Milken and his department should be exonerated for the role they played in the failure of the thrift industry, but no one was personified more unfairly than Milken and Drexel. They were convenient scapegoats for regulators and policymakers to deflect criticism from their own role in the thrift industry's demise. Congress wanted us to believe that it was those bad "banksters" making all that money from Drexel.

Junk bonds were often demonized as the major cause of the demise of thrifts. True, high-yield bonds were a meaningful contributor to the downfall of some of the large, more notorious S&Ls, but contrary to conventional wisdom, junk bonds were not widely held in the industry as a whole. High-yield bonds were concentrated in a few institutions. The final tabulation indicated that junk bonds accounted for far less of the total losses among the S&Ls than previously proclaimed.[15]

The problem the thrift industry was having with high-yield bonds was just a symptom, not the cause of bigger problems. Economists and analysts often contended that the amount of regulatory capital within the savings and loan industry was insufficient to cover the impending losses. Nonetheless, policymaking mechanisms handicapped regulators from keeping abreast of financial evolution. Policymakers are inherently reactive (as opposed to proactive) and should not be expected to foresee changes and appropriately reshape regulations. Congress rarely revisits rules frequently enough to stay abreast of the evolution of markets. Only a crisis prompts action. Policymakers are content to enact post-crisis legislation that suffices for a decade or so—or until another disaster elicits a response.[16]

For whatever reason, most likely because of insufficient deposit insurance funds, policymakers dragged their feet and failed to address the problem, presumably hoping that interest rates would fall and bail out a failing industry. Instead, their tardiness fostered excessive-risk taking and extreme levels of leverage. Most S&Ls became growth-driven without the capacity or experience to assess the risks they were taking. Hope had replaced logic in the regulatory process!

FIRREA had established more stringent minimum statutory capital standards. When determining compliance, lawmakers explicitly specified that certain investments required greater capital. In addition to imposing restrictions on junk bond investing, other assets—such as commercial real estate loans, construction loans, and consumer and business loans—all were assigned the highest risk-weighting. This meant that carrying these types of assets required higher capital ratios to cushion against losses.[17]

Furthermore, FIRREA greatly reduced and eventually eliminated the amount of supervisory-goodwill that could be used to satisfy the new minimum capital standards. The lengthy time frame to write-down supervisory-goodwill was reduced significantly. Ordinarily goodwill is perceived as valuable because a rational buyer would not overpay for assets were it not for some of its intrinsic value. Supervisory-goodwill, on the other hand, was a sort of perverted goodwill created when federal regulators supervised the acquisition of failed savings institutions. The purchase price is sensible only because of the accounting treatment, not because of some intangible benefit.

The FSLIC permitted thrifts that acquired failed entities special accounting treatment regarding the shortfall of the actual versus the book value of insolvent institutions. Shortsighted regulators granted these acquiring entities the right to record supervisory-goodwill as a "paper asset" or substitute for capital. This was most likely because the deposit insurance fund had insufficient monies to cover the short fall between the assets and liabilities of the insolvent thrifts.

This capital substitute was used to persuade healthier institutions' participation in supervisory acquisitions. In lieu of recognizing the loss immediately, the FSLIC deposit insurance fund allowed thrifts that assisted FSLIC and acquired insolvent savings institutions to treat supervisory-goodwill as regulatory capital, a form of capital forbearance or capital gimmick that disguised inadequate capitalization. The acquiring thrift was happy because the inflated regulatory capital allowed greater leverage and presumably more profits. In essence, supervisory-goodwill allowed the FSLIC to shield their deposit insurance fund from having to go to Congress for additional government funding. The need for a taxpayer bailout rested on a "wing and a prayer."[18]

This was not the only gimmick clever lawmakers devised or employed to bolster the thrifts' capital ratios at the time. To put it briefly, when Wall Street bundles mortgage-backed securities to create a REMIC, a byproduct of the process is "phantom income" (reportable, taxable income without any cash flow). This phantom income resides in the REMIC's noneconomic residual (NERD). To assure that the associated taxes were paid on the income, the IRS imposed requirements clarifying the transfer of a NERD. The party that transferred was obligated to "reasonably believe" that the taxes linked with the NERD would be paid by the transferee. Net operating losses (NOLs) could not be used to offset this phantom income.

Naturally, in order to incur this negative tax treatment, the buyer required compensation, which was referred to as an inducement payment. Creative policymakers (not an oxymoron) deduced that if thrifts were allowed to utilize their abundant NOLs to offset phantom income, the inducement fees would be a convenient way to prop up the thrifts' capital. In addition, only profitable thrifts would meet transfer restrictions—a bailout in disguise.

What a convenient way to turn widely held deferred assets, net operating losses (NOLs), into capital via the income statement—a creative contribution from the taxpayer to thrifts' capital. For those select few S&Ls that were profitable and understood the dynamics of the NERD market, there was a brief window of opportunity to expeditiously recapture NOLs. And let's not forget Wall Street, the REMIC issuers. For the issuers, it created with a significantly lower tax rate a very motivated buyer. Everyone, save the IRS, went home happy.

Yet it all proved to be insufficient. The crux of the problems for most of the industry was bloated overhead costs. Many of the thrifts had overhead costs somewhere in the vicinity of 100-150 basis points (1 to 1.5 percent). Also the financial service industry was becoming more competitive and less fragmented. At the same time, communications and technological advancements were increasing the efficiency of the financial sector. Subsidiaries of automobile companies were offering car loans; mortgage bankers and commercial banks were increasingly originating a larger portion of single-family residential housing loans more efficiently; and financial subsidiaries of large conglomerates like GE Capital were in the commercial loan and real-estate lending business. Perhaps the thrift industry's regulatory structure needed updating to incorporate the new market realities?

Regulatory bodies, as history has proven again and again, were mostly unable to keep pace with the rapidly changing financial terrain. Individual borrowers now had broad access, via non-deposit-gathering entities, to funding from global markets remarkably close to levels previously enjoyed only by larger entities.

Soon a chorus of economists was expressing deep concern regarding the amount of risk harbored on the balance sheets of thrifts. They argued that allowing thrifts to use federally insured deposits to purchase such risky assets went against common sense. The delinquency rates on these new loans accelerated. The realized returns from land, commercial real estate, commercial loans, and junk bonds proved less than expected and in most cases lower than their traditional assets. It was becoming evident that the longer regulators delayed, the greater the potential cost to the taxpayers.

The policymakers' forbearance policy, like an ostrich with its head buried in the sand, did little to solve the industry's long-term financial problems. Political interest often trumped vigilant regulators as they tried to deal with the problem. The hope of buying time until a secular trend of lower interest rates would lessen the cost, proved to be foolhardy. The cost of closing the insolvent S&Ls did not serendipitously recede, it swelled.

The low capital requirements coupled with forbearance; induced technically insolvent and inefficiently run thrifts to portfolio investments that were excessively risky, at least from FSLIC's or the taxpayers' point of view. Though this had been common knowledge for some time on Wall Street, it was finally becoming apparent to regulators that for thrifts to survive, they needed to become more efficient.

For practical reasons, Congress needed to address the growing problems within the thrift industry. The Financial Institutions Reform, Recovery and Enforcement Act was that crucial response by Congress to the large number of insolvent thrifts. The pendulum had swung from one extreme to the other. As the political forces shifted, the opinion among lawmakers turned away from supporting existing inefficient institutions at the expense of more promising enterprises.[19] One of my S&L clients appropriately lamented; Like a drug dealer ratcheting up the cost of drugs, Congress's new definition of capital removes much of supervisory-goodwill immediately and by 1994 completely excludes its use in capital compliance. According to FSLIC data at the time, supervisory-goodwill represented more than one-third of all thrifts' capital.

Few in the thrift industry perceived the impeding write-down of supervisory-goodwill. Yet at that time the predictive failure was not their main concern; instead, their focus was finding an immediate source of capital. As a consequence, many in the thrift industry were no longer in compliance and insolvency became common, if not the norm. Also for those thrifts whose leverage ratios were scarcely in compliance, the higher standards compelled them to reduce their leverage, raise capital, or fall into insolvency.

There was widespread anger among the entities that fell short of capital requirements because of the phase-out of supervisory-goodwill. They had accommodated regulators by taking questionable assets of failed S&Ls in return for what they deemed was a promise that supervisory-goodwill would be allowed for the purpose of meeting regulatory capital. Policymakers' overtures quickly turned to condemnation. Unfortunately, regulators chose to paint all thrifts, well managed or not, with the same brush and showed little sympathy.[20]

When defending the government's action, William Seidman, then chairman of the FDIC, stated: "The government cannot be bound to cancerous products, even though the government said before that it was okay."[21]

Regulators failed to differentiate between recoverable and non-recoverable goodwill. Loans whose values were reduced solely because interest rates moved higher, ultimately recovered the resulting goodwill after the principal was repaid. Goodwill, created by performing securities being marked down to reflect higher interest rates, was recaptured dollar for dollar when these assets reached maturity and the principal was repaid at par value. On the other hand, if the underlying assets backing a loan fell in value, it may be expected that the accompanying goodwill most likely was not recoverable.

Once the initial shock wore off, there were numerous court filings from the thrifts who felt deceived, asserting that the government had breached their contractual promise. The courts eventually ruled that the federal government had indeed breached its obligation with some acquirers of failed thrifts when the FIRREA mandated supervisory-goodwill write-offs. The *Journal of Financial Research* reported, "On July 1, 1996, the U.S. Supreme Court in a 7–2 decision ruled that the U.S. government had violated contractual obligations through the 1989 passage of the FIRREA."[22] Thus the attendant regulatory enforcement may have been premature. This odyssey does not demonstrate a spirit of partnership nor create a foundation of trust in the financial sector. The opaque process fostered mistrust and cynicism within the financial community.

The lessons are a stark reminder that policymakers can be as capricious and punishing as the markets themselves. The S&L crisis makes clear that bureaucratic self-interest is a real threat. Policymakers proved very capable of disguising their role in the demise of the industry while magnifying their successes.

Congress understands that most of the results of regulations only become apparent over long periods. Those thrifts that were solvent when supervisory-goodwill was counted should have been allowed either to negotiate the return of the questionable assets or be allowed a longer transition period. Yet what should have been was now of little consequence to the industry. In aggregate, the thrift industry did not satisfy the requisite capital ratios to be able to survive after the government clamped down and imposed tougher treatment of goodwill. The lessons for Lehman should have been clear: the government was not a dependable business partner and was ill-equipped to make prescient decisions regarding individual financial institutions, absent of political influence.

When political tides change, the whim of the government can shift quickly. Politically popular policy is much easier to deliver to politicians' constituents. Lehman should have understood that the government is prone to interpret ambiguous market information as validation of their decisions when political calls for scalps are popular. Apparently the consequences of the financial excesses (and subsequent abandonment of the thrift industry) proved not to be unforgettable enough to prevent Lehman from making some of the same mistakes.

Hedge funds in disguise!

Select large S&Ls with efficient deposit and consumer franchises survived and maintained adequate value to compete under the more stringent requirements. In time, many would be bought, others would grow through acquisitions, and some would serve as precursors to mortgage hedge funds. These financial engineers argued that they provided liquidity indirectly through the capital markets instead of directly by lending, but with one significant difference: their funding was at least partially FSLIC-insured.

In lieu of relying solely on borrowing from depositors, these new hedge fund-like thrifts would sell portfolio assets or use assets as collateral to self-fund. Instead of making loans, they purchased tradable securities. Just as a conventional S&L attempted to earn the interest rate spread between their loans and their cost of deposits, the intention was to realize a greater return from the assets they purchased versus the assets they sold. I would like to see James Stewart explain that one to the community in a remake of Frank Capra's *It's a Wonderful Life*!

Long before the government understood that the role of the small S&Ls was increasingly becoming archaic, these entrepreneurial thrifts took advantage of their expanded investment authority to push the investment boundaries. In many cases they were pioneers in developing sophisticated computer models to identify value in the mortgage market. One of the first such thrifts to value mortgage-backed securities using quantitative mathematical measures was American Pioneer Savings Bank. Jon Knight, the chief investment officer and a PhD, had recently hired a NASA mathematician to focus on reducing the number of iterations (geek-speak for repetitions) "Monte Carlo simulations" needed to maintain accuracy when calculating the option-adjusted spread (OAS).

Monte Carlo simulation was the common method used on Wall Street. It imitated the sources affecting the value of a mortgage-backed security (MBS) and calculated its value expressed as an OAS. The OAS is the net yield advantage after compensating for the value of the inherent prepayment option or right of the borrower to repay the mortgage loan. A MBS's cash flows are contingent upon the option of the lender to refinance: the more volatility in interest rates, the greater the cost.

As you would expect, this requires a large sample of future yield environments to be robust enough to accurately capture this expected cost. The number of evaluations at that time often exceeded 10,000 iterations. Knight's new hire, Ali "Alp" Kerestecioglu, PhD, was, via his work at NASA, uniquely suited to solve the problem of reducing the requisite number of repetitions. If Alp could accomplish the task, it would provide American Pioneer with a significant advantage over its rivals by more quickly identifying and taking advantage of market anomalies.

Most of the mortgage valuation models at the time incorporated several common features: interest rate distributions were proportionate to the relative level of rates or "lognormal," in the terminology of "quants;" the model was constructed not to introduce a bias (i.e. "arbitrage-free"); and the bench marks were the current U.S. Treasury rates or "on the run," as Wall Street referred to them. Got that? Don't worry!

A common problem among the models was that the lognormal distribution, especially in a steeply sloped yield curve, often produced unreasonable levels of interest rates, perhaps a 20 percent interest rate on a thirty-year mortgage. To compensate for the abnormality, most researchers arbitrarily lopped off some of the exceedingly high and low rate levels that did not make sense; not quite a purely scientific solution, but it seemed to work. At least it would do until someone discovered a more eloquent or robust solution.

The distribution problem had been the subject of extensive research for several years without a concrete solution. Then two Salomon PhDs, Janet Showers and Mark Koenigsberg, completed work on a new valuation model applicable to mortgage-backed securities that purported to address this issue. Knight along with Alp contacted me and requested an audience with either Showers or Koenigsberg to discuss their findings, so I arranged for us to meet Koenigsberg in his office in Salomon's New York office building.

After the customary introductions, Koenigsberg first described the current lognormal distribution problem with most OAS models. His supposition was that the flaw "rested within the assumptions of volatility." The term Koenigsberg coined was the "term structure of volatility" (TSOV), which in layman's language means that the volatility varies with the term of the security.

As he described it, short-term rates historically were significantly more volatile than long-term rates, and it was intellectually appealing to assume the condition would continue. To dramatize his point, he showed a short film comprised of a series of actual yield curves dating back several decades. As Knight, Alp, and I watched the film, the curves looked like a whip with long term rates as the handle and short term rates as the whip's end. Koenigsberg's point was crystal clear.

Koenigsberg logically reasoned that if you incorporated the TSOV or the respective volatility level to each part of the yield curve in the model, unreasonable interest rate levels outside of historical norms were no longer a problem. He used the term "mean reversion" and explained that when interest rates spring to either very high or low levels they would recoil to a more historically normal range. I still followed his supposition, I think.

Koenigsberg then began to construct a differential equation to describe their findings. That is where he lost me, and my mind began to wander. Alp and Knight, however, followed intently. After Koenigsberg completed the equation, Alp made the comment, "I am not certain the *sigma* in your equation is unique." Without having anything intelligent to say, I quickly added, "Yeah, I was thinking the same thing; maybe you should use colored chalk?" I don't think they appreciated my attempt at humor.

As the conversation was ending, Koenigsberg and Alp agreed to share their research to determine if *sigma* in Koenigsberg's equation was unique. In a few weeks they determined, *sigma* was indeed unique. What a relief for me! I don't think I slept through the night during that time worrying about *sigma*.

Jon Knight, along with Anthony Huggins and several mathematicians, including Alp, eventually transferred their expertise and launched the hedge fund Atlantic Portfolio Analytics & Management, Inc. (APAM). The story may be instructive and I hope amusing, but the lesson is clear. Thrift policymakers had little understanding of the risks being taken by the institutions they were charged with regulating.

Lawmakers would like us to believe that the demise of thrift industry was a result of inept financiers. Although the industry had its share of less than competent managers, the problem was largely structural: federally insured deposit should not be used, either alone or commingled, to fund what are really only trading bets on relative value—something today's policymakers should keep in mind.

Along with a number of other ill-conceived regulations, allowing insolvent thrifts to continue to take new deposits resulted in unintended consequences that exacerbated the problems. Bureaucratic forbearance, along with the new investment powers presented by the Garn-St. Germain Act and the liability deregulation of the early 1980s presented a perverse incentive for insolvent thrifts to attempt to gamble their way to solvency. Seek risk in a desperate effort to survive!

As the George H. Bush administration implemented FIRREA and sought solutions to resolve the increasing number of insolvent thrifts, it faced numerous challenges. The most complicated were liquidating an immense number of assets and avoiding serious disorder in the fixed-income markets, while containing the cost to the federal deposit insurance fund. To accomplish these often conflicting goals, the government created the Resolution Trust Corporation (RTC), a limited life federally owned asset management company. Congress was concerned about creating another large bureaucracy—as well it should have been.

At the time, several recent problems with some government-led efforts shook public confidence. As a consequence, the RTC had a short life. Given its unparalleled mandate, the RTC had the capacity to foster abuse as well as favoritism. To ensure accountability, the administration established an oversight board which served as the RTC's board of directors. Significant safeguards addressing contracting partners, soliciting competitive bids, and rescinding contracts were established. Extensive auditing and reporting requirements were imposed. Uppermost in the minds of legislators was "a fair and competitive bidding process" that minimized the cost to the taxpayers. No one was keen on having the government manage an asset liquidation company.

As legislators are prone to do, they also sought to intercede and leave their footprint in the RTC's management. Correctly or incorrectly, they had no confidence that the government had the expertise or manpower to undertake such a massive disposition of assets. Several wise regulators believed it was necessary to set up a system that used the private sector in the disposal of thrift assets. But soon political goals began to creep into the debate.

Eventually Congress and the first Bush administration came to some agreements, and the RTC began to confront the difficult task of liquidating assets. At first, the RTC organized several bulk sales of assets. Soon the worst fears of creating a government entity ill-equipped to dispose of assets in a cost-effective manner were coming true. The pricing on most of these portfolio sales was disappointing and discounted substantially more than anticipated.[23]

A stark example is the package of whole loans purchased by Cen Trust, I referred to earlier. At the time there was no common system to decipher whole-loan mortgage tapes. These tapes stored the essential information about the characteristics of the loans in the pool. So despite the requirement of soliciting multiple competitive bids, few outside of Salomon's mortgage structuring group were equipped to understand what was contained within the tape. The cost of re-engineering the infrastructure to read a tape was far too large to incur just to bid in competition for an isolated loan package. For Salomon's whole-loan trading desk, it created the potential to profit mightily, far more than in a fully competitive marketplace.

Policymakers soon concluded that the RTC was woefully understaffed and poorly trained. Regulators realized the RTC was at a substantial disadvantage in the process and began to engage the private sector. Consolidating these portfolios of distressed assets and partnering with experienced private-sector managers was more cost-effective. At the same time these changes made the RTC a less convenient target of criticism.

From then on, the RTC primarily acted as conservator of failed thrifts contracting out much of the assets management and selling. To accomplish a more favorable execution, the RTC pioneered what they referred to as "equity partnerships," where they retained an interest in the assets. The remaining interest was acquired by a private sector partner, who directed the management and sale of the assets.[24]

The private-sector partners provided experience in managing and disposing of distressed assets and capital. The profit-sharing structures of the private/public partnerships assured a balanced alignment of incentives. The lesson learned is simple enough: the cornerstone of managing large-asset disposition is best done in partnership with the private sector, including private equity funds designed to invest in distressed government assets with the taxpayer maintaining sizeable ownership.

* Investopedia explains **call protection** as "advantageous to investors because it prevents the issuer from forcing redemption early on in the life of a security."

** A tolerance or delay in meeting capital standards.

ß The nominal or face amount that is used only to calculate payments and does not change hands.

ßß Bond convexity is an arcane finance concept that Wikipedia defines as "a measure of the sensitivity of the duration of a bond to changes in interest rates." In plain English: As interest rates change, the price of the bond does not change linearly.

6

THE ROLE OF THE FHA, FNMA, AND FHLMC

"A Wolf in Sheep's Clothing" Aesop.

After lawmakers formed FHLMC in the early 1970s and GNMA and FNMA separated in the late 1960s, each performed distinct secondary market functions. GNMA's main responsibility was to act as guarantor for residential mortgages insured by the Federal Housing Administration (FHA) and Veterans Administration (VA). FNMA functioned largely as a portfolio investor for the FHA/VA mortgages and other conforming loans* originated by the mortgage banking industry. And FHLMC acted as a conduit for the thrift industry's conforming origination. Thrifts would deliver their conventional residential mortgages into FHLMC, which would convert the mortgages into participation certificates (PCs) and sell them into the capital markets.

As a consequence of the burgeoning mortgage market, FHLMC and FNMA evolved and expanded their secondary market efforts. The two began to compete for the wave of thrift securitization. Both entities designed new programs to assist the thrift industry restructure and to provide liquidity for their residential loan origination. FHLMC was first out of the blocks to introduce their guarantor program. Within a few months FNMA followed with their mortgage backed securities (MBSs) program. Thrifts were now able to exchange seasoned, as well as newly originated, mortgages for FNMA and FHLMC guaranteed pass-through securities. The swap provided thrifts with securities in a more fungible or exchangeable form.[1]

FNMA and FHLMC both rightfully claimed that the new, more liquid securities allowed access to previously untapped institutional pools of money—foreign investors, public and private pension plans, and insurance companies, to name a few—to fund residential mortgages. Supply and demand, enhanced by the quasi-government support, was balanced by interest rates. Consequently, FNMA and FHLMC accelerated the increase in their qualifying loan limit at a pace that exceeded the rise in median house prices. The federalization of the mortgage market began in earnest as the pooling of thrifts' residential housing loans into FNMA and FHLMC securities exploded. FNMA and FHLMC morphed into the government's off-balance sheet funding vehicle to transfer wealth from taxpayers to homeowners via mortgage interest deduction.

Some would like to broaden the debate regarding the merits of the tax preference to homeowners and the housing subsidies provided by FNMA and FHLMC. The issue of whether or not keeping mortgage rates lower than they otherwise would be via FNMA's and FHLMC's subsidization is topical in light of their recent role in the financial crisis. Many other countries with advanced economies have relatively high levels of home ownership without offering tax preference for mortgage interest or the implicit support FNMA and FHMLC furnishes.

Canada's home ownership rate, for example, is nearly equal to the U.S. rate; yet it has no quasi government-sponsored entities (GSEs) like FNMA or FHLMC, mortgage interest is not tax deductible, and mortgage lenders have full recourse to the borrower's other assets. Instead, Canada has reconciled the importance of a liquid mortgage market in its economy and chooses to back most of its housing finance through a 100 percent government-owned credit insurer, the Canada Mortgage and Housing Corporation. Canada provides an explicit government guarantee and any subsidies are transparent to the taxpayers.[2]

In the recent crisis, the roles of FNMA, FHLMC, and GNMA have escalated. Today the three account for the overwhelming majority of mortgages. Few among the general public are aware that FNMA and FHLMC currently guarantee or own roughly half of the United States' $11 trillion mortgages. If policymakers chose to use the taxpayers' credit card, doing so should be transparent. The government agencies are already in place to accomplish their political housing agenda.

The role the government has the Federal Housing Administration (FHA) playing in the current crisis may provide us with an example. The New Deal-era agency does not purchase loans; it only insures them through FHA-approved lenders. These FHA insured mortgages are then packaged into Government National Mortgage Association (GNMA) backed securities. The reader may recall that GNMA's mission is to help direct global capital into the U.S. housing market for low- and moderate-income borrowers. GNMA guarantees the timely payment of interest and principal which makes them the only MBS to bear the full faith and credit of the federal government, hence a lower or, more aptly stated, subsidized cost of funds.

To date, the FHA has proudly been a self-funded government agency. The income from the insurance premiums is held in a separate reserve account and has been sufficient to meet all obligations. Like any insurer, loans must meet the FHA's established requirements to qualify. Ironically, before the crisis the FHA was a relatively insignificant player in the housing market. As private lenders loosened standards, the FHA continued to require minimum down payments and documentation of incomes for loans they insured and seemed to have dodged much of the subprime bust.

As the crisis unfolded, however, the private label mortgage-backed securities market ceased to function and the FHA's role increased significantly. FHA figures show that in fiscal year 2008 it guaranteed nearly $205 billion in mortgage loans compared with $85 million in 2007. Under the guise of helping to steady the struggling housing market and ease the downturn, policymakers have pressed the FHA to offer credit on easier terms. These relaxed lending standards are where the problems and lessons lie.

Congress increased the loan caps and the FHA is currently insuring loans with down payments as low as 3.5 percent to borrowers whose credit ratings are often below average to poor. With private lenders tightening standards and increasing down payment levels, new borrowers as well as those wanting to refinance are flocking into FHA-insured mortgages. GNMA President Joseph Murin indicates that GNMA expects the value of outstanding MBSs it guarantees to exceed $ 1 trillion by the end of 2010, which is more than double their 2007 level.[3]

Not surprising, the quality of its portfolio is deteriorating. A whopping 24 percent of the 2008 FHA-backed loans were past due as of September

2009. When you account for the $8,000 refundable tax credit which for all intents and purposes funds the down payments, owners have little or no money at risk. And we all are perfectly aware of what that means: subprime, in case you forgot.

The FHA plays down the notion that they may require a taxpayer bailout, though weekly capital reports show that the agency's reserves are declining. In late fall of 2009, the FHA reported that its cash reserves had fallen below the 2 percent required by federal law. What may save the FHA, however, are falling housing prices relative to personal income. If employment starts to rise and household formations begin to catch up to supply, a floor in housing prices may mask the loosened underwriting standards and low down payments.[4]

Every borrower who refinances into an FHA-insured loan from a private-sector loan shifts the risk out of the financial system into the FHA insurance fund. Any subsequent foreclosure costs are then borne by the insurance fund. Should the fund's equity run out, the taxpayer shoulders the cost of the bailout. Result: Congress's pressured changes to underwriting standards are funded by a government agency, not by the private sector.

Though this may prove to be a subprime lesson revisited, it is not about the FHA tightening their lending standards, nor is it meant to debate the merits of social programs designed to increase home ownership. Those arguments are better left for the academic economists to fret over. It is about the risks that government mandates designed to advance political agendas pose to the larger financial system.

The FHA is just a microcosm or laboratory of the role government policies have played in the recent crisis. The 1992 Federal Housing Enterprises Financial Safety and Soundness Act was designed by Congress to force the government-sponsored enterprises FNMA and FHLMC to acquire "affordable" housing loans.

To comply with the law's requirements, FNMA and FHLMC had a seemingly insatiable appetite. This dovetailed with another federal law, the Community Reinvestment Act (CRA). The CRA pressured large banks to boost lending in low- and moderate-income communities and generated aberrant demand, in this case a voracious appetite for mortgages that qualified to meet low-income lending mandates.

When the supply of worthy borrowers was exhausted, lenders relaxed underwriting standards which increased CRA lending substantially. To meet FNMA's and FHLMC's turbo-charged demand, Wall Street eagerly produced increasingly riskier assets. Combine a secular decrease in mortgage rates from roughly 10½ percent in spring 1990 to 5½ percent in 2004 according to HSH Associates Financial Publishers, and you get an unprecedented housing bubble—the foundation for the subprime panic.[5]

These dynamics were widely understood on Wall Street, especially among FNMA and FHLMC portfolio managers. Few predicted that the increased amount of subprime loans would trigger what resulted in our financial system teetering on the verge of collapse, but many understood the driving forces behind the deterioration in substandard mortgages. Congressional induced demand would lead to increasingly looser underwriting standards and lower down payments.

During part of this process, I had both former customers who were FNMA portfolio managers and current customers who previously managed mortgage portfolios at one of the agencies. Their stories were the same. "You would not believe the junk we have to buy." Pressing market-distorting policies on the private banking system stood at the root of much of the subprime problem.

The lesson is clear: Shoving Congress's social agenda through the private sector had a destructive influence on financial markets. If Congress chooses to enact lending mandates to achieve political agendas, government agencies are much better suited to fill the role. The FHA's public-private partnership is an example of using government agencies as vehicles to remedy what policymakers deem social inequities. GNMA's advantage of a government safety net provides an inexpensive funding source for the low- and moderate-income homeowner. The catch: Together the FHA and GNMA provide a clear accounting for the cost and much easier way to measure the success or failure of the low- and moderate-income housing programs. It is time for policymakers to admit the importance liquid mortgage markets play in the economy and bring the debt of FNMA and FHLMC back onto the federal balance sheet.

If administered effectively, and absent congressional influence, agencies can serve as valuable tools for the Federal Reserve in their oversight duties. As the housing market begins to overheat, the agencies can easily turn the thermostat down by curtailing their purchase program, hence reducing demand. Likewise, should market participants start to flee en masse, the agencies can ratchet up purchases to stave off a panic and restore order and confidence to the market. Taxpayers can then see how much of their money goes to support the housing market and judge whether this is how they want their dollars spent. Congress may not be as eager to further political causes when there is a price tag directly attached to its budget.

* **Mortgages** that meet both the quality guidelines and amount limit established by FNMA and FHLMC.

7

SALES, TRADING, AND RESEARCH PARTNERSHIP

"If we are together nothing is impossible. If we are divided all will fail."
Winston Churchill

Banks might do well to delineate more clearly the roles and responsibilities of the sales, trading, and research partnership. Salomon's training class continually emphasized that the most successful traders were excellent sales-people and the most successful sales-people were excellent traders, though the concept did not become clear until one understood how the markets functioned. After all, there are basic traits that separated the two. Savvy traders, at their core, are market savants. Their passion and focus are markets, particularly their sector. The best traders have the capacity to sort through mounds of data, quickly quantify its influence on their sector, and then judiciously put the firm's capital at risk.

A proficient sales-person, on the other hand, is a market generalist and the trader's and firm's spokesman to the market participants. His responsibility is to ensure the long-term relationships of the firm. Adept sales-people understand the firm's strengths, identify the client's needs, and facilitate transactions. In the right environment, neither sales-people nor traders are successful alone. The trader needs to persuade (or sell) the sales-person on the value within his or her sector. The sales-person must know where markets are trading in order to manage the firm's relationships and reveal to management where there may be excess risk.

A trader's primary, even if not sole focus is his own profit and loss (P&L) statement. At the end of each day, how well he sleeps depends on his P&L. Traders are wired to take risk—manageable risk. The best traders learn to harness this faculty to their benefit. Traders generate profits from two sources: mostly by making markets but occasionally by proprietary trading. As a market maker, the trader stands ready to buy or sell at the client's request and take out the bid/ask spread for his efforts. When a trader maintains a position and puts the firm's capital at risk, it is referred to as proprietary trading. At the core, the functions appear to be polar opposites, but at the margin, they overlap. In properly functioning markets the two cannot be separated.

Research's responsibility is to innovate and disseminate market information that provides a fair and consistent framework for analysis. Along with investment innovation, they develop valuation methodology, identify applications and attendant risks, explore market mispricing, introduce standard bench marks, discuss accounting and tax complexities, and independently determine value. Without regard to trading desks' positions, research should opine on where it sees value in the market. A trader's shortsighted view may tempt them to sway research. Yet most successful traders realize this causes market participants to lose confidence in the veracity of research; and they would lose the most from the misstep.

For a sales-person to be successful, it is imperative he or she possesses strong and current understanding of all three positions: trading, research, and sales. It is vital for a sales-person to understand the increasingly sophisticated securities and the attendant tax and accounting issues affecting his or her clients; to know the mathematical concepts behind valuation methodology and the attendant bond theory; and to be cognizant of valuation anomalies in the various markets, but not, of course, to the detail of the respective specialists. Executing this task requires constant, meaningful, and focused dialogue among the three to gather pieces of market intelligence that may prove valuable in formulating strategies for both the desk and the clients. It is important that in partnership with the desk, a sales-person is astute enough to ascertain when the customer is either a competitor or a partner in the trade, and when a trading desk is exceeding its limits. As a stakeholder—and preferably a shareholder in the partnership—it is incumbent upon sales to recognize and convey when one or the other is out of bounds.

Sales, trading, and research people are coordinated risk-takers tenaciously seeking irregularities to exploit in their respective markets. It should not surprise anyone that this balance is fragile. Fixed-income's profits come from the trading book, so traders are closest to the money, a fact that leads many inexperienced sales-people to conclude that the trading desk holds sway over them. Like a recent addition to the club, for a new sales-person there are elements of truth to the supposition. But when the process works best, it is a partnership.

The first time a sales-person approaches the desk for an offering (buy request) and the trader says, "The trade fits me, I don't want to lose the trade" and a second later the sales-person responds, "The best he's seeing away is par—match it and you're done," he's the man. But if the trader says, "The trade fits, don't fuck it up" and the sales-person comes back with, "Done away on a tie breaker," the sales-person is a schmuck. Few if any traders gave me the "don't fuck it up" line, probably more because of my wrestling skills than my perceived sales skills. There always was a "the strongest survive" atmosphere on Wall Street and maybe they feared I would take it literally. The thought makes me cringe.

The relative contribution of sales versus trading is not the important issue. Compensation committees should be organized and equipped to sort through the process. What's important is that the structure empowers the sales-person, as a stakeholder, to offset risk and research to maintain its independence. When the scale tilts to the trading desk, it invites excesses. Financial institutions may restrain risk by emphasizing to the sales force that the trading desk may have input into their compensation, but how well they manage the relationships and risk profile of the firm are measures that directly affect compensation.

Allowing a trader to run roughshod over a sales-person or researcher is untenable. Despite Salomon's reputation as a testosterone-driven trading floor, in the mid 1980s its position was that under no circumstance was it sales' and/or research's responsibility to bail out a trader's ill-conceived position. Sales-people were always encouraged to vent their concerns. Perhaps an example would be helpful.

The following episode involves what was at the time a recent mortgage market innovation: interest only (I/O) and principal only (P/O) STRIPs. As explained in Chapter Five, interest-only and principal-only STRIPS are created by dividing the monthly principal and interest cash flows from a mortgage security into two classes. The I/O class received a percentage of the interest payments and the P/O class received a percentage of the principal payments. In this case the percentage was 100 percent each of their respective monthly payments.

This was a first. Other firms dissected the monthly cash flows into various proportions but no one had divided them into virtually 100 percent I/O and 100 percent P/O. This attribute made the other structures obsolete. Clients could now reconstruct any coupon that fit their investment needs. By mixing with other I/O–P/O STRIPS or with pass-throughs, virtually any hybrid security could be constructed. This quickly became the new norm.[1]

I also explained in Chapter Five that Salomon's research noticed, the current prices of GNMA 11.5 percent I/Os and FNMA 9 percent P/Os were in disequilibrium and underestimated their true value. And that after visiting several accounts, Dick Jaegel from Salomon's asset/liability group and I found a fit.

What I did not mention was that when Salomon's research group began to reconstruct the respective I/O–P/O proportions to meet the account's duration, a problem emerged. Greg Hawkins, later with Long Term Capital, and Nathan Cornfeld, the I/O–P/O traders, balked at selling the GNMA 11.5 percent I/O without having a respective P/O buyer in place. Jaegel and I appealed to Mike Mortara, the head of mortgage trading. Unfortunately he sided with Hawkins and Cornfeld.

Our only avenue remaining was Lew Ranieri. Ranieri sided with Jaegel and me, clarified the rules of engagement, and directed Hawkins and Cornfeld to do the trade. Ranieri said something to the effect that it was not the sales-person's job to bail out the desk. If you make the offer, either find a buyer for the other side or figure out how to hedge it. Perhaps he used a few more choice words or even expletives as adjectives.

The system was in balance and it worked. Research's assessment of value was accurate, the I/O–P/O combination, when matched against the client's liability structure offered superior returns, and Salomon issued its first high coupon I/O–P/O, adding to the efficiency of the mortgage market. And the trading desk had no need to worry. They realized a requisite return for their market-making risk.

Unfortunately in the late 1980s the culture at Salomon began to change. As a Salomon associate said at the time, several events should have warned us that our sales, research, and trading balance was beginning to break down. Salomon's chairman and CEO John H. Gutfreund—armed with his corporate warfare experience acquired while wresting control of Salomon Brothers from Philipp Brothers—wanted no rivals for his sole control. A Salomon manager made the accusation that after installing himself as Salomon's sole leader, Gutfreund felt a need to neuter his competition, even at the expense of the firm.

At Gutfreund's urging, Salomon lost two of its key vice chairmen, Ranieri and Henry Kaufman. Ranieri was labeled a "restless innovator" and Kaufman a "risk-adverse researcher." Together they formed the internal conscience of Salomon's executive committee, but unfortunately they were deemed dispensable and forced out. No one was left to fight the internal war of restraint and a short time later John Meriwether negotiated an unqualified fixed percentage payout for the arbitrage desk. Kaufman's* and Ranieri's departure appeared to mark the end of a remarkable run for Salomon Brothers' mortgage department.

> Questions I'd like to ask **Henry Kaufman**: As a Lehman Director, did he ever sense Fuld was making the same mistake? And did he feel a tinge of déjà vu as Fuld made sure he maintained his tight hold on Lehman and weeded out any rivals?

After Ranieri's and Kaufman's exit, several key talented mortgage traders and researchers followed. Soon, Salomon's mortgage traders began to spread their expertise throughout Wall Street. Mortara joined Goldman Sachs and eventually became a partner. Andy Stone left Salomon to recreate a mortgage desk at Prudential. Lehman recruited Nathan Cornfeld to help them design their mortgage strategy. And Jeff Kronthal eventually went to Merrill Lynch, where he became a managing director and head of global principal investments. Also Marty Leibowitz , who was Salomon's director of global research and led its early efforts to bring sophisticated quantitative methods to fixed income markets, joined TIAA-CREF, where he eventually was named vice chairman and chief investment officer.

Salomon had a strong bench in mortgage trading, sales, and research; nonetheless the exodus was difficult to shrug off. Many of Salomon's mortgage department professionals who stayed were talented and tried to ignore the departures. Nonetheless, there was no denying that Salomon's mortgage trading desk was pressed to maintain its dominant position.

Subsequently, the relative status within the firm of the arbitrage desk increased.

Evidence that the arbitrage desk had cemented its position of importance at Salomon surfaced when Salomon agreed to a payout formula based on a percentage of the group's revenues. Under the guise that several key players threatened to depart after a highly profitable year, rumors quickly spread that Larry Hilibrand was paid $23 million. Most of Salomon's professionals expected the arbitrage desk to be paid handsomely. As a group, it provided substantial profits to the firm. Yet few felt that the amount would have been a specified percentage of one year's earnings without a cap or cost of risk-adjusted capital. When the rumor leaked, no one was aware of any other department at Salomon having such a plan.

With the firm supplying space, vital market information, essential models, and a substantial amount of extremely cheap capital; an unconditional 15 percent payout was viewed as excessive even by Wall Street's standards at the time. If a majority portion of their compensation had been retained and at risk along with the firm's capital for an extended period of time or until actually realized, a 15 percent payout over and above an agreed-to hurdle return would have seemed reasonable. Instead, it was the firm's capital at stake, and few were confident that management understood how much.

A Salomon trader aptly stated that it's more intellectually appealing to argue that if the arbitrage desk was truly confident in its ability to generate consistent above-market returns, it would have preferred its compensation to be retained within the capital pool at risk. In such a structure, the group's net worth would increase along with the earnings of the firm. What's more, the ability to retain key people would have improved as an increasing amount of their net worth was retained.

Many at the firm conjectured that had Ranieri and Kaufman still been vice chairmen, both would have vehemently opposed any such arrangement. Resentment began to stew among Salomon's employees. Some were more outspoken than others. One in particular was Paul Mozer. Mozer was at one time part of the arbitrage desk but now he was running the government desk; at the time of his appointment, this was viewed as a promotion.

Mozer was slight in stature and perceived by most as high-strung but abrasive by the rest. As a trader he was focused, capable, and composed even under intense stress. And, although most hated to admit its influence, his trading book, for which he was paid generously, was very profitable. Still he was not paid as much as Hilibrand.

Among other things, Mozer's responsibilities included bidding the U.S. Treasury auctions. Prior to the summer of 1990 Wall Street understood, via a "gentleman's agreement," that no bidder in any government-bond auction would exceed 35 percent. In the summer of 1990 the Treasury converted the gentleman's agreement into an official restriction. Mozer vehemently opposed the bid limits and was publicly critical of both the restriction and the deputy assistant secretary of federal finance, Michael Basham, who was responsible for the Treasury auctions. Within Salomon, it was common knowledge that Mozer battled with Basham and despised the auction limit. Because of the stir, we referred to it as the Mozer/Basham rule.

The details of the squeeze are not important. What is important begins in February 1991 at the government bond auction, where Mozer ignored the restriction and submitted a bid that exceeded the authorized limit. In addition to a 35 percent bid he placed on Salomon's behalf, Mozer submitted bids for 35 percent each in the names of S. G. Warburg, then one of the largest investment houses in the U.K., and Quantum Fund. Both were Salomon clients and neither gave Mozer authorization to bid on their behalf.

As a fellow sales-person bluntly remarked, it was sheer audacity. As if to flaunt his contempt, Mozer left no room for error. Either because he was caught up in his own self-interest or was so angry, he failed to take into account that one of the entities may submit a bid on their own. The smallest of bids by either party would expose his ruse. What arrogance!

My cohort was correct. Warburg submitted a relatively small order, revealing Mozer's attempt to manipulate the government bond auction. Following an investigation, Treasury officials notified Warburg of the infraction and as a clue to their suspicion copied Mozer. Mozer's only option was to notify Meriwether of the letter, but as later described to the employees, Mozer maintained that it was an isolated incidence, an aberration.

Equally puzzling was that after senior management Gutfreund, Strauss, and Meriwether became aware of the incident, they failed to grasp the gravity of the situation, to discipline Mozer, or to address the issue with the Treasury and/or the New York Federal Reserve. A few months later, after discovering that the infraction was not an isolated incident, Gutfreund notified the authorities. By then it was too late. Gutfreund, Strauss, and

Meriwether were forced to resign and Warren Buffett became interim chairman and overseer of the stakeholders' interest. As a major equity holder—and ironically, at the urging of Gutfreund to stave off a takeover attempt by Ron Perelman—Buffett was brought in to rescue the firm.

When word of the illegal bids first surfaced, most of the rank and file was shocked and baffled. Even those Mozer may have rankled did not contemplate that he would engage in illegal activities. As a Salomon researcher said, it unfortunately appeared that Mozer was not as principled as he was intelligent.

Over the next several months, the firm tried to right the ship and reconcile the fact that a manager of a trading desk could single-handedly jeopardize the entire franchise. Further examination of Mozer's bidding in government-bond auctions revealed a systematic practice of false bids. By year's end regulators had accused the firm of submitting, via Mozer, false bids in the two years leading up to the May 1991 auction.

Customer trust was compromised and defections were widespread. The risk of a panic and a massive sell-off of Salomon's stock was a real threat. Loyal customers were dismayed. Either out of fear that Congress might press regulators to close Salomon or because of its inability to fund itself, clients defected. As Salomon employees we lamented that the damage a single person's transgressions could do to a firm's reputation, was frightening.

Restoring Salomon's reputation was urgent. Buffett's unique skills were critical to Salomon's survival; his successful navigation through congressional hearings rescued Salomon from possible criminal charges, and failure. After the Treasury banned Salomon from bidding in government bond auctions, Buffett convinced policymakers that a ban would force Salomon into bankruptcy with potential worldwide consequences for the financial system. Treasury rescinded the ban and the Federal Reserve announced its plan to retain Salomon as a primary dealer. Salomon did not go unscathed, however. It paid a $290 million fine, the largest ever levied against an investment bank at the time. A hefty cost for misguided confidence!

The Myron Scholes Irony

But for the Mozer debacle, the following event most likely would not have occurred. During the turmoil that fall, I was in Salomon's New York office with a customer. As we sat on the mortgage trading desk conversing with one of the traders, someone from the arbitrage desk yelled over, "Stan,

Myron Scholes is on line three for you." Scholes was one of Salomon's mild-mannered finance professors turned Wall Street rocket scientist. He is a Nobel laureate in economic science and along with Fischer Black, then employed by Goldman Sachs, co-originated the Black–Scholes options pricing model, a formula they derived to accurately calculate the price of options. The standard is still in use today.

I was aware that Myron Scholes was a special consultant to the office of the chairman at Salomon but could not imagine why one of the more brilliant minds in finance wanted to speak with me. The customer seemed astonished. I turned to him and said, "Not again—when is he going to stop pestering me with these questions?" and quickly picked up the phone.

Our discussion revolved around an arcane class of a collateralized mortgage obligation (CMO) referred to as a residual. As you may recall from Chapter Five, a CMO bundles mortgage loans and issues a mortgage-backed security. The CMO servicer collects the monthly principal and interest (P&I) payments and then directs the cash flows—not pro-rata, but in a rule-based sequence—to create different classes of securities. By prioritizing the cash flows into consecutive classes, a CMO creates tranches (another term for class) with various maturities, coupons, and risk profiles. The issuer's main rationale is to profit by capturing the differential between the cash-flow yield of the mortgages contained in the deal and the weighted-average cost of the series of classes. The residual owner was last in line and received whatever was remaining between the cash flow from the mortgage collateral and the cash flow used to fund the serial classes of the CMO.

If you think about it, a pattern emerges. The weighted-average cost of the serial classes of the CMO increases through time while the mortgage collateral remains constant. This dynamic aspect has tax implications for the residual owner. In the early years of the CMO the residual owner's taxable income generally exceeds the accounting income and in the later years the accounting income is greater. The residual owner will recognize taxable income quicker than accounting income. In Wall Street jargon it is appropriately referred to as "phantom income." Generally speaking, this is income that does not generate cash flow but is reportable for tax purposes.[2]

In 1986, REMIC provisions were authorized as part of a tax reform bill. These changes removed certain constraints in the existing tax laws. The removal of these restraints in the legislation and some Wall Street structuring wizardry created a new class of equity interest—a sort of residual on steroids. The Wall Street quants anointed the "noneconomic residual" with a fitting acronym: NERD.

Owners of NERDs generally receive no cash flows but are responsible for the tax liabilities created in the structure: phantom income. A REMIC modeler cleverly described phantom income as "A pernicious byproduct that because of its timing disparity between the reporting of income and expense produces taxable income, yet no cash flows."[3]

As one may surmise, the homeowner's option to prepay magnifies the effect of phantom income. This is where Myron Scholes's expertise came into the discussion. Besides being the world authority on options, Scholes has substantial tax knowledge. Later I discovered Scholes's passion for minimizing taxes. As a researcher once remarked, Scholes viewed the tax code as a fiendish Sudoko puzzle. His challenge: to sort through the complex provisions of the tax code and uncover ingenious or creative strategies to maximize after-tax returns.

Scholes's grasp of the arcane relationship between the prepayment option and attendant tax implication make him uniquely qualified to develop a model to determine the option-tax adjusted spread of residuals. And that is exactly what he planned on doing. What did I bring to the discussion?

At the time I had several accounts that were active in residuals. I placed many of the firm's residuals, so Salomon's arbitrage desk suggested Scholes might want to contact me. He was interested in the particular tax circumstances that made residuals appealing to my accounts. I told him that over time, the federal tax code provided exceptions to certain categories of residual owners—and in some cases state and local taxes as well. I suggested that, as a general rule, net operating losses (NOLs) could not be utilized to offset phantom income but that under a few obscure circumstances some owners were exempt from this restriction.

A unique treatment for insurance companies with assets below a set limit seemed particularly to pique his interest. He said, "I am not aware of any such preferential tax treatment, I will get back to you." By now, of course my customer had figured out the jest. As soon as I hung up the phone, he appropriately said, "You jackass."

A few weeks later, Scholes called me in Atlanta confirming that indeed the current tax code provided an exception for certain small insurance companies. Curious, I inquired, "Why are you working on such an insignificant issue? After all, deriving an elegant mathematical formula that completes the puzzle of option pricing seems far more exciting." He answered, "I was retained as a special consultant by the office of the chairman, John Gutfreund, in an attempt to assign the appropriate cost of capital for the various divisions within Salomon Brothers. With John Gutfreund's departure, I am attempting to constructively use my expertise during my tenure at Salomon."

On occasion, especially in tumultuous markets, a thought occurs to me: What impact on the global financial markets might Myron Scholes have had had he successfully completed the appropriate "cost of capital" conundrum among the various divisions of an investment bank? We will come back to this later.

Final wrestle-offs to make the 1976 Olympic Team against Lee Kemp, an eventual 3 time World Champion

1977 World Championships in Lausanne, Switzerland: Hand raised in victory over Monsoor Barzegar, Olympic silver medalist and 1973 World Champion of Iran

1977 World Championships' award podium: Left–Barzegar, Iran; Center–Stan Dziedzic, USA; Right–Nanev, Bulgaria

Interview with ABC sports following 1977 World Championships

White House reception with President and Rosalynn Carter following the 1980 Olympic boycott: Lee Allen shaking President's hand, President Carter, Rosalynn, Dziedzic, Gable, and Baughman

1999 New York Athletic Club Hall of Fame induction with my wife Arlene and friend Paul Kieblesz

Atlanta managing director's antique double-front desk originally used by Henry and Emanuel Lehman in their Montgomery, Alabama office.

Stan Dziedzic
OLYMPIAN

1976 Olympic Games in Montreal: Dziedzic en route to victory over two-time world champion, Ashuraliev of the USSR

8

TRANSFER TO LEHMAN BROTHERS

"Change is hard because people overestimate the value of what they have—and underestimate the value of what they may gain by giving that up." James Belasco and Ralph Strayer, Flight of the Buffalo (1994)

The fall of 1991 was a tumultuous time at Salomon Brothers. The once venerable firm was embattled and undergoing a financial contraction. The SEC investigation of Paul Mozer for violation of Treasury bond market rules; the subsequent resignation of CEO John Gutfreund, President Thomas Strauss, and J. M. Meriwether; and the congressional hearings were more than your normal distractions. Rival dealers who lost money in the "Mozer squeeze"* did not, as one would expect, take it lying down. An associate lamented that they are both the victims and stand to gain the most from crippling Salomon.

The lawsuits began to mount and the publicity was particularly negative. Both Moody's and S&P downgraded Salomon's debt rating, which increased its borrowing costs and limited its ability to function effectively in several key markets. Confidence in Salomon was eroding, and its future relied heavily on new (although interim) chairman Warren E. Buffett's unique ability to restore its reputation and navigate through Congressional hearings as well as the court of public opinion. A few years earlier Buffett had acquired a 12 percent stake in Salomon in order to help fend off a takeover move by Ronald Perelman, ironically at John Gutfreund's request.

Whenever possible, most of us at the firm watched Buffett's testimony on C-SPAN via our internal processor, which was high-tech for the day (computers and the internet were not yet common). The congressional panel was uncharacteristically respectful toward Buffett. The inflammatory statements so common in congressional hearings seemed noticeably muted. As one would expect, Buffett was contrite and admitted that Salomon's senior management, especially Paul Mozer, had erred.

Buffett's opening remarks before the September 4th, 1991 House of Representatives subcommittee captured the essence:

> **"Mr. Chairman, I thank you for the opportunity to appear before this subcommittee. I would like to start by apologizing for the acts that have brought us here. The nation has a right to expect its rules and laws to be obeyed. And at Salomon, certain of these were broken. Almost all of Salomon's eight thousand employees regret this as deeply as I do. And I apologize on their behalf as well as mine.**
>
> **My job is to deal with both the past and the future. The past actions of Salomon are presently causing eight thousand employees and their families to bear a stain. Virtually all of these employees are hardworking, able and honest ...."**[1]

Nonetheless, it was both the panel's and the press's duty to get answers, especially regarding the role of what they rightly characterized as the lavish bonus structure. I recall one of Buffett's responses when queried about Larry Hilibrand's extraordinary $23 million bonus. Buffett dodged a direct answer by suggesting a baseball comparison. In his folksy, Will Rogers-like style, the "Sage of Omaha," as Salomon employees referred to him, described Hilibrand as the closest thing Salomon had to a .400 hitter.

Most Salomon professionals were keenly aware that Buffett himself questioned the size of Hilibrand's compensation package, and that posing a balanced response to such inquiries would be difficult for him. Though Buffett planned to overhaul Salomon's employees' pay structure, he was wise enough to know he needed to retain flexibility to determine compensation if he were to maintain the franchise value of Salomon—and his investment.

About the same time, Lehman approached me to ask if I would be willing to explore the possibility of moving to its Atlanta office as senior mortgage salesman. Given the circumstances, many Wall Street firms were seizing upon the weakened morale within Salomon. Even Salomon's most committed workers were embarrassed and dismayed by the deportment of Paul Mozer and the inexcusable decisions made by top management. As a cohort wisely noted, "How can the actions of so few taint so many? It's becoming increasingly more difficult to defend."

What once was perceived as a team had become an amalgam of individual fiefdoms, rife with deception, conflict, and discontent. The chemistry created by assembling a uniquely talented group of people with mutual respect for one another, had evaporated. The atmosphere of energy and optimism had grown destructive. The whole episode posed an interesting lesson: No matter how difficult it is to build, the structure of an investment bank is fragile and depends on the confidence of its customers.

Ray Struble, who managed Lehman's Atlanta office, was Lehman's main spokesman in the transition process. He started in Lehman's Boston office in 1982. He was candid regarding both the firm and himself. Struble was a recovering alcoholic and openly gay, a rarity on Wall Street at the time. He was unpretentious, friendly, well prepared, and comfortable with himself. Struble earlier had attended Catholic seminary and reconciled any conflict he may have had with his devout religious beliefs. He seemed devoted to Lehman and spoke proudly of its tolerant culture.

In our first meeting I needed to be certain not to waste anyone's time. I wanted Struble to be aware of the previous conversations I had had with Lehman. I told him that a few years ago Steve (Stephen) M. Lessing, then head of mortgage sales at Lehman, had convinced me to move to Lehman. After agreeing to resign from Salomon, I changed my mind and at the last minute decided to stay. The strong business ties I had built within Salomon, the knowledge of how to bring the firm's resources to customers, and my allegiance to Salomon for the invaluable training provided me, made it too difficult to leave.

Struble indicated that he was fully apprised of the situation; Lessing, now global head of fixed income sales and research, was supportive. Struble assured me, "Some trepidation is expected. But there's no denying the treasury scandal has changed Salomon. It's my job in the vetting process to demonstrate that Shearson Lehman more than ever is committed to building the preeminent fixed income franchise on Wall Street." At the same time, he was equally responsible to determine if I would fit on their team. This was a timely and refreshing thought, with Salomon's team concept in shambles.

Struble began with a more detailed history of Lehman than I wanted to hear. With seemingly genuine pride and a storybook cadence he emphasized that Lehman was a legendary firm with roots dating back to the pre–Civil War south. In 1844, the Lehman patriarch Henry was part of a vast wave of German immigrants searching for a better life in America. He emigrated to a small Jewish community in Montgomery, Alabama, and opened a general merchandise establishment catering to the nearby cotton farmers. When his two brothers, Emanuel and Mayer, joined Henry in 1850, they aptly named the business Lehman Brothers. Shortly after its founding, Lehman expanded to commodities brokering. In 1858, in what proved to be a prescient move, Lehman opened a New York office.

Struble paused and then continued, "And now being a resident of Atlanta, I have a greater appreciation that because of Lehman's presence in Montgomery, it did not avoid the misfortunes of the Civil War." He said that Lehman's New York office allowed them to rebuild and concentrate its operations there. Leveraging its commodities expertise, Lehman spearheaded and helped found the New York Cotton Exchange in 1870. This gave Lehman a permanent presence in the New York financial community. A few years later Lehman became a member of the New York Stock Exchange, marking its emergence from commodities broker to investment bank.[2]

I indulged Struble as he continued the chronology. "Lehman began to reinvent itself as a financial firm, expanded into trading, financial advising, and international investment banking. Lehman played an instrumental role in funding emerging industries. It underwrote, either solely or jointly, some of industry's most famous names: Sears, Roebuck, RCA, Paramount Pictures, and 20th Century Fox, to name a few. Did you know Lehman was among the earliest firms to deploy private placements during the Depression?" he asked. Answering his own question, he said, "Though they are commonplace today, at the time private placements were very innovative. Without private placements many of the blue-chip borrowers might never have been able to raise capital in the thirties."

Despite Struble's obvious enthusiasm and sense of pride, I interrupted him. "How did Lehman get to where they are today?"

"I am getting there, be patient," he responded. He pointed out that after merging with Kuhn, Loeb & Co. in the late 1970sLehman became the fourth-largest U.S. investment bank behind Salomon Brothers, Goldman Sachs, and First Boston. The merger increased Lehman's international stature and with it expanded its financial advisory efforts both domestically and internationally. Lehman acted as an advisor on several noted cross-border transactions; namely Chrysler-American Motors, Bendix-Allied and General Foods-Philip Morris.[3]

As Struble began to describe Lehman's more troubled period his enthusiasm began to wane. His mood turned somewhat somber as he described how in the mid 1980s Lehman began to unravel. "Lehman developed a highly competitive internal environment, which finally grew dysfunctional. A war of stereotypes developed between banking and trading. Those of us who experienced the battle refer to it as the 'Great War of '83.'" He continued, "These stereotypes permeated the firm all the way to the co-CEOs: Peter G. Peterson, a former secretary of commerce and investment banker, and Lewis Glucksman, a consummate trader. Though successful in their respective areas, both failed to create an environment of teamwork either in their individual office or across the firm. A power struggle between the firm's investment bankers and traders ultimately resulted in Lehman being acquired by American Express."

Struble closed solemnly, "In 1984 Lehman, once the longest perpetually surviving investment bank, succumbed." American Express combined Lehman's investment bank and institutional sales with Shearson, known primarily for its retail sales expertise. A later acquisition of E. F. Hutton & Co. formed Shearson Lehman Hutton, an American Express company.[4]

At one point Struble began to describe the Lehman families' private art collections and business aristocracy history. I told him that a personal friend, Henry (Hank) Goldman had fully apprised me of the Rembrandts, Matisses, and other old masters that had at one time decorated the Lehman offices and were now displayed in the Robert Lehman Wing of New York's Metropolitan Museum of Art. Hank had often spoken of his father's friendship with Bobbie Lehman. Hank said that his father described Bobbie as "demanding" but emphasized that he was both a "man of stature and an uncanny judge of talent"—traits I would later find lacking in Dick Fuld. But now it was more important for me to acquire information about Lehman's current mortgage efforts.

Struble agreed that it was time to get down to business, "Today we have the full support both financially and conceptually of American Express's management. They share our goal of rebuilding a preeminent investment bank. And the mortgage department is one of the cornerstones of that strategy."

Struble was right. Lehman's trading desks had some talent and in several areas were more developed than Salomon. Michael Gelband, then head of the structured product desk, had hired several experienced traders from around Wall Street; among them were Alan Galishoff and William Mok. Wes Edens, founding principal, chairman, and CEO of Fortress Investment Group LLC., was then a managing director and ran Lehman's mortgage trading area. Michael Mazzei and Mark Walsh were responsible for the commercial mortgage desk, a new yet growing area. Mazzei directed the trading while Walsh handled the acquisitions.

The commercial real estate group's most noted transaction was an early 1990s partnership with Westinghouse Electric Corporation. The partnership was 51 percent owned by Lehman. It purchased, at a significant discount, a portfolio of commercial property loans originated by Westinghouse Credit Corporation, a Westinghouse Electric subsidiary. As Edens described the strategy in our first meeting, "The intention was an expeditious liquidation through securitization and other accelerated disposition avenues." In the process Lehman hoped to earn a generous profit and gain valuable commercial real estate experience in what Lehman viewed as the next burgeoning segment of the mortgage market.

Struble told a great story of what he viewed as the ongoing saga of Lehman's rebirth. Like a classic folk tale, Struble's accounts of Lehman's reemergence as a preeminent investment bank were graced with fairy-tale endings. He painted a colorful picture of what Lehman had learned from the past so as to better reorganize under a strong team concept. The history of internal feuding between banking and capital markets gave the impression of being the wakeup call Lehman's management needed. In order to succeed as a full service investment bank, it was necessary to forge a culture of teamwork. Increasingly I became more comfortable with Lehman's culture, personnel, and operating style.

Some of Struble's recounting of Lehman's history was instructive. It helped me develop a more informed view of how previous events and decisions influenced Lehman's current culture. I learned how lessons from past successes and failures seemed to provide Lehman with vital information to address its current problems. Nonetheless, the final decision was gut-wrenching.

That may sound a bit harsh to the reader—at the time; it did to me, too. As I tossed during sleepless nights, I remember thinking, "Why am I torturing myself about this decision?" Lehman's two-year offer included a significant increase in compensation which would have taken me a lifetime to earn as a coach and teacher. On the other hand, if I chose to stay at Salomon Brothers, I might have been paid less (but still handsomely) for my efforts and I already knew how to navigate the firm in order to meet my customers' needs. Why was I anguishing over a decision when either outcome was attractive?

Ralph Waldo Emerson eloquently captured the essence of my anguish in numerous lectures when he proposed: "One thing is forever good; that one thing is success."[5] And I understand and believe the concept. After graduating from college I devoted the next five years of my life to winning a wrestling gold medal, not solid gold, just gold plated—a coveted, not valuable precious metal.

The sport of wrestling is not a precision or garden-variety sport. It demands as much physical preparation, if not more, than any other Olympic sport. In a typical two-hour practice at the Olympic training camp, most of the team would lose roughly 8 percent of their body weight. And there were two practices a day, plus individual workouts. Imagine a 400-pound *Biggest Loser* contestant losing sixty-four pounds, not after two months in a controlled, structured environment, but just from a couple of two-hour practices where no one cries after being weighed!

Not that any sane person would suggest such a punishing exercise regime for the average person, especially *Biggest Loser's* Dr. Rob Huizenga, himself an NCAA All-American wrestler at the University of Michigan. It takes years of progressively pushing to new horizons for Olympic-level wrestlers to master exhaustion at that capacity.

Wrestling as a competition weighs relative performance, not absolute performance. It is not how high, how far, or how fast, but how much better you are than your opponent. As in most highly competitive international contests, there are occasional moral transgressions such as a corrupt official selling his ability to influence the match outcome, or even the desperate wrestler who is willing to trade his performance for money. But in almost all cases, if a wrestler loses he has no one to blame but himself. And all of this for a medal: success!

In Olympic wrestling there is neither fame nor money, just the satisfaction that accompanies accomplishment. Fortunately or unfortunately, on Wall Street the metric of success is not a monetarily insignificant gold medal, it is compensation. In an effective meritocracy, compensation takes care of itself. Investment banking is not the only career where compensation is correlated with creating value. Steve Lessing summed it up effectively. "If personal monetary gains are distasteful, no need to worry, there are more than enough worthy charities willing to put it to good use. Contrary to popular opinion, many successful investment bankers are quite altruistic."

Most of us did not delude ourselves; we understood that by any absolute measure, Wall Street professionals were egregiously overpaid, but the focus was more on how much we were paid relative to our peers, not on absolute levels. Emerson's quote was germane. Just like wrestling, if one were going to succeed, he better choose his coach, workout partners, and training conditions wisely. So I had to ask myself: Did Lehman provide a structure where I could succeed? Was Lehman committed to building a preeminent investment bank? Given my skills, could I play a meaningful role and flourish in the environment?

After concluding that Lehman was committed to building a world-class investment bank and that the fixed-income department was going to be the cornerstone of that effort, I was convinced. I believed, not exactly innocently, that the experience had left Fuld and his merry men with the wherewithal to lead Lehman to its destined greatness. In January 1992 I left Salomon Brothers for the challenge of joining Lehman's team.

* See earlier discussions regarding Salomon's illegal bidding in government-bond auctions

9

LEHMAN AS A STAND–ALONE

"To see what is in front of one's nose needs a constant struggle." George Orwell

When I first arrived, I found that its history of internal strife and its subsequent acquisition in 1984 by American Express had put Lehman behind some of its major competitors. The primary measure for Shearson Lehman was revenue as opposed to productivity. Higher revenues resulted in additional compensation dollars for Lehman employees. Sales credits, supposedly a measure of relative contribution, were mostly standard, and any differentiation among the quality of sales credits was left to the subjective judgment of sales management—a practice Wall Street continues to downplay. At that time Salomon had a more advanced system of recognizing relative contributions by its employees. In both cases there were more elements of self-promotion than Wall Street admits or that one would expect in a meritocracy. American Express's arrangement, however, seemed particularly disjointed.

In 1993 the landscape changed. American Express, Inc., under newly appointed CEO Harvey Golub, began to shed noncore businesses. It first sold the Shearson's asset management and retail brokerage business to Primerica. At the same time, it began to organize Lehman Brothers Kuhn Loeb for a divestiture. Dick Fuld and J. Tomilson Hill were co-presidents. Perhaps because his fixed-income division made most of the money—but more likely, as rumor has it, because Hill challenged Golub in earlier disputes—Fuld was chosen as the sole leader. Soon, the responsibility of restoring Lehman to its former self would rest with Fuld and his loyal acolytes.

In 1994 American Express invested roughly $1.1 billion, and spun off the Lehman Brothers Kuhn Loeb division in an initial public offering. The $1.1 billion injection was meant to ensure that Lehman as a stand–alone investment bank was viable and had sufficient capital to maintain a single A credit rating. At the time, a single A rating was the minimum necessary to function properly within the credit-sensitive areas of fixed income. American Express negotiated for Lehman to purchase space in the American Express Tower at One World Financial Center and to receive a sizable percentage of Lehman's profits above a certain target level for a stated period, in return for the capital. One thing the reader can be sure of: Lehman was keenly aware of the end date for this profit-sharing arrangement.[1]

The limited capital put Lehman at a disadvantage compared to its more capitalized competition, especially at the end of each quarter when its trading desks scrambled to shed assets in order to meet balance-sheet bench marks. Lehman was not the only Wall Street firm to boost its leverage ratio* *intra* reporting periods and then "manage" the size of its balance sheet down just before filing to the public. The practice was common and within standard accounting practice. Yet for the foot soldiers, Lehman seemed to be the poster child of balance sheet management and the quarterly exercise was an unwanted diversion. As Lehman's capital grew, however, window dressing, as the sales force dubbed it, became less fashionable and was no longer a regular part of Lehman's quarter-end routine.

Despite initial struggles, the capital injection proved sufficient to build a franchise, and few complained. The internal mantra was that the dream had become reality. Lehman was free from the bondage of American Express and controlled its own destiny. The newly formed Lehman Brothers Holdings, Inc. had rid itself, apparently with egos intact, of American Express. Lehman, as it was called, was reborn and its modern era had begun—a rebirth that many in the firm only dreamed would happen.

The "Lehmanites" who had worked both in the independent structure and as a vassal of American Express clearly preferred Lehman as a stand–alone. On the day of closing, every employee received a commemorative t-shirt and the fortunate among us received a portion of the initial shares to be considered "part of something special—'One Firm' Lehman." With the reincarnation, however, came new responsibilities.

Some of Lehman's warts, hidden during the bondage, began to surface. All of a sudden the kinder, gentler Lehman was unshackled from American Express and as a pay-for-performance entity had to learn how to measure performance. There was a clear mandate for a more effective corporate governance and performance evaluation framework. The stakeholder's measure of success was not simply revenue but productivity or "return on equity"**. The competency bar would be raised and the bloated system—including many friends, cousins, and nephews—needed to be trimmed.

In Lehman's fixed-income department, the original responsibility for delivering a cohesive effort rested mostly with Stephen M. Lessing and Joseph M. Gregory, both Lehmanites and part of a close-knit, ruling-elite group who in less kind terms were dubbed the "Long Island Mafia." Lessing, the lesser in the powerful partnership, joined Lehman in 1980 while Gregory had started in 1974.

As partners responsible for Lehman's fixed income department, Steve Lessing and Joe Gregory shared some common traits: both were energetic, optimistic, and passionate—not revered—leaders in their respective roles. Lessing was a dispatcher who thought in relationships, not numbers. His ability to identify sales talent and his more affable nature made him well-suited to be the firm's representative to the clients and cheerleader to the sales force. On the other hand, Gregory's strong sense of self and his tenacity allowed him to gain the attention (and some might say, fear) of the trading desks.

Gregory's and Lessing's critics often portrayed them as less than astute regarding the modern, more complex financial markets. Also, Gregory was particularly quick to pounce on anyone he viewed as an adversary. Neither accusation was completely inaccurate. Like many if not most of the ruling elite on Wall Street, Lessing and Gregory were unschooled and lacked experience in the rapidly expanding securitization process and in the over-the-counter derivatives market. Both portrayed the image that they did not have the time for such minutiae. Whether the reason was time or intellectual capacity, it made them particularly vulnerable to criticism among the troops.

Likewise, nothing would seat you as squarely in the cross-hairs or elicit a more fervent response from Gregory than what he viewed as not being "on board" or in placing Lehman's brand at risk. Also, it was an era when a sophomoric notion of a ruthless management mentality prevailed—spawned at least in part by the media's "Masters of the Universe" depiction of Wall Street. And Gregory thrived in playing the role, especially if he viewed you as a threat. After sorting through the rubble later, it remains a matter of opinion when Gregory acted like a henchman or when he was a responsible partner in building the franchise. Most able mercenaries capable of advancing Lehman's franchise had nothing to fear from Gregory. But any Lehmanite with ambitions of supplanting Gregory ought to beware.

Lessing and Gregory had grown up at Lehman and conveyed the impression that they were committed to excellence and intensely loyal to what they would characteristically call "the franchise." Everyone was part of something special and had to be on the team—"One Firm." At the time, both guarded Lehman's reputation as much as its earnings and often echoed, "integrity, communication, and teamwork are nonnegotiable values at Lehman." Lessing and Gregory understood well the need for harmony between sales and trading. If Lehman were to be a viable investment bank and manage risk effectively, input was welcome, encouraged, and in many cases needed.

Lehman had neither a sophisticated training program nor a stable of loyal alumni. Instead, it had in place misdirected incentives, and it tolerated far too much nepotistic hiring, a practice which resulted in a somewhat bloated infrastructure. This lack of an advanced training program to indoctrinate and educate new employees, and few faithful alumni to serve as an adjunct source of new business made Lehman's task of building a world-class investment bank a challenge. It would be like trying to develop a major league baseball team without a mature scouting or farm system.

In this situation, one had better be good at identifying and poaching talent from the competition. Lessing and Gregory were effective judges of expertise, and with promises of guarantees were at first successful in luring talent from other firms. Regrettably, as they jockeyed for position, their commitment to excellence and to the firm gave way to installing loyal acolytes. In the end, Gregory and Lessing joined Lehman's sycophantic royalty and appeared more loyal to Fuld than to "the franchise." As the remnants of the Long Island mafia succumbed, "One Firm" eventually morphed to "Our Firm."

During most of the early rebuilding of Lehman's fixed-income department Jeffery Vanderbeek, currently chairman and largest shareholder of the NHL's New Jersey Devils and at that time global head of fixed income, commanded its risk management. Vanderbeek, not a Lehmanite, joined the firm from Donaldson, Lufkin & Jenrette (DLJ) in 1984 as a managing director and COO of central funding. Following his central funding duties, Vanderbeek was promoted to COO of the fixed-income derivatives division, which supplied him with invaluable experience in the arcane world of derivatives.[2]

Energetic, confident, and demanding, he brought candor and refreshing debate to the fixed-income division. Vanderbeek was stocky and had played football at a small college, though my sense was that he longed to have had the opportunity to test his mettle at a larger Division I program—if only he had been bigger.

Vanderbeek believed a management practice that incorporated a sports-like competitive structure, best enhanced performance. His contention was that the bottom five percent was best persuaded to pursue a career in another industry or with a competitor. Despite Vanderbeek's high-pressured style, never were the relationships of Lehman's customers compromised. He listened to people and what he didn't understand, he learned. Repeatedly Vanderbeek reminded his underlings, "Don't tell me what you think I want to hear; tell me what you really think. The truth, even if ugly, is invaluable. Without it I can't make good decisions." It wasn't that he just routinely took your advice, but the debate provided him the requisite information to make informed decisions.

When a disagreement between sales and trading arose, Vanderbeek did not shy away and most often instructed us to "Work it out between you and we shall discuss it at the next meeting." The serious discussions somehow helped dispel misinformation and assisted in identifying opportunities, attributing performance, and uncovering risks. Vanderbeek understood that an open-minded culture that fostered debate created a healthy environment in which to manage risk and build a franchise.

An anecdote may be instructive of Vanderbeek's management style and approach to the business. Adams, Viner, Mosler (AVM) an investment advisor based in Boca Raton, had an offshore fund, III Offshore Advisors (called III or III Advisors), an active worldwide money manager known for their innovation and long-term superior returns.[3] III was a global account with sales coverage in several of Lehman's offices including Atlanta, New York, London, and Tokyo. I was assigned to cover their global mortgage arbitrage group run by Ivan J. Ross and Donald S. Uderitz in AVM's Boca Raton headquarters.

Ross's group capitalized primarily on variations in the option-adjusted spreads (OAS) among the various GNMA, FNMA, and FHLMC coupons. Simply speaking, the OAS is the net expected yield advantage over the corresponding federal government bond, adjusted for the vagaries in prepayment rates. Ross and his talented group—whom I counted as friends—had a proprietary OAS model. Don Uderitz concentrated on bond structures and arbitrage opportunities resulting from abnormalities in the relative pricing of the multiple classes. Since I was the office manager of the Atlanta office and sales coverage for Lehman's southeast region, overall client relationship responsibilities rested with me.

Early in Vanderbeek's tenure there was a trade dispute with III, not emanating from Atlanta but from a trade facilitated out of Lehman's Asian office in the Japanese government bond (JGB) market. Nonetheless, damage control and resolving the issue were up to me. Without experience in the JGB market or the transaction in question, the learning curve was steep. As it was described, the system to borrow bonds in Japan relative to the U.S. Treasury market was less advanced. But more important, the JGB market was a "no fail" market. This meant failure to deliver JGBs as promised held the risk of serious sanctions—a risk apparently no one wanted to test.

Warren Mosler, a founding partner of III, pointed out that their trading desk had repeatedly warned Lehman's Tokyo office that the reaction of the repo markets signaled the development of a shortage of the specific JGB in question. If Lehman was short, the advice was, "cover your short." Lehman's traders in Tokyo ignored the warnings, and as the settlement date approached were having a difficult time acquiring sufficient bonds to deliver against the short. As settlement approached, the shortage of the specific JGB pushed the price to levels beyond any semblance of relative value. A game of "chicken" ensued. Lehman's trading desk signaled to III Advisors that they planned to fail.

Mosler and Cliff Viner, AVM's partner in charge of the overseas markets, felt allowing Lehman's threatened failure to deliver to occur was not prudent. The costs, distractions, and uncertainty of arbitrating in front of the Bank of Japan (BOJ) were not worth the potential reward. III blinked and closed out the shorts without any premium. The outcome: from then on no one at AVM, III Offshore Advisors, or affiliates was to do business with Lehman.

Lehman's version differed slightly. Lehman's Tokyo trading desk, headed by Mike Gelband, viewed III's backing down as an indication of culpability. The trading desk contended that III caused the shortage by their excessive concentration in the specific JGB, something Lehman's Tokyo desk referred to as a "squeeze" and maintained that it was against the spirit of market protocol. Lehman's trading desk felt strongly that Lehman had no obligation to pay the excessive premium for the JGB. The Tokyo traders further noted that, technically, the trade was executed off-shore, giving Lehman possible relief from the "no fail" rule and any sanctions.

For those two reasons, Lehman's Tokyo office was willing to go in front of the BOJ for a ruling on the issue. On internal calls describing the details, Thomas A. Russo, Lehman's chief legal officer, consistently handicapped the outcome of any hearing at better than 80 percent in Lehman's favor. Assuming Russo's assessment was dependable, for the next few months Mosler and I debated the merits of the issue virtually every day. After these discussions, Ross, Uderitz, and I would lament that we were the only ones suffering, and yet we had nothing to do with the trade.

Mosler and I eventually reached an impasse. Despite the insistence of Lehman's trading desk's vaunted position, it became clear that the issue could not be resolved unless the debate was expanded. The contention that Lehman would receive consideration from the Bank of Japan because the trade originated offshore was weak. Likewise, III's warnings to cover any short were only deceptively attractive.

The core argument centered on the assertion that III's concentration in the specific JGB violated the spirit of the rule, and that therefore the BOJ would waive the no-fail restriction and admonish III Offshore Advisors for their excessive concentration. As I indicated to Vanderbeek, it was Russo's task to convince Mosler that the probability of the trading desk's argument prevailing was much stronger than III's assertion. Vanderbeek agreed and instructed me to organize a conference call between Russo and Mosler.

The call could not be arranged quickly enough. Mosler, philosophical, polite, soft-spoken, and uncommonly composed, was the antithesis of the typical Wall Street trader. On occasion Mosler could be eccentric, yet he was very bright and always understood the nuances of an issue. Likewise, Russo conveyed confidence in his assertion of Lehman's position and was well versed in the technicalities of the Japanese bond market. When I scheduled the call, I anticipated a spirited exchange with cogent reasoning and earnest debate, but I was disappointed; the call was relatively brief.

After exchanging some informalities and brief descriptions of their respective roles within the firms, Mosler asked Russo a pointed question: "What do you think the odds were of your argument persuading the BOJ to abandon the no-fail policy?" Russo deftly danced around and argued the premise of the firm's trading desk's position, trying to avoid a direct answer. Mosler pressed, "What percentage?"

Russo hesitated, and then reluctantly said, "Fifty-fifty."

I could not believe it. For a moment I was speechless as I remembered his previous confident assessment of a better than 80 percent chance of success. I said, "Warren, we will get back to you shortly."

While I sat at my desk, fuming about how I had been hung out to dry, my memory drifted to an earlier wrestling experience, one that required serious self-restraint. Some may think that wrestling and restraint are incompatible. Not so! The essential mission in wrestling is to dominate your opponent without injuring him. It is about refining techniques, strategies, and mastering exhaustion; it is not about injuring someone. Restraint is the primary difference that separates wrestling from ultimate fighting. Think intelligent self-interest versus untrammeled greed.

The following incident exemplifies this kind of extraordinary self-control. Some background first: In the fall of 1979, angered by President Carter's decision to allow the deposed Shah of Iran into the United States for medical treatment, thousands of Iranians protested in front of the Embassy in Tehran. A militant Islamist group broke from the demonstration, stormed the United States Embassy, and took more than sixty Americans hostage.[4]

A few months later, in February 1980, the United States freestyle wrestling team traveled to the USSR to participate in the annual Tbilisi tournament in the Soviet Republic of Georgia, and I was the coach. We arrived in Moscow on February 21, one day past the ultimatum date of another of President Carter's foreign policy initiatives. Earlier, in response to the Soviet Union's military intrusion into Afghanistan, President Carter had promised that if the Soviet army did not withdraw from Afghanistan by February 20, 1980, the United States team would boycott the 1980 Olympic Games scheduled in Moscow.

While we were en route to Moscow, President Carter, in his state of the union speech, made it crystal clear that this was no idle threat. Until the president's ultimatum of 20 February, most of the U.S. wrestlers believed the boycott would not actually take place. The athletes were convinced that because the president faced reelection in the fall, he was obliged to proclaim the United States' objection to the Soviet incursion. The American wrestlers held onto the belief that common sense would prevail and that they would be allowed to march under the Olympic flag and participate in the games. (Many U.S. allies allowed their athletes to compete under the Olympic flag.)[5]

The Soviet Union took its sports seriously, and there was national pride involved in showing the prowess of its athletes. Yet sports were never the cold-war military proxy that the media proposed. None of us with even limited experience with the Soviets ever believed that boycotting the Moscow games would affect the USSR's military policy. The U.S. wrestlers perceived the whole episode as an idealistic rather than strategic reaction. A symbolic protest that hurt so many athletes who had committed years to their Olympic guest!

The fact that leading up to 1980, the United States freestyle wrestlers had some of their best performances ever, made the situation particularly difficult for the team. For many, the biggest hurdle to winning an Olympic medal would have been making the team. In the 1979 World Championships, the United States freestyle team won seven out of a possible ten medals, and was second only to the USSR in team scoring. Also, for the first time since the Soviet Union entered international competition, the U.S. team defeated the Soviet's strongest team in the World Cup. All of these factors made it that much more difficult for the wrestlers to refrain from expressing their feelings.

Aware of the potential for propaganda by the Soviets, I hastily called a team meeting and instructed them that because we were representing the United States, everyone was to refrain from expressing their personal sentiments publicly.

One team member asked, "Coach, what do you think President Carter would do if the Cuban army landed in Miami?"

Another team member quickly responded, "Cancel the World Series."

"Keep that among us," I advised. As much as I shared their sentiment, I borrowed a phrase and counseled them to remember that united we stand, divided we fall. If the president says we're boycotting, we're boycotting; enough said. Needless to say, morale was low.

Prior to the Islamic Revolution of 1979, the United States and Iranian wrestling teams generally got along. The Iranian wrestlers were viewed as being part of an informal alliance to balance the more structured Eastern Bloc nations' sports machinery. The Japanese, Western European, Iranian, and American wrestlers were the counterforce to the state-sponsored communist sport programs and prevented them from running roughshod over the international wrestling community.

That all changed when the Iranians took the Americans hostage. This was the U.S. team's first contact with the Iranian wrestlers since the Islamic students had stormed the embassy building. Most of the U.S. team members were naturally apprehensive and avoided any contact in the days leading up to the competition. Likewise, the older, experienced Iranian wrestlers appeared to be cautious, but the younger wrestlers seemed almost cult-like in their behavior. Yet, nothing could prepare us for what happened next.

International wrestling protocol calls for each country to march under their respective flag in the opening ceremonies of any international tournament. As we lined up, I noticed the Iranians did not have a flag; instead they carried a picture of the Ayatollah Khomeini. My first reaction was an instinctive, primitive response: my pulse quickened, my heart raced, and my adrenaline surged. The hairs on my arm and back of my neck stood up. For a moment I wasn't thinking rationally, and I had to step back in order to clear my mind. Then I looked at the U.S. team to see if anyone else had noticed. One had, Gene Mills.

Mills wrestled in the fifty-two-kilogram weight category and I had assigned him to carry the United States flag for the ceremonies. As I walked up to him, he asked, "Coach, do you see that, do you see that?"

"Yes, I do, and I know what you're thinking, but don't do it," I advised. "You wrestle the Iranian first round, just wait. In an hour you can beat the hell out of him on the mat. You may feel better if you do what I think you want to do with that flag pole, but in the long run it is better to restrain yourself."

By then a few others had also noticed, and I cautioned them all: "Don't even think about it." Though I was having difficulty containing my anger, protocol called for restraint.

Later, the Iranian Wrestling Federation was sanctioned and fined (And if you care, Mills mauled—within, or should I say, at the edge of the rules— his Iranian opponent.) More importantly, an international confrontation was avoided and a lesson in restraint learned.

Despite the lesson I walked away with from my quasi-diplomatic wrestling experience, I still hesitated to discuss the results of the conversation with Russo; instead, I called Vanderbeek. Though it might have sounded more like ranting, I recounted the highlights of the discussion between Mosler and Russo. I described in detail the dialogue regarding the relative chance of the Bank of Japan ascribing to Lehman's position. When I got to the punch line and told Vanderbeek that Russo answered "Fifty-fifty," he responded, "That pussy. Let me schedule a conference call with Gelband, Lessing, Russo, Gregory, you, and me sometime in the next few days. I'll get back to you."

Several days later Vanderbeek convened the group to discuss how best to proceed. Aside from some tentative dissension from Gelband in defense of his Tokyo trading desk (read profits), the group agreed that the customer had the stronger argument and the proper course of action was to mend our relationship with AVM/III Advisors. Still, it was my sense that had Gregory not been so absolute in his proclamation, Gelband would have protested more forcefully. Nevertheless, Lessing, Vanderbeek, and I would go to Boca Raton and negotiate a fair settlement.

I was confident we would reach an amicable resolution. Mosler was fair and looking for a more symbolic than punitive restitution. After all, if Russo's fifty-fifty assessment was accurate, there was still reasonable doubt in Mosler's assertions. So even if a few of his cohorts would be looking to pounce on the opportunity, Mosler was the ultimate arbiter and would prevail.

Lessing's strengths were more in motivation and the customer relations areas and less in nuanced debating, so Vanderbeek and I handled most of the discourse. Aside from a brief diatribe by one of Mosler's minions, the meeting was congenial. After we resolved the main issue, Vanderbeek, Viner, and Mosler digressed to examine several international market irregularities that might offer reason for Lehman and III Advisors to coordinate more in the future.***

In sum, the process was longer and more wrenching than it needed to be, but the vetting process produced the anticipated outcome. The "One Firm" partnership between sales and trading functioned effectively. The client-driven business model under Vanderbeek's leadership remained intact.

---

* The simplest explanation of **leverage ratio** is total debt divided by equity. It is often referred to as debt to equity ratio.

** Earnings or revenue divided by **equity**.

*** These discussions ultimately led Lehman to an ill-advised investment in III's High Risk Opportunities Fund, a prominent victim of Russia's 1998 default that led to a worldwide financial crisis—a subject to be addressed later.

10

GLASS–STEAGALL

"All the king's horses, and all the king's men, couldn't put Humpty together again."

E ven prior to the repeal of Glass–Steagall (a depression era act that prohibited commercial banks from participating in investment banking activities) in 1999, the evolution of securitization and derivatives blurred the lines dividing the financial service industry. Aside from underwriting equities and bonds, there were few things that large banks did not do. And despite conventional media rhetoric, banks are still limited by law and regulation as to their activities. The bank holding company is where the expanded investment privileges reside.[1]

Unless the government is able to break up the too-important-or-interconnected-to-fail financial institutions by both size and function, what is accomplished? Simply splitting Bank of America into three, five, or even seven smaller entities without dividing functions accomplishes little, aside from creating inefficiencies and adding to the difficulty for the Federal Reserve to identify problems. The same amount of capital is supporting the same amount of assets.

When the functions of commercial banks were distinct from those performed by investment banks, there were some inherent checks and balances. Take for example the commercial mortgage-backed securities (CMBS) market. In the early stages of the CMBS market, large investment banks had the technology to securitize commercial loans and the global sales force to distribute the securities. Big banks, on the other hand, had an army of lending officers with a diverse customer group and a stable retail deposit base to finance the loans during the warehouse period.*

In 1996, First Union Bank (later Wachovia), hired Richard Owen Williams from Bear Stearns. First Union created a new position in its Capital Markets Corporation, head of fixed income, and Williams assumed the responsibilities. First Union Capital Markets was a division of a nonbank affiliate of First Union, Wheat Securities. First Union acquired Wheat First Butcher Singer in the summer of 1997, after Bankers Trust purchased Alex. Brown & Sons and their cross town rival, NationsBank (later Bank of America), bought Montgomery Securities.[2]

Global banks felt a sense of urgency and were eager to build full-service investment banking divisions. Non-banks were steadily encroaching on their business. Savers could realize better returns with only marginally more risk in money-market funds. And corporations that previously relied on banks for funding could easily tap the global bond markets.

Williams and I knew each other from Salomon Brothers, where we both started. A few months after Williams had settled into his new position, I contacted him and suggested that it might make sense for Ted Janulis, the head of Lehman's mortgage department, and I to visit Charlotte and explore areas in the mortgage effort where our firms might have reason to work together. Williams agreed.

Before moving into his current position, Janulis worked as a collateralized mortgage obligation (CMO) and asset-backed securities (ABS) trader. From the trading desk, his responsibilities expanded to include the new issue market. Janulis then moved off the trading floor to run Lehman's mortgage finance department. In 1996, he returned to head up Lehman's entire mortgage department.

Janulis's calm, unassuming yet focused demeanor and detailed understanding of the new issue securitization market mixed well with Williams, a more quintessential Wall Street ego type. Accompanying Williams at the meeting were his heads of structured finance, asset-backed lending, and commercial real estate. The meeting went as I expected and First Union Capital Markets' division desired more advanced discussions in the ABS and commercial mortgage-backed security (CMBS) areas.

As a follow-up, Mike Mazzei, co-head of Lehman's commercial real estate group, and I met with Williams and several of his key commercial real estate employees. Mazzei played a vital role in building Lehman's CMBS effort into one of the most respected on Wall Street. He started on Lehman's commercial desk in 1986 and was viewed as one of the pathfinders of the CMBS market. Mazzei was not a compelling presence but as we would find out later, it was his intricate knowledge of CMBSs that First Union cared most about.

By the end of the discussions, Lehman and First Union had agreed to pursue a joint CMBS. The agreement called for Lehman to be the lead underwriter; each would contribute a portion of loans into the pool. The efficiencies came from the makeup of loan type, property type, and geographic distribution. As statistics urged, rating agencies required less subordination with more diverse collateral, and the combination of First Union's and Lehman's loans, as it turned out, was the most geographically diverse pool to date.

What's more, the collateral included multifamily housing, retail, office, hotel, and industrial warehouse properties. Lehman and First Union would save millions in legal fees, warehouse lending costs, and subordination levels from the added efficiencies. But more importantly from a risk perspective, a cadre of Lehman and First Union underwriters would comb through each other's loan documents to assure their veracity and add an element of risk management as each protected their respective franchise.

In the end, Lehman and First Union collaborated on a few deals—including a landmark $2.24 billion joint conduit deal in 1997—before the relationship began to exhaust its usefulness. First Union had ulterior motives, as Williams admitted: "To capture not just the origination fees but the profits that come from securitizing and distributing as well. Partnering with Lehman was the entry fee or tuition." The key point here is that through evolution, the levees between banking and investment banking eroded well before the repeal of Glass–Steagall in 1999. Today the Glass–Steagall Act would be enormously difficult to reconstruct effectively.

* The **time period** between making the loans and selling them as securities.

11

CENTRAL BANKERS

"There is nothing more difficult to take in hand, more perilous to conduct, or more uncertain in its success, than to take the lead in the introduction of a new order of things." Niccolo Machievelli, The Prince (1532)

Central bankers worldwide are patting themselves on the back. Commonly one hears claims such as *The financial officials of the world's biggest economies acted quickly and forcefully. The programs we launched have successfully diffused a rapidly deteriorating and potentially dangerous situation. We averted a panic almost miraculously.*

And proudly they offer the formula: "Collectively following the collapse of Lehman Brothers we committed to prevent any other large financial institutions from failing. We instituted a litany of bold programs, including purchasing mortgage-backed bonds and debt issued by FNMA and FHLMC; guaranteeing debt for several large banks; opening the discount window for select at-risk investment banks; and providing rescue capital to faltering financial institutions such as Citigroup and AIG, to restore frozen credit markets. Our injection of funds via frozen fixed-income markets restored confidence. With aplomb we brought our economies back from the brink of disaster."[1]

Naysayers argue that more could have been done and that some policy choices were mishandled. Yet, even if a less tardy response or a more orderly failure of Lehman may have saved taxpayers billions of dollars, few have reason to argue with the central bankers' assessment or offer superior alternatives. Nonetheless, if indeed central bankers believe their actions were responsible for keeping the global economy from sliding into the abyss or for the so-called miraculous recovery, then by extension they should assume market participants will interpret their actions as a formula for success—a template or tool kit for handling future financial crises.

The once implicit government protection for the too-big-or-interconnected-to-fail is now explicit. Otherwise the very confidence among market participants that is essential in establishing stability in the financial system may evaporate–unless, of course, the Federal Reserve derives a new model to tame the boom-and-bust cycle.

Preventing another even larger crisis might require fixing the structural problems at the micro level. The mispricing of assets needs to be subdued before it reaches levels that threaten the stability of the financial system. Monetary policy is a blunt tool. A far sharper instrument might be tightening leverage ratios where the bubbles originate.

The skills that allowed the Fed to steer the financial system through the chaos, however, differ vastly from those required in oversight. Executing a macro-economic rescue program to stem a calamitous financial system collapse differs from designing meaningful and comprehensive supervisory reforms to avoid a repeat of the recent disaster. Offering prescriptions predicated on a misunderstanding of the nature of the problems might worsen future crises.

This is not to suggest that the Federal Reserve is ill-suited to oversee systematic risk, but to emphasize that the super-regulator, whoever it may be, requires independent authority and expertise to regulate all large financial institutions on the micro level. How the oversight function is administered is far more important than where it is housed.

The rescue of LTCM, AIG, FNMA, and FHLMC makes it clear that systemic risk is not confined to large commercial or investment banks. It includes hedge funds, insurance companies, government-sponsored-entities (GSEs), or any financial entity large or interconnected enough to impose systemic risk. As economists have pointed out, the too-big-or-interconnected-to-fail financial entities are bigger and more interconnected now.

Today, to arrive at an assessment of systemic risk the Fed has to rely on a sketchy surveillance system and insufficient authority to intervene. Currently our federal supervisory system is too disjointed to discern systemic risk. As nonbank financial entities expanded into various components of the global financial system, the regulatory structure became increasingly ill-equipped to oversee risk. Market strategists point out that currently, multiple government agencies developed haphazardly over the past seventy plus years often have oversight responsibilities for different functions within the same financial institution. Hardly a model constructed to produce a comprehensive response to risk.[2]

The challenge of sorting through reporting data from various agencies complicates efforts of any new super-regulator and the ability to arbitrage regulator restrictions compounds the problem. When risky units are deemed to require additional capital to restrain systemic risk, altering ownership structure (regulatory arbitrage) does not lessen the risk and needs to be deterred. The argument for independence of the resolution agency to impose restriction harmoniously among all large financial entities is compelling. The conclusive possibility of some sort of conservatorship or receivership might reintroduce the discipline that eludes our current structure.[3]

A regulatory structure that offers no credible alternative to intercede as we race toward a collision course with financial Armageddon seems enormously irresponsible. Lawmakers and the executive branch should consider setting strict directives giving the super-regulator discretionary authority to access financial information and make defensible and principled recommendations. As the experts have noted, the circumstances and uncertainty surrounding Lehman's demise and its subsequent bankruptcy proceedings vividly illustrate the need for the super-regulator, in due process with its oversight committee, to have full statutory powers, a clear path to intervention.[4]

Several critics have observed that given its way, congress seems destined to turn our financial system into one big government-sponsored entity. This reinforces something we should have learned from previous crises: Independence for those responsible for overseeing systemic risk in our too-important-or-interconnected-to-fail institutions is paramount.[5]

As many economists have noted, history is replete with the adverse consequences of politicizing the Federal Reserve System. Defending against Congress's infringement on the Fed's ability to manage monetary policy and authority to oversee the super-regulator is central to the market's confidence.

Likewise, of the various agencies, the Federal Reserve appears to have the most compelling argument to host the oversight and supervisory group, even if it consolidates more authority. The Fed's responsibility as the institution in charge of maintaining the safety and soundness of the financial system as a whole, argues for a comprehensive involvement in the oversight and supervisory functions. Along with its lender-of-last-resort responsibility, the oversight responsibility provides another tool to intercede when markets behave irrationally and threaten the financial system. The authority may prove vital for the Fed to guide the economy when reacting to financial stresses in the future.

12

"TOO-IMPORTANT-OR-INTERCONNECTED-TO-FAIL"

"Be careful what you wish for; it just may come true." Anonymous

The Federal Reserve's stated litmus test for too-important-or-interconnected-to-fail remains: Will the shock of failure jeopardize the entire financial system and hence devastate the broader economy? When faced with the collapse of several of the larger U.S. financial institutions, federally assisted consolidation was one of the more effective tools used by the Federal Reserve and Treasury to stem the financial crisis. When Merrill Lynch, Bear Stearns, Washington Mutual, Wachovia, and others teetered on the brink and the financial system was precariously close to the precipice, it was the too-important-or-interconnected-to-fail banks—J. P. Morgan, Bank of America, and Wells Fargo—that the government depended upon for help. These firms acquired the faltering entities, helping diminish the magnitude of the crisis. And many if not most would agree, had the Treasury been able to orchestrate the same for Lehman, the crisis would have been far less severe and less costly to the taxpayer.[1]

The meshing of these entities has resulted in a substantial increase in the share of deposits controlled by the largest banks. According to several financial information services, the three largest control 33 percent of U.S. deposits at the end of the first six-month period ending in June 2009, compared with roughly 22 percent at the close of 2008. And the top five largest banks' assets exceed $8.5 trillion, which is greater than 65 percent of the U.S. gross domestic product (GDP). Bank of America's quarterly reports show it has grown from roughly $1.8 trillion at the end of 2008 to almost $2.6 trillion as of September 30, 2009. And Citigroup continues to be an expansive financial conglomerate, with operations all over the world and hundreds of millions of customers.[2]

The contention that the recent government intervention will lead these now much larger banks to take more risk has led many central bankers and government officials around the world to conclude that the best way to protect taxpayers is to limit the size and scope of banks. One proposal advancing among policymakers is to give governments the authority to preemptively dismantle even healthy institutions they deem too big as well as to separate commercial banking from investment banking. A number of the most respected economists have indicated they agree with the concept, and yet they have not explained how to accomplish it.

Forcing large bank holding companies to split into smaller institutions may do little to reduce the chances of another crisis, but may thwart one of the options needed in remedying it. Without the too-important-or-interconnected-to-fail-institutions, who will the government turn to for assistance in crises? Perhaps as important, it removes vital sources of profit. Requiring large, interconnected global banks unilaterally to reduce their size or to become "disentangled" so that they do not fail may just legislate the economy back to the Dark Ages of savings and loan companies.

To paraphrase economists who oppose dismantling large financial entities, taxpayers may have far more at risk if the banking system again freezes and prevents money from being channeled to productive enterprises. Remember, many of the benefits of consolidation among bank holding companies have accrued to the borrower.

Starting in the early 1970s and gaining traction in the 1980s is a secular trend toward financing assets in the global capital markets thru securitization. Rather than funding assets with deposits or selling individual loans, banks currently bundle loans into securities and sell them efficiently to global investors. These assets include almost all types of lending: credit card, auto, home equity, commercial real estate, and residential mortgages, to name a few. Most often, securitizing assets and selling them in the capital markets is the least expensive method of funding and frees up valuable capital for other lending. Splitting up bank holding companies would increase the cost of funding and eliminate a valuable source of profits.

Large bank holding companies can shed businesses that are nonessential to their core function and simplify their organizational structure. Whittling down their sprawling franchises to reduce their importance, or "disentangling," is another story, however. It ignores the advantages of economies of scope and scale that larger diverse banks provide in today's global economy. The current globalization of financial markets requires a full spectrum of banking activities. Senior management of large global companies continually emphasize that the role that large integrated banks play in the financial irrigation system of the global economy serves a vital commercial function. The benefit of foreign exchange services and accessing global capital that accrue to customers of a global financial institution are key examples of integration leading to economies of scale.[3]

To overlook the benefits of large banks to provide expedient global processing of currency and other commercial payments and transfer transactions seems short-sighted. Imposing restrictions may reduce these efficiencies and will significantly handicap U.S. banks' abilities to compete against their foreign competitors. The growth and consolidation of the financial sector occurred in tandem with globalization and is a primary part of the evolution, not a change in ideology. In today's economy, large corporations and equity, fixed income, commodity, and foreign exchange markets operate on a global scale. This requires the same global scope from financial institutions.

One problem with imposing boundaries on the size of financial entities is that no one has the faintest idea of what the boundaries should be. Systemic risk is as much a function of how interconnected these financial institutions are as size is. Lehman's assets totaled less than $700 billion at the time it filed for bankruptcy protection. The turmoil created in the aftermath of this event should provide ample evidence of the fragility of our financial system. It is possible to solve the problem without dismantling large financial institutions.

As policymakers struggle to design changes so that future crises do not require taxpayer money nor disrupt the broader economy, a restriction to limit size might not prove to be the best answer. Policy heads and bank managers might do better to learn from Lehman's demise and focus on structures that muffle the vicious cycles. But in doing so, it will be important to remember that adequate capital does not change proportionately with size. When credit spreads narrow, margin requirements lessen and asset size approaches systemic risk levels; the capital required to forestall another financial crisis grows exponentially. Once some exogenous event triggers massive deleveraging, there is little time before contagion sets-in.

Consolidation of assets at both bank and nonbank financial institutions contributed to more violent asset price swings in the recent crisis compared to the 1998 crisis. Going forward, the prudent assumption should be to expect increasingly violent price swings unless irrational asset prices are moderated. The best preemptive measure to accomplish this discipline may be reducing leverage, not dismantling our large financial entities. Requiring increasingly larger margins and risk-based capital within the financial units taking the risk may be the best tool.[4]

The firewalls that were installed to segregate bank subsidiaries from non-bank subsidiaries in a holding company structure could easily extend to individual risk units. Lehman's non-bank subsidiaries were easily separated and sold—in several cases to existing management—when it failed. Lehman's structure allowed regulators, for example, to extricate the money management and private-equity units from the failed entity. In short order, the broker-dealer, investment banking, and asset management businesses were acquired by several global financial institutions. If similar firewalls with individual capital had been in place for the trading units, Lehman's failure may have been more orderly and significantly less costly.

Since the current "great recession" began with many Americans acquiring houses they could not afford, the housing market provides an easy illustration. When housing prices advance at a rate faster than average income, larger, not smaller down payments are the prudent course. Unfortunately, there were no firewalls within the broader investment banks or capital restraints to curb the prodigious cycle. Even if one had seen the subprime panic coming, little could have been done to stop it.

There was no framework to curb the aberrant demand. Paraphrasing remarks made by some prominent economists encapsulates the thought:

> **Under the guise of advancing homeownership rates, the amount of mortgages with sub-par equity and credit standards escalated, leading up to the crisis. Affordable-housing mandates added fuel to the fire. Though it did not comport with sound financial**

management, Congress, at the behest of advocacy groups, continued to pressure the GSEs (FNMA and FHLMC) to meet their affordable-housing goals. To fill the government-enhanced demand, lenders loosened credit standards. The result was a massive expansion of low down payment mortgages at a time when down payments should have increased.[5]

And the problem was no secret. From its inception, subprime mortgages meant exactly that; subprime—shorthand for junk. I recall parts of a particular conference call between Lehman's non-agency trader* and Wachovia's investment department. Wachovia was reviewing the subprime collateral in a Lehman deal when subprime was still a small but expanding fraction of the U.S. mortgage market. Michael Buttner, Wachovia's head portfolio manager, worked on Wall Street before joining Wachovia and required meticulous due diligence before acquiring any non-agency collateral.

At the time, the disclosure material describing the pool data or term sheet, as it was known, supplied a larger picture of the loan characteristics—such as average FICO scores, average loan-to-value (LTV) ratios, or the percentage of mortgages that were primary residences—but not a detailed view of each loan. The investors, to take but one example, had access to the percentage of loans with private mortgage insurance** (PMI) whose LTVs are greater than 80 percent, but not which loans.

Mike Buttner, after combing through the documents—searching microscopically, traders would complain—for discrepancies, wanted more information as well as the traders' perceptions. Buttner was particularly focused on the percentage of limited- or no-doc loans and the geographical makeup of the pool, if possible with a breakdown by zip codes.

As the conversation continued, one of Wachovia's investment managers noted, "This is junk." The Lehman trader candidly responded: "Right, it is all crap. That's why it's called subprime. We are only trying to figure out if enough subordination and diversification will alter the fact, or if the yield is high enough to warrant the risk."

After a thorough review, Wachovia's investment department astutely concluded that they did not want any part of subprime nor, for that matter, any non-agency mortgage security with more than just a minimum of California, Nevada, or Arizona loans. Though Buttner's group held a gloomy outlook, they did not predict a collapse of West Coast real estate prices, just that the additional yield was not sufficient to warrant the risk in what they perceived as a frothy housing market—especially when the loans were underwritten using substandard guidelines.

Imagine how Buttner's desk felt when Wachovia's senior management acquired Golden West Financial Corporation. A Lehman trader jumped all over that one. "It's ironic, Buttner's group concluded that California, Arizona, and Nevada mortgages were crap, yet senior executives bought the outhouse."

* A **trader** who trades mortgage loans that do not conform to FNMA, FHLMC or GNMA underwriting standards.

** Supplemental insurance lenders often require from homeowners whose mortgages are more than 80% of the house's appraised value.

13

THE BAILOUT OF LONG TERM
CAPITAL MANAGEMENT

"Danger breeds best on too much confidence." Pierre Cornielle, in Le Cid (1636)

In the late summer and fall of 1998, Lehman faced its greatest threat since being spun off by American Express. Russia defaulted on its debt, which would eventually lead to the near collapse of Long Term Capital Management (LTCM). Convinced that governments did not fail or default, investors disregarded prudence and become less vigilant. Lenders overextended and underplayed the attendant risk within emerging markets. An astute trader noted that as market participants extrapolated healthy returns and a rational response to market anomalies, the risk/return did not adequately compensate for the risk. When the bubble burst, market participants fled en masse. Restoring confidence became much more difficult.

At first, the world markets' reaction to Russia's debt moratorium was muted. Several emerging stock markets fell and several lesser countries' bonds widened, but no major dislocations appeared to be unfolding. In fact, U.S. equity markets ended higher on the day and most of the major U.S. banks confidently provided perfunctory statements assuring markets that their exposure to Russia was insignificant. The conventional wisdom on Wall Street was that just as they did for Mexico, the IMF (International

Monetary Fund), or the G-7 (Group of Seven Economic powers) would come to the rescue.[1]

In a few days, when the markets realized no rescue was imminent, the exodus from secondary credits began. There was a frenzied flight to quality and an exit from risk, any risk. All over the world investors sought safe havens and sold risk. Market participants were buying only the most liquid "on-the-run" (recently issued) government securities and selling all other spread product. No fixed-income market was spared. And the traders reinforced the idea that their bids and offers were indications-only.

Spreads in the entire credit sector, including agency and FNMA and FHLMC mortgage-backed securities (MBSs) gapped to unprecedented levels. The "off-the-run" versus "on-the-run" treasury spreads nearly doubled, reflecting not only a flight to quality but also an extraordinary premium for liquidity. As a Lehman mortgage trader complained, "Risk models were not calibrated to this level of volatility or absolute spreads. Spread relationships among credit markets have become distorted, rendering hedges mostly ineffective." As more and more market participants fled, the exit wasn't large enough. The lemming-like response by market participants began to appear ruinous.

Regulatory responses that in normally functioning markets would have calmed them and allowed them to trade in a more orderly way had little effect. Macroeconomic policy seemed to have a distorted or mitigating effect on modifying market participants' behavior. Firms could not count on their customary relationships with other dealers during the steep slide. Market participants, even those as large as Lehman, found a contraction in financing and larger hair-cuts. A larger amount of capital was required to support the same asset base, which exacerbated the decline in asset prices. The sequence of events would strain the crisis management of Lehman.

As with most Wall Street trading desks in late summer, Lehman was staffed with just a skeleton crew. Many of the senior traders and managing directors were whiling away the dog days of August on their customary pre-Labor Day vacation. Whether one was enjoying the quiet solitude that came from watching the sun rise on a beach in the Hamptons or the tranquil sense of relaxation that accompanied a leisurely stroll along a mountain trail in the Adirondacks, these were abruptly interrupted. Sales and trading management, as they sauntered back from the quaint coffee shops with their cappuccino in one hand and *The Wall Street Journal* in the other, were summoned to return as soon as possible.

Like a general going into battle, Fuld convened all the business managers. As he was prone to do, Fuld peppered the meeting with sports or battle metaphors: "Everyone needs to give a hundred and fifty percent." "We need to rally the troops." "This is an epic battle for survival." The war analogies were particularly annoying and I was never a soldier. I kept thinking, "We are not preparing to wrestle for an Olympic medal and certainly not readying for battle. Skip the hyperbole and just get to the task." And in this case the list of tasks was long.

Wary of mounting losses and widening credit spreads, a detailed review was ordered. "All clients' assets being funded are to be priced conservatively. Any exposure demands an immediate margin call. If margin calls aren't met, portfolios are to be liquidated." Banks everywhere were tightening credit lines. As portfolios were liquidated, prices fell, and banks retracted. Markets were sinking so fast, trading desks had a difficult time providing accurate pricing. Maturing repos were not renewed unless management approved.

As the self-fulfilling destruction continued, Lehman had a bigger worry: funding itself. Rumors of Lehman's impending demise began to swirl on the Street and customers reminded me of this several times a day. Given the real or perceived leverage, relative size, and asset mix, Lehman was deemed to be the most vulnerable. Senior management made it clear that all of Lehman's assets—commercial real estate, credit card, and auto whole loans being warehoused for securitization—were being dusted off and used as collateral.

The margins were severe and the funding rate punishing. Yet when compared to the alternative, the cost looked attractive. Funding trades once viewed as routine were celebrated. While Lehman was bailing water to keep afloat, LTCM, comprised mostly of ex-Salomon arbitrage group members, was hemorrhaging money.

In the early part of September, rumors of LTCM's demise surfaced on Wall Street. The word was that the highly-leveraged hedge fund's capital had tumbled from roughly $2.3 billion to just over a half billion dollars. Fearing LTCM's failure would spark an even more vicious cycle of liquidation and a possible seizing up of the entire financial system, the Fed hastily called a meeting of all the major Wall Street banks to discuss possible solutions, particularly a private-sector solution.

The call from the Fed fell on receptive ears. All the participants, painfully aware their losses were mounting, understood the system was vulnerable and were eager to find a solution. Under the guise of expediency (read self-interest), bankers dispensed of any broader discussion of the finer points of global capitalism. As Vanderbeek recalled, "Rest assured, there was nothing benevolent about the bailout."

Eventually the various institutions agreed to contribute a combined $3.625 billion to bail out LTCM. Eleven banks would agree to contribute $300 million each. Although no one framed it this way, Lehman would have been pressed to allocate $300 million to saving LTCM. Instead, Lehman successfully argued its exposure to LTCM was minimal and contributed $100 million. There was a sense of relief among Lehman's managers and product heads, as the $200 million could be put to better use elsewhere. Bear Stearns was the only institution to decline to participate.[2]

Although the Federal Reserve lowered interest rates quickly following the agreement, LTCM continued to lose money. The world financial system's worst fears were coming true. Troubles continued to soar for the large Wall Street banks, and the bailout did not cauterize LTCM's bleeding. Firms whose quarter ended in September reported large losses in the early part of October. Even Wall Street banks with relatively small proprietary trading desks lost money. Banks' and investment banks' stock, including Lehman's, fell precipitously. The bailout did not restore confidence in Wall Street.

In response, the Fed lowered interest rates again in mid-October and Federal Reserve Chairman Alan Greenspan announced emphatically that the Fed was ready to continue cutting rates until the market began to function more normally.[3]

Soon after that announcement the markets, starting with credit, began to gain confidence and mend themselves. One Lehman trader proffered that the same market participants whose pessimisms drove spreads to unprecedented levels are suddenly prone to the herd mentality of optimism. Credit spreads tightened, LTCM stabilized, and equity markets rallied. Volatility was redefined and markets were indeed global.

The most stressful and intense period in the capital markets since the Great Depression would subside. The once-in-a-lifetime financial crisis (as it was referred to at the time) would pass and too soon would be forgotten. Little did we know it was not the once-in-a-lifetime crisis we all thought. Instead it was only a precursor of a more vicious financial tsunami. Policymakers take heed!

For the quarter ending September 30, 1998, Lehman eked out a $74 million profit and the rumor mill was silenced. In the first nine months of 1999 Lehman would report record earnings.[4] A sizeable portion (as rumored among insiders) was from the nimble and timely trading by Jeff Vanderbeek. The most prescient was buying back Lehman's debt. When Lehman's debt tightened a few hundred basis points, income soared.

In a harsh irony, Lehman's success in 1998 instilled a false sense of confidence in the market's ability to right itself. Lehman's robust revival seared in Fuld's psyche the notion that panic-driven sell-offs were buying opportunities and blinded him to the potential of collapse. Fuld began to believe he and Lehman were invincible. What he failed to grasp, however, was the most important premise: adequate capital was first needed to survive the crisis. The strategy of buying on severe weakness would later turn out not to be the treasure trove Lehman once thought. Instead it provided the lyrics for Lehman's dance with delusion.

Lehman's near-death experience during the LTCM crisis sent a message and management took steps to establish a sturdier risk management structure. Lehman and other Wall Street banks introduced some risk and credit management changes. Larger margins were required; debt terms were lengthened; and exposures across trading desks were aggregated and priced timelier, at least at first.

As Maureen Miskovic, Lehman's then chief risk officer, so aptly put it to its managers, "Models designed to foretell risk are going to be viewed in a different context. A .5 percent chance of occurrence will no longer be looked to as unlikely or remote; instead it will be interpreted to mean: be prepared for it to occur once every 200 days."

Equally important adjustments were made in the way trading desks hedged their positions and viewed market-making. Conventionally, when bond traders took principal positions and risked capital in executing trades, they shorted the like duration treasury as a hedge. As a Lehman mortgage trader complained: "Shorting treasuries protected the price movements associated with interest rate moves, but left us exposed to adverse credit-spread changes."[5]

As the volatility and historical relationships of credit spreads changed during the LTCM crisis, the mortgage trading desk altered its hedging strategy. From this point, shorting assets—whose credit spreads would likely move in tandem—quickly became the norm. Regrettably, the diminished profitability resulting from higher hedging costs persuaded Lehman and others on Wall Street to reduce the capital allocation to the market-making business and devote more capital to proprietary trading.

The major mistake or lesson lost, however, was to only re-calibrate risk models to withstand the new extremes of 1998. The ability to endure financial crises should have been viewed not from the historical perspective of the recent once-in-a-lifetime 1998 catastrophe, but prospectively. Continued securitization, globalization, and consolidation of assets among global financial firms would mean fewer market participants moving larger amounts of money more easily and quickly. Lehman should have learned more than anyone from the lessons of the Russian default and subsequent LTCM collapse and concluded that viewing the past as a dependable forecaster of the future may prove catastrophic.

14

LEHMAN BEGINS TO LOSE ITS BEARINGS

"In the field of observation, chance favors the prepared mind." Louis Pasteur

After Vanderbeek was promoted from head of global fixed income to head of capital markets, Lehman's fixed-income division started to lose its bearings. Without his leadership, the institutional memory began to fade. Lost were his experienced hands at the wheel, which marked the beginning of a downward path toward irresponsible risk taking. The firm's creed had not changed just management's implementation of it. Without exception, Dick Fuld's letter to the stockholders and customers in Lehman's annual report emphasized the culture of commitment to the clients. In Lehman's 2000 report, for example, Fuld wrote:

> "Our clients are the heart of our franchise–they define our purpose and, ultimately, the strength of our Firm. We regard our client relationships as partnerships, where the excellence of our ideas, advice, products, service and execution determine the quality and longevity of these relationships. As a partner, we look to help our clients achieve their vision, sharing in their success through our efforts."[1]

In 2003 he wrote:

> "Our results again demonstrated the Firm's ability to deliver strong performance across market cycles and reflected our commitment to client service and our customer-driven business model. Our business relies on our commitment to find the best solutions for our clients."[2]

The message of a culture built around "client relationships as partnerships" was clear enough, but I began to question whether Lehman's current fixed-income management had instilled the concept to some of the traders. For all of the high-minded rhetoric, it appeared that no one had bothered to inform several trading desks that they were not just giant hedge funds.

A few traders on the mortgage trading desk were particularly Machiavellian. David Sherr, the global head of mortgage structured product, to take but one example, seemed unusually callous to the clients. He was incapable of disguising his views and any attempt to reason with Sherr seemed to make him more defiant. He had developed the Wall Street trader's pot belly and along with it, a disdain for the customer.

Dave Sherr was a competent trader but his wariness of clients clouded his judgment. He failed to recognize the role the customer played in the trading desk's success, an attribute that may work in a hedge fund but not as a market-maker on Wall Street. In his mind the customer was disposable.

Sherr looked and acted eerily similar to Austin Powers in the James Bond movie spoof, *The Spy Who Shagged Me*. As in the movie, Sherr was the British super-spy and the customers were Dr. Evils, the arch-villains plotting to extort the desk's money. Sherr had a cynical wit and, just for effect, was often prone to say something juvenile that would have been insulting if overheard by anyone other than the trading desk staff. Sherr's recalcitrant attitude reminded me of wrestlers who had a distorted need to dislike their opponents.

Don't get me wrong; there were personality traits among some of my most ardent opponents that heightened my competitive spirit, yet few ever invoked anger or disdain. More appealing was resisting disliking my opponents, not for magnanimous reasons or sportsmanship, and certainly not because wrestling was not fiercely competitive (wrestling a Chechen in a filled-to-capacity arena in Grozny is competitive). Rather it was because, as wrestlers, we had a lot in common, including respect for each other's preparation and competitive spirit—the more competitive; the more we appreciated each other. Besides, anger was a distraction and a waste of energy, energy required to compete effectively.

Mutual respect among wrestlers transcends nationalism, religion, ethnicity, and government ideology. Wrestling's competitive internationalism makes the world seem smaller and often trumps sectarian and even national interests. I recall vividly the night before the final day of competition at the 1977 World Championships in Lausanne, Switzerland. I was sitting in the sauna. The last weigh-in was the next morning and I needed to lose just a few pounds. My next opponent was Monsoor Barzegar of Iran. Barzegar was a 1973 world champion and had beaten me in a close match in the round-robin the year before at the Montreal Olympics.

As I was contemplating my strategy and tactics for the most important wrestling match of my career, Rouslan Ashuraliev, the Russian in my weight class, entered the sauna along with an interpreter. Ashuraliev was a medalist in the Munich Olympics and world champion in 1974 and 1975. In the Montreal Olympics the year before, both Barzegar and I had defeated Ashuraliev, dropping him to fourth. On this particular day he had been beaten and eliminated from the competition.

Through his interpreter, Ashuraliev proceeded to provide me with a detailed scouting report and the attendant strategies and tactics I would need to defeat Barzegar. Whether Ashuraliev's tactics helped in my victory the next day was not the point; what was important was the fact that my Russian competitor, at the height of the Cold War from the USSR's Muslim republic of Dagestan, would seek to deliver his privileged scouting information on the Iranian.

Although Sherr may have benefitted from such an experience, expecting such a noble gesture from a trader would have been naïve. Trading desks' eyes should be focused on making money. Yet I would expect that traders know not to breach the trust of either the customer or the sales force. Expecting the trading desks to understand the vital role the customers play in indentifying opportunities or allocating capital efficiently in the market seems sensible.

Traders falling short of this principal concept of partnership should have been reined in by senior sales and trading management. Unfortunately sales and trading management, particularly in mortgages, was becoming noticeably lax at Lehman under Herbert (Bart) McDade III and Alan Marantz.

The following vignette is an example of the role client interaction plays in identifying opportunities. Until the late 1980s private issuers, mostly investment banks such as Shearson Lehman, were responsible for issuing the lion's share of CMOs. As the reader may recall, these are pools of mortgage-backed securities (MBSs) divided into sequential pay classes of various average lives. Eventually, because the outstanding amount of bonds becomes so small relative to the ongoing administrative cost, CMOs have clean-up call provisions. This allows the deals to be collapsed before all of the underlying pass-throughs have completely paid down, which is the focus of this story.

Normally, when a CMO was collapsed, the issuer took delivery of the remaining FNMA pass-throughs, which was contemplated and painstakingly delineated within the legal documents. What might not have been adequately considered was such a large secular reduction in interest rates and the effect that would have on the value of this option to call the underlying premium coupon FNMA pass-throughs at par.

Either because of the perceived administrative hassle or a lack of foresight, when structuring a particular series of CMOs, Shearson Lehman oddly attached the call provisions to the residuals. So, collectively the residual holders, not the issuer, held the right to collapse the deal. All these Shearson Lehman series of CMOs preceded the current traders, so the desk was unaware of the nuance. These particular Shearson Lehman CMOs were structured under the auspices of Steven Carlson, a Lehmanite who many felt floundered among the more intellectually agile traders now populating Lehman.

Donald Uderitz of AVM's global mortgage arbitrage group, after combing through the prospectuses* concluded the market was not pricing the call provision properly in several of these Shearson Lehman CMOs. As the call provisions approached, the combination of the residual and remaining CMO tranche should trade at a cost similar to the underlying MBSs. Otherwise rational market participants would buy the combinations, collapse the deals, and then own the underlying FNMAs at a significant discount to the market price.

Don Uderitz had a calm demeanor, was forthright in his dealings with Wall Street's trading desks, and understood the nuances of structured product. His supposition was that the owners of the residuals were either not aware that collectively they possessed the rights to capture the premium or did not own a majority interest. There was some risk, of course. If Uderitz was unable either to acquire the majority interest, or mortgage rates were to rise sufficiently before the call was exercised, the option might have been rendered worthless.

After assembling the majority interest in several of these residuals, Uderitz brought it to Lehman's attention and asked if Lehman would work an order to acquire the residuals. He naturally figured, as issuer, that Lehman would have the best handle on who owned the residuals and the percentage of ownership. What he didn't take into account was Sherr's cunning attitude.

A trader once described "working an order" as similar to dealing at a high-stakes private poker table in Las Vegas. The dealer doesn't play; he just takes something out for the house in every ante. In this case, the Lehman trader would carve a handsome piece out of the transaction for the home team without ever holding the bonds or risking capital. For having the institutional knowledge of where to secure the specific bonds, the desk realized an ample finder's fee. Sounds like quite a racket; and if one deals or works customer orders long enough, he ends up with all of the money.

Lehman's residual trader Timothy Brown was naturally anxious to take the order and get started. Tim Brown, a principled trader by the standard of Wall Street, understood that if Lehman purchased the residuals, it was a no-win proposition. If Lehman exercised the call provision, some premium coupon bond holders might feel slighted and decry the idea. Yet if Lehman failed to collapse the deal, the residual owners would cry foul and press him to exercise the call. By gathering a sufficient amount so that Uderitz accumulated the requisite majority, all the residual holders were assured a market-based exercise of the call by a third party.

Pulling it off, however, required some deft trading. If Brown divulged the strategy, he ran the risk that competitors would learn of the price disparity and step in front of the trade. Or if he acquired bonds from the firm's clients without disclosing the strategy, he ran the risk of being viewed as favoring one customer at the expense of another. This left two choices: either to purchase securities in the open market or form partnerships among the residual owners to consolidate a majority interest.

Forming partnerships among competitors on Wall Street is extremely difficult, so Brown opted first to try to free up willing sellers in the open market via the dealer desk. Typically, fixed-income dealers function as independent agents to facilitate transactions on behalf of their customers, mostly among clients that are either too small or too inactive to justify direct Wall Street coverage. Rarely do dealer firms risk capital and position (inventory) assets.

Advocates argue that dealers broaden the market and that their sales force adds another set of professional eyes to scour portfolios to uncover value. Critics describe them as purveyors or outlets for Wall Street trading desks to unload the unwanted to the less informed. In reality there are elements of truth in both suppositions.

Yet, regardless of which side of the argument you adhere to, the dealer community plays a valuable role for both the buyers and sellers in the marketplace. They often dislodge pockets of hidden or otherwise untradeable assets and act as intermediaries between nameless buyers and sellers, providing anonymity among market participants. The dealer community allows sophisticated investors—money managers, trading desks, and hedge funds—to either accumulate or divest positions without revealing their strategy to the competition.

Before Brown could engage the dealer desks to locate sellers, Sherr got wind of the order. He decided, despite the fact that Uderitz had discovered the price discrepancy and brought it to Lehman's attention, that it was more profitable to take the entire trade for Lehman's desk. As I remember my exchange with Sherr, he asked, "Why would Lehman accumulate residuals for AVM when we can acquire them for ourselves?" "How about, it fails the smell test?" I responded. In my mind, Sherr had crossed the line between proprietary trading and customer activity. He put his own interest ahead of Lehman's long-term financial interest. Any hope of maintaining the customer's—or my—confidence vanished.

Sherr's unapologetic willingness to breach the trust of the customer and the sales force was not only shortsighted, it was bad business practice. Left unchecked, it ran the risk of imperiling relationships with key clients and jeopardized Lehman's franchise. Instead of assisting clients navigate through market uncertainties, Sherr chose to be a competitor—and the behavior was ignored or at least quietly tolerated. Ultimately, it was my contention that McDade and Marantz were responsible to put guard rails on the practice.

McDade was generally well thought of within sales and trading. He had an earnest manner, and by Wall Street's standards did not seem overly preoccupied with his own advancement. Most, including myself, understood why Lehman chose McDade to lead its global fixed-income department. He had the aura of the one in charge and in the broadest sense understood the business and the firm.

Unfortunately, McDade's outward assurance belied the fact he rarely requested feedback or criticism and preferred to delegate implementation to his loyal minions. Instead of being open to tough questions, McDade turned a blind eye and dodged accountability. He fell short of creating an environment of teamwork and never provided a platform nor guided sales and trading to exchange or come up with fresh ideas to solve problems.

McDade failed to heed the lessons from the 1998 financial crisis and mistakes of LTCM. He did not exhibit the hard edge so common among trading leaders and he lacked an understanding of the complexities of mortgage-backed securities. His apparent confidence in the mortgage desk's management and his unwillingness to enter the arena of debate spawned risk taking. Unlike Vanderbeek, who insisted on hearing real thoughts, McDade preferred to hear what he wanted to hear; and every time he was promoted, it seemed to reinforce these inadequacies. Lehman's mortgage desk no longer resembled the disciplined unit Vanderbeek had established.

McDade and Marantz were in senior enough positions during the LTCM crisis to have understood its lessons and the relevance to the current situation on Lehman's mortgage desk. Regrettably, McDade and Marantz were either skeptical of or didn't appreciate the role the customer played in the complicated mortgage market. The era when Lehman's key stakeholders had a seat at the table was beginning to evaporate. Lehman's culture of "One Firm" began to derail.

---

* Mind-boggling documents, written in legalese, that provide detailed material information about the securities.

15

PAY-FOR-PERFORMANCE

"As iron sharpens iron, so one man sharpens another." Proverbs 27:17

The issue of compensation in a meritocracy is a complex one. There are those who view the bonus discussions as just a distraction from the real issue of too-important-or-interconnected-to-fail. Yet together, they are the cornerstones of managing risk. The public is naturally frustrated, and offended at Wall Street's excesses that led to the financial crisis. Uproars over bonus payments should be expected. Lehman's management had the opportunity to lead and set the tone, but failed to capture the importance of pay in managing risk in a meritocracy. Warren Buffett, if you recall, faced a similar quandary after the Paul Mozer scandal at Salomon Brothers.

Buffett's distaste for the levels of compensation at Salomon Brothers during his tenure as interim CEO was well known among employees. Yet his assessment at the time, as difficult as it was for him to swallow, was probably the prudent approach. Salomon, like any competitive investment bank, needed the flexibility to maintain or lure the wisest and brightest minds. Summarizing Buffett's sports analogy is particularly appropriate: No one was suited to justify what Wall Street pays its best performers any more than professional sports owners can justify the outsized salaries awarded to professional athletes. Buffett understood that the industry did a poor job of aligning the shareholders' interests with those of the employees, and compensation practices needed to be reconfigured; but he did not want to be handcuffed.

Professional sports offer some interesting comparisons. When professional sports facilities need reconstruction or renovation, the debate over the taxpayers' share of the financing is rekindled. The owners argue job creation and presumed economic impact. They contend that their sports teams are a source of civic pride and have even shown studies alleging to quantify the value fans realize from donning the team's symbol, such as Green Bay's cheese heads.

On the other hand, critics provide evidence showing professional sport teams provide little additional economic activity to an area. They cite a slew of studies confirming that publicly supported sport facilities seldom generate the economic returns originally promised. Critics say that, absent the sport franchise, the public would spend their entertainment dollars elsewhere in the community and argue that funding professional sports arenas is a poor use of public funds.

To illustrate, the critics offer examples such as the empty Pontiac Silverdome, former home of the Detroit Lions. After the taxpayers of Detroit offered a more appealing lease, the Lions moved back. Pontiac's taxpayers were left with an empty municipal stadium and ironically had to offer further tax incentives in order to sell the wasted arena.[1]

In the end, the arguments are mute and the process becomes a bidding war. Cities elsewhere in the country seeking a professional sports franchise provide attractive packages. Local authorities and business leaders cave in and match with similar enticements. Considering money is fungible, the net effect, whether the team stays or moves, is that taxpayers subsidize most of our professional sports organizations. All the while, owners' franchise values increase dramatically and players' salaries skyrocket.

Yet any uproar from the public usually revolves around the loss of a team or key player and not the level of taxpayer support needed to acquire new players or teams. There is hardly a peep from taxpayers when drug tests reveal an elevated level of testosterone or other performance-enhancement substances among prominent players playing in taxpayer-subsidized stadiums. Instead it is more likely to draw criticism from fans as too harsh a punishment.

This is not to say Wall Street's so called pay-for-performance policies, as currently used, properly account for the levels of risk and does not need fixing. Before you label me a Wall Street sympathizer, let me say I harbor as much disdain for those who risked taxpayers' money on ill-advised risk taking as anyone. The current bonus structure is grossly skewed to reward questionable or unrealized profits.

Even today's banking management acknowledges that the method used to pay sales and trading encouraged excessive risk-taking and contributed to the crisis. Any disagreement on adjusting warped incentives is not with the goal, just with the most effective method of accomplishing it. Government-imposed restrictions or pay caps would create a real risk of an exodus of talented employees-those not responsible for the losses–to unrestricted financial entities and create potentially grave consequences for taxpayers.[2]

Likewise, the notion that bank executives (or even traders) wittingly gambled the destruction of their firm for the sake of annual compensation remains a mystery—or makes little sense. Lehman and Bear Stearns employees had among the highest percentage ownership on Wall Street. Most of the highly paid investment banking employees had far more to lose from an erosion of the stock price than gains from any annual increase in income. As Fuld testified to Congress, "I could have sold that stock [ten million shares]. But I did not, because I believed we would return to profitability."[3]

The decline in value of their restricted stock and/or options holdings for most of management and senior traders far exceeded any annual pay package. In most cases, a large portion of the net worth that employees accumulated over their lifetime was at risk. As an ex-frontline trader stated succinctly, management may have been ignorant to the extent of the risk their firms were taking, but deliberately jeopardizing destruction for the sake of compensation is a difficult argument.

The challenge for management now is to design a compensation structure that is risk-adjusted, aligns personal reward with realized (not interim) marked-to-market profits, and compartmentalizes the risk. Lehman's mistake of letting one department bring down the entire firm is unacceptable. More than bankers' compensation hangs in the balance. The smooth functioning of the global banking system is at stake.

The typical partnership's earning distribution structure offers insights and lessons for aligning consequences of risk-taking with the risk-takers. Over time, a major percentage of a partner's net worth is retained in the equity of the partnership. Each partner receives his portion of the firm's earnings, which aside from a relatively small cash payment, remains as equity in the firm. Only after retiring are partners generally allowed access to his equity. And that usually is distributed incrementally over time. It is easy to imagine how intensely the partners focus on risk and wealth creation. The asymmetry in the current system does not exist within partnerships.

Lehman, in a veiled attempt to replicate the discipline of a partnership, required management to emphasize the importance of relative performance, teamwork, and client relationships in their annual compensation process. The firm would distribute the "Global Sales Organization Talking Points" as if it were some managerial genius. The process was shrouded in secrecy.

The following are a few examples of the talking points

> *We have the industry leading Fixed Income Sales Organization, with record client revenues.
> *Fantastic job! It could not have been done without our Research, Trading, Structuring and Origination partners...with whom we have a unique relationship versus all other sell-side models.
> *We perform in a Meritocracy...which provides the best working environment for our Sales organization.
> *The Firm's focus on becoming a more client-centered organization makes our role in impacting the organization more significant than ever before.

The communiqué included discussion points for special cross-selling bonuses. Specific instructions not to commence with compensation talks until receiving official word from Bart McDade were included.

Lehman purportedly used a multipronged compensation program. Management was instructed to remind their sales-people, traders, and researchers that their total pay was based on how well Lehman, the Fixed Income Department, their respective business unit (i.e. mortgages, corporate, treasuries, etc.), and of course the individual performed. A detailed review of Lehman's fixed income and the particular business unit's performance were included. Highlights of the individual's performance were the responsibility of the manager to know. And finally, "Suggestions for Responding to Employee's Questions/Concerns and Special Situations" were included. Most of these suggested responses were designed for those who failed to manage expectations properly or for employees who had delusions about their skills—journeymen who thought they were Hank Aaron.

When faced with such a situation, I always liked to look at the salesperson and ask a direct question: "How much did you think you would make?" You would think most people would get somewhat uncomfortable and at least hem and haw just a little. Not on Wall Street—immediately they would blurt out some number, usually about three or four times what the president of the United States was making.

For those so proficient in math, it seemed a bit puzzling that everybody was above average. "At least be creative," was my first thought. When a reporter questioned Babe Ruth's demand of a salary higher than President Hoover's, he responded, "But I had a better year than Hoover."[4]

The recurring scene epitomizes how imbedded the attitude of entitlement or privileged interest had become on Wall Street. The Street is replete with inflated egos, which only heighten the need to measure performance accurately, an area where Lehman's fixed-income management increasingly faltered.

In case you haven't figured it out, I had little sympathy for the pervasive attitude or inflated egos on Wall Street. It was the same with the traders who took themselves too seriously. Allow me a short narrative. There was one mortgage trader, Rick Redmond—consistently cantankerous Rick Redman—whose attitude was particularly annoying. The glass was always half empty. When asking Redmond for a bid, a typical retort was: "That better be all this guy is selling."

My usual response, as I waited impatiently for his bid, was, "Rick, if I thought he was going to sell more I would tell you. Have any of my customers ever not respected market protocol?"

I was not alone in my assessment and on one particular occasion I seized the opportunity and used Rick's obstinate attitude to add a little levity. Deepak Narula, PhD and former research analyst turned mortgage trader was in Atlanta to meet with ING's fixed-income investment group. Upon our return to the office I decided to show off my recently installed voice-activated car phone, something relatively new at the time. I said, "OFFICE." The phone responded and called the office. I informed the office that we were on our way and that Deepak needed transportation to the airport; would Erik (my sales assistant) please call the car service.

After I instructed the phone to disconnect, Deepak said, "Neat, I have never seen that before."

I responded, "But it has its kinks."

"What do you mean?"

"Yesterday, I was driving home from work and some guy cut me off. I yelled, 'YOU ASSHOLE' and the phone dialed Rick Redmond," I told him. Deepak thought it was hilarious. I never gave it another thought—until the next morning.

Early that day Deepak decided to recount the story over the "hoot and holler," the firm's intercom system, for the entire global mortgage department. Afterwards, Deepak called me and said, "Rick didn't seem to mind until everyone kept laughing." No need to worry. Just like Rod Tidwell said in *Jerry Maguire*, "Show me the money!" As soon as one of my customers had a profitable trade, Rick and I were like buddies.

Lehman's final compensation documents contained valuable and useful facts that impacted unique situations, including an "Equity Award Schedule" for eligible employees that provided the detailed proportion of the bonus that was cash, restricted stock units (RSUs), or options. In some cases the greatest percentage was in either RSUs and/or options. At the conclusion of the discussion, the employee was handed his or her detailed RSU and option sheet, including the vesting and termination provisions.

This compensation system appeared to work reasonably well in the early years, after American Express spun off Lehman as a stand–alone entity. Yet the process began to show fractures as Lehman grew and management became disjointed. Skepticism and cynicism spread as more and more employees lost faith in sales management and realized the largest component of compensation was not performance but rather, "What was the bid away." Of course it is easier to measure the "bid away" than to risk adjusted contribution to profits.

From the rhetoric surrounding Lehman's compensation process, it was understood that pay should correlate with a multipronged incentive system. Yet management failed to implement a meritocracy that reflected the respective risk among individual divisions and aligned with the long-term fortunes of the shareholders. By incorporating the elements of a partnership that its multipronged compensation espoused, Lehman could have segregated a portion of the earnings within each business unit.

Like small partnerships, a percentage of the profits of each division, after taking into account a cost of capital adjusted for the respective risk, would be distributed to sales and trading and retained in the unit's capital, hence fastening full responsibility on those incurring the risk. Lehman already calculated detailed P&Ls by units, so earmarking a portion of an employee's restricted stock in the capital of his or her unit would not have been difficult. Nothing but leadership—or lack of it—prevented Lehman from setting up such a compensation structure that more effectively managed risk.

16

GLOBAL FOCUS

"Don't mistake wishes for facts." Bertrand Russell

A current concern seems to be the global imperative to adhere to a set of guiding principles. The cultures and political aims of Europeans and Americans are different, yet everyone seems to hold hope that in our global economy there is enough common interest to advance policies to collectively strengthen the entire global financial system. Unfortunately, Europeans have a tendency to interject a moral issue into the argument and promote a global tax as the solution. They tend to prefer more regulation and intervention in financial reform. The U.S., on the other hand, might be more concerned about constructing policies that protect the soundness of the banking system than closing the gap with Europe's more congenial approach or "soft moralism."[1]

Under the surface there may be more resentment regarding our status as the reserve currency than policymakers may realize. Europeans have long bristled at the immeasurable benefit, as well as the potential conflict of interest the world's reserve currency status affords the U.S. government. Since worldwide cash reserves have grown substantially following the 1997–98 Asian financial crises, essentially the reserve status allows the U.S. Treasury to print dollars, and any attendant fall in the exchange rate simply devalues foreign dollar reserves.[2]

A plausible anecdote: The notion of how deep the world's animosity toward America runs and how differently we, as Americans, view things occurred to me while attending the Denver 2009 SportAccord International Convention held in March. The SportAccord gathers the leaders from the International Olympic Committee (IOC), National Olympic Committees (NOCs), and over 100 international sports federations, including all those responsible for organizing their respective events at the Olympic Games. The predominant issue or topic of discussion at the forums as well as the social gatherings was a lifetime profit-sharing contract signed between the IOC and the U.S. Olympic Committee (USOC). Under the agreement, the USOC's share of the global marketing revenues and television fees from the Olympic Games is roughly equal to the share received by the other 204 NOCs combined. Obviously lopsided!

Before you jump to any conclusions, understand where the revenues are generated. According to the *Baltimore Sun*, the U.S. broadcaster for the 2008 Beijing Games, NBC, paid roughly $894 million, almost twice the amount paid by the European Broadcasting Union ($443.5 million) and Chinese networks ($7 million) combined.[3] Also obviously lopsided! The IOC members, save the U.S. representatives, argue that the percentages paid by the U.S. broadcaster and the marketing sponsors are down substantially from when the original contract was signed. Fair enough.

What they fail to point out is that greater than 60 percent of the revenues still come from U.S. sponsors and TV rights. None of this seemed to matter when the dollars were relatively small and the Olympic movement struggled. The IOC members conveniently forget, despite a boycott by most of the Iron Curtain countries, the 1984 Los Angeles Olympic Games under the leadership of Peter Uberoth developed a new model and demonstrated to the world the value of hosting the event.

At the SportAccord in Denver, Hein Verbruggen, IOC member and the association of summer Olympic sports federations' vice president stated the IOC members' position bluntly: "The USOC's share is an immoral amount when compared to what the rest of us receive." Darryl Seibel of the USOC was more conciliatory: "The USOC wants to discuss the issue in a fair and equitable manner. This is not a time to be divisive." Both the USOC and the IOC membership want to renegotiate, but what each considers fair and equitable remains far apart. The devil is in the details.

The IOC's bargaining chip: who hosts the Olympic Games? The IOC members, via the selection process in Copenhagen, demonstrated that they intend to hold the United States hostage until they get what they want.

Without regard for what holding the 2016 Olympic Games in Chicago may have done to advance the Olympic movement, the IOC sent a clear message. Dick Ebersol, NBC Sports chairman, summed it up perfectly in *The Baltimore Sun*. "This was the IOC membership saying to the USOC there will be no more domestic Olympics until you join the Olympic movement [shorthand for "renegotiate the contract"]. Chicago never had a chance, it turns out."[4]

Of course, the world is inextricably linked economically and has far more at stake in international banking coordination than holding the United States hostage over who hosts the next Olympics. Nonetheless, underestimating the resentment among Europeans toward the residual privilege the United States receives as the reserve currency may prove to be an error. Anti-Americanism is widespread and real, including in the financial sector. Copenhagen's Olympic vote, and more recently the attempt to reach a climate pact, demonstrates the difficulty in reaching global consensus.

This is not to marginalize EU countries, but their political differences and division create a cumbersome financial system. Until the EU's economic efforts are more coherent, the challenges to reaching a meaningful common global banking foundation are substantial. Even more difficult will be adequate verification and supervision.[5]

Given that our economy is the largest in the world, our financial institutions and policymakers should know by now to take the lead and introduce sound capital and risk management policies. With so much at stake, protracted delays while locked in a stand-off waiting for other governments' policymakers to initiate change only prolongs the time until the recovery is complete. The uncertainty surrounding the future regulatory environment fosters risk taking. If the U.S. drags its feet too long, it may run out of time.

Imposing onerous restrictions that handicap U.S. financial entities vis-à-vis their foreign competitors would obviously be foolhardy. The experts have rightfully noted the merits and benefits of a global focus. Absent worldwide agreement and a level playing field, the risk of regulatory arbitrage is real. Yet if U.S. policymakers introduce effective financial overhaul with broad authority to stabilize before a crisis arises, our foreign competitors would recognize the advantages and follow suit. Global investors rely on transparency and a sound financial system. Global capital would flock to the new structural integrity in the U.S. financial system.[6]

17

NONECONOMIC RESIDUALS

"The only source of knowledge is experience." Albert Einstein

Because of the complex and revealing nature of the following anecdote, I thought it might be helpful to review several key concepts. One is "phantom income," the other is "deferred tax asset."

Phantom income, broadly defined, is any income that does not generate cash flow but is reportable for tax purposes. A zero coupon bond, for example, does not pay interest but instead is sold at a discount. Yet it accrues or realizes reportable income but pays out no cash until it reaches maturity. In this sense, phantom income is produced in the noneconomic residual of a real estate mortgage investment conduit (REMIC), the investment vehicle normally used for the securitization of mortgage loans.[1]

In 1986, as part of the Tax Reform Act, REMIC provisions were first authorized, which removed certain constraints in the tax law. The removal of these restrictions allowed Wall Street modelers to create a new REMIC class that had no cash flow but in the early years produced phantom income. Wall Street quants appropriately anointed this class with the moniker noneconomic residual (NERD).

A REMIC bundles a group of mortgage loans and issues a multiclass security in which cash flows are directed to individual classes of varying coupons and maturities. The servicer of a REMIC collects the principal and interest payments (P&I) from the borrowers and then allocates the cash flows to create different classes of securities. By prioritizing the cash flows, a REMIC creates a staggered series of short-, mid- and long-term classes, with various coupons and risk profiles. The residual classes are ownership interests, with unique tax features, created in the REMIC securitization process.

A pattern emerges: As the shorter, lower-yielding classes are retired, the weighted-average cost of the REMIC classes increases through time while the yield of the mortgage collateral remains constant. This dynamic aspect of a REMIC has tax implications for the NERD owner. The timing difference between the taxable and economic (realized) income creates phantom income. Eventually the economic income exceeds the taxable income and phantom income gives way to "phantom loss." Over the life of the REMIC, phantom income and phantom loss will sum to exactly zero.[2]

A modeler, a nerd himself, cleverly described a REMIC's phantom income in an easy to remember way: A pernicious byproduct that because of its timing disparity between reporting of income and expenses, produces taxable income yet no cash flows—technically an interest-free loan to Uncle Sam.[3]

The other critical principal that needs delineation is an obscure accounting concept referred to as a deferred tax asset/foreign tax credit. A deferred tax asset is a balance sheet item that is deemed usable to offset a company's income tax expenses in future reporting periods. Deferred tax assets might arise due to a variety of reasons, such as operating or capital losses and tax credit carry-forwards. The most common is net loss carryovers (NOLs). In this recount, the deferred tax asset is "foreign tax credit."

Generally speaking, a foreign tax credit is a credit granted to avoid double taxation on income already taxed in a foreign jurisdiction. It is generally more valuable than most deferred tax assets because it reduces a company's tax liability on a dollar-for-dollar basis instead of just a deduction. Unfortunately it can only be carried forward for the succeeding ten years. Simply put, it is a delayed tax benefit with a finite life.[4]

If the reader visualizes phantom income as a pernicious byproduct that produces taxable income yet no cash flows and a deferred tax asset/foreign tax credit as a delayed tax benefit with a finite life, it should be easier to focus on Lehman's flawed risk management within its fixed income division in the following anecdote.

In 2001 a long-time customer of mine, Donald Arndt, took a position at J. P. Morgan (JPM) to trade and manage its REMIC residual interest portfolios. Following the dismantling of Glass-Steagall, banks were seeking experienced mortgage-backed securities expertise. Don Arndt was an ideal candidate. He was a Georgetown ROTC graduate and had served on active duty as an armor officer with the 1st Infantry Division in Germany. He was disciplined, focused, and willing to share his views. Most importantly, he was one of the most knowledgeable and technically proficient traders in his field.

Arndt's wry sense of humor appeared to some as wise-cracking, but he was really just frank. He had begun his career at Ocwen Financial at a time when the REMIC residual market was going through a series of innovations. The changes improved on the structural efficiencies, but complicated the transfer and reporting requirements. After Ocwen, Arndt moved to First Union, where he gained valuable experience establishing its residual trading desk within its structural product group. I first got to know Arndt when he joined Ocwen, and our sales-client relationship continued while he was at First Union. The years of interaction helped instill a mutual level of confidence; both of us remained abreast of the detailed reporting requirements needed in the esoteric world of REMIC residuals.

After several months at his new firm, Arndt called, indicating that he did not have the inclination or time to establish the trust required with new sales coverage. He said that if it were at all possible he wanted to speak with me instead of a salesperson from Lehman's New York office. I informed Arndt that it was probably a moot point since Lehman was currently retaining all of its residuals. Lehman's last NERD transaction was the trade he and I completed in 1999.

Arndt knew Lehman retained its residuals in-house but persisted, "Please pursue the issue; I am confident Lehman will recognize the mutual benefits. Over the years, our allegiance has given Lehman the best execution in terms of pricing, transfer risk, and analytics. Given the arcane nature of the current regulatory environment, it would take me too long to become comfortable with a new salesperson."

Periodically I had quizzed the mortgage trading desk, "What is Lehman doing with its NERDs?" Yet no one was able or willing to give me a satisfactory answer. Given my lack of trust in Sherr, I decided the more prudent course was to avoid any conversation with the trading desk. Instead I called Chal Taylor, then head of mortgage sales. Taylor was aware that few within Lehman's sales force had any experience with residuals. He said, "Give me a day or two and I'll get back to you."

Taylor did a quick search of the records and concluded no one was covering JPM for residuals; nor was he aware of any prior NERD transactions. He had no objection to me speaking with Arndt regarding residuals. "Morgan's derivative desk is all yours; go for it. You know we retain all of our NERDs," he added.

"I have a few ideas to explore. If they don't make sense, we will know quickly enough," I responded.

After receiving the okay to pursue the residual market with JPM, my first call was to the tax strategy group (or the financial engineering group, as they preferred to be called). I asked, "What role if any did the financial engineering group play in the managing the noneconomic residuals Lehman retained?" I intentionally refrained from using the term NERD, fearing they might think I was referring to them and take offense. They indicated they had no expertise in noneconomic residuals and referred me to the firm's tax department, specifically to Joe Monico.

I called Monico and introduced myself. I told him I was a managing director, in charge of Lehman's Atlanta office. I gave him a synopsis of my background in mortgage-backed securities, particularly NERDs and indicated, "I have a few questions regarding noneconomic residuals." Monico hesitantly responded, "Okay, I may have some questions of my own."

I said, "A brief review of the past few consolidated financial statements leads me to believe Lehman might have excessive foreign tax credits. If these continue to grow, would that risk a valuation allowance?"

At first Monico seemed wary, but after some deliberation he explained that if Lehman no longer had a sufficient amount of taxable income to utilize our foreign tax credits, accounting provisions would require a valuation allowance. Any tax credits deemed to expire would force Lehman to take a charge-off to reflect the reduction in the value of the deferred tax asset—in this case the loss of the foreign tax credits. It was a "non-cash" charge, meaning we did not need to write a check, but it was still a charge that could impact earnings.

I responded that I was under the impression that tax laws prohibit using normal tax deductions, like net operating losses to offset phantom income, but utilizing foreign tax credits was in accordance with general accounting principles.

Monico tersely responded, "That's my understanding as well."

Monico didn't say anything else, so I quizzed him further, "The last several consolidated financials indicate that our foreign tax credits appear to be increasing. Is that correct?"

"Yes, a larger portion of our taxable income the past few years has come from overseas operations," he replied.

Then I said, "Retaining our noneconomic residuals must help?"

"Of course," Monico replied. "We might have had to take a write-down, were it not for the phantom income REMIC residuals."

I sensed Monico was beginning to hesitate. I asked only one more question. "If the foreign tax credits are increasing each year, do you worry that Lehman's internal production of noneconomic residuals will not be sufficient to meet the firm's need for phantom income?"

There was a long pause before Monico asked, "Why? Can you acquire phantom income?"

"Sure, how much do you need?" I responded.

"What will it cost us?"

"Nothing—the issuer pays us an inducement fee to take the tax burden off its hands," I said.

"The issuer pays us? I'll get back to you," he snapped.

That Monico was neither aware of outside sources of phantom income nor that Lehman would receive an inducement payment for assuming the tax liabilities puzzled me and further fueled my suspicions about Sherr's trading desk.

A few weeks later, Monico called and indicated that indeed the firm could use additional phantom income. "How much?" I asked.

"More than you can get," Monico responded with confidence.

Unsure whether Monico understood the size of the market, I threw out a few numbers to gauge Lehman's needs: "$300 million, $400 million, a half-billion?"

"More than you can acquire," he reiterated.

I suggested a target. "It may take a year, but let's shoot for $650 million."

The main point to grasp is that Lehman's deferred tax assets resulting from foreign tax credits could be used to offset the phantom income produced from the noneconomic residual of a REMIC and reset the expiration date. In other words, the phantom income saved Lehman from having to adjust the value of its deferred asset, resulting in charges that might erode earnings.

To ensure it receives the due taxes, the IRS has established guidelines that address safe-harbor, or legitimate NERD transfers, lest it lose its interest-free loan. To summarize the IRS' reasoning: If either party knows, or should have known, that the transferee is a foreign entity not subject to U.S. taxation and unable or unwilling to pay the taxes due, the transfer is to be disregarded for tax purposes.[5]

Before the more onerous guidelines were introduced, several dubious transactions occurred where the transferor claimed to have satisfied safe harbor, but the economics proved otherwise. The alleged culprits purportedly involved a domestic partner receiving an inducement payment where ultimate ownership resided with a foreign partner, not subject to U.S. taxes.

This put the IRS in a tenuous position. On the one hand the issuers argued that if the IRS forces legitimate transfers to fall outside the protection of safe harbor, it unduly impedes the mortgage markets by forcing issuers to retain ownership. At the same time, the IRS had to introduce more stringent procedures that addressed the perceived abuses. Ultimately, the IRS put in place more restrictive limits, and burdens were placed on the transferor to establish that the transferee indeed had the ability (as well as the intention) to pay the taxes associated with ownership of the residual interest—a sort of "know your customer" rule.[6]

Needless to say, both Arndt and I were especially sensitive to avoid what the market referred to as fraudulent conveyance. The last thing either of us wanted was for safe harbor to be denied and the transfer disregarded. Arndt and I spent the later part of 2001 educating Monico on the NERD's secondary market conventions, including the new safe harbor rules. In the early part of 2002 we hammered out a deal.

The assumptions for calculating the inducement fee, purchase and sales agreements, master agreements, and other relevant due-diligence factors had to be negotiated to assure safe-harbor transfer under the new, stricter regulations. JPM felt comfortable that Lehman's strategy of using the phantom income from the NERDS to offset foreign tax credits met safe-harbor standards. Monico indicated that Lehman, to avoid incurring a charge to profits, wanted a deal by the start of the second quarter.

In early April 2002 Lehman concluded its first portfolio transfer. The projected taxable income was roughly $280 million, with Lehman receiving an inducement fee of slightly more than $12.5 million. Deloitte was chosen to validate the accuracy of the inducement payment.

Deloitte had just completed their audit when coincidently Bart McDade and Alan Marantz visited the Atlanta office. Strangely, neither Marantz nor McDade were even remotely aware of the transaction, so I walked them through a condensed version describing the genesis, evolution, motivation, and the benefits to the firm. Since they were unschooled in the details of the mortgage securitization process, our discussion regarding the character of the NERD interest was largely abstract. McDade acknowledged his deficiency, saying "It may make more sense for me to discuss the issue with Ted Janulis [McDade's then co-head of fixed income]."

The fact that McDade, global head of fixed income, and Marantz, global head of fixed income sales, were not even vaguely aware of the transaction was perplexing. Yet the dereliction of Sherr or the mortgage trading desk to advise Lehman's tax department that there was an active secondary market to acquire additional phantom income was still deeply troubling, and I emphasized this point to McDade and Marantz at the time. Perhaps their thoughts were elsewhere?

Earlier in the conversation with McDade and Marantz, I pointed out, "The antique double front desk in my office is purportedly the original desk used by Henry and Emanuel Lehman in their Montgomery, Alabama office. Legend has it that through various moves, it eventually landed in Atlanta." It certainly looked the part. Unable to provide the chronological details of how it arrived in Atlanta, Marantz surveyed the desk and suggested, "It appears to be genuine reconstruction era."

Turning to the more substantive issue of the residual interest portfolio trade, I did not give it another thought until Marantz and McDade were departing for the airport. As Marantz was about to enter the elevator he said, "I'll get back to you next week." The statement made me think he was referring to the NERD trades until he added, "I'll talk to Dick [Fuld] to see what he wants to do with your desk." Unfortunately his comment was not a verbal misstep and it underscored my previous suspicions.

Marantz was a Lehmanite, and before becoming head of fixed-income sales in 2000, he had held numerous positions during his career at Lehman. After managing Lehman's global foreign exchange division, he moved to Tokyo, where he was head of fixed income for Asia. Prior to his service in Asia, he led several sales units including foreign exchange, central funding, commodities, and government bonds. Unfortunately, none of Marantz's previous positions provided the requisite experience in the complex world of securitization.

Marantz understood the politics within Lehman, but not securitized assets. This was excusable, but his indifference to its basic precepts was most disturbing. Given the desire, Marantz had ample intelligence to grasp the concepts, but was preoccupied with managing his career. The thought of seeking product managers to walk him through the process in order to acquire the basic principles of securitization must never have occurred to Marantz. Regrettably he seemed to care more about promoting himself than forging a balanced sales/trading environment. Marantz's sole priority appeared to be career advancement, even at the expense of his sales management duties.

The following week, McDade, Janulis, Gerard Reilly (CFO of the fixed-income division), and I had a conference call to review the transaction. As I mentioned earlier, Janulis had joined Lehman in 1985, trading asset-backed securities (ABSs) and REMICs, including the residual interest classes. After trading, he ran Lehman's mortgage finance group and ultimately the mortgage department. Now he and McDade were co-heads of fixed income. Janulis's experience made him fully conversant with residual interest, if a bit rusty with the nuances of the most recent safe harbor. Unfortunately, shortly afterwards, Janulis* took over Lehman's investment management division and the securitization experience and residual interest understanding went with him.

During the call I took the opportunity to express a concern: "Isn't anyone puzzled that during the course of all the internal transfers, no one on Sherr's mortgage structuring desk ever mentioned the ability to acquire phantom income from outside sources?"

After an uncomfortable pause, they assured me that "nothing was as it seemed," yet offered no meaningful explanation. Sherr's desk hardly needed the assistance of Lehman's tax department. Yet there were numerous creative trading strategies to reduce the cost of NERDs, so for the moment I felt it was best to leave well enough alone. Nonetheless, it heightened my suspicions and left me wondering what had happened to the Vanderbeek days when the issue would have been quickly addressed in an open forum.

Early in the second and third quarters, I arranged for the transfer of two more NERD portfolios. Shortly after completing the third-quarter transaction, the financial engineering group (tax strategy) expressed interest in reviewing the portfolio. They were curious to see if, within the tax code, they could more skillfully exploit the taxable income to broaden the gains for Lehman. Fortunately, after completing their analysis in early 2003, they concluded that they did not have the models or expertise to proficiently manage the portfolio and the character of residual phantom income was too restrictive. Of course, I had suggested this at the outset.

During the fourth quarter, several changes occurred. Lehman's balance between domestic and foreign earnings began to shift and mortgage-backed securities prepayments were much higher than originally projected. Lehman was no longer generating excess foreign tax credits. At the same time, mortgage rates fell during 2002 and into early 2003 from somewhere near 7 percent to the mid 5 percent range. The lower mortgage rates spurred a refinancing wave and reduced the expected phantom income relative to the original projections.

The key point: Faster mortgage prepayments meant roughly 70 percent of the acquired NERD portfolio had reached or were about to reach their crossover point—the magical juncture where phantom income reverts to phantom expense. Many of the residuals would soon be generating phantom expense and compel Lehman to transfer them in order to recapture the tax basis. For Lehman, the benefit of receiving the additional after-tax income at year end, as opposed to a period of several years, was substantial.

In order to recapture this built-up tax basis, eliminate funding the deferred asset, and realize the profits within the portfolio, it was time to seek a counterparty who met safe-harbor transfer rules. Lehman's next taxable reporting juncture was at fiscal yearend in November, so there was little time to waste.

In the fall of 2003, as Lehman was preparing for the NERD bidding process, Thomas Humphrey was named to replace Alan Marantz as global head of fixed income sales. Tom Humphrey was verbose, ambitious, and energetic, with a prodigious ego. He worked hard and most found him genial and focused. Unfortunately, he could not imagine consequences well and confused reality with what he wanted an outcome to be. He did not possess the certitude for eye-to-eye debate required with trading.

The following story may help the reader acquire a sense of Tom Humphrey: At the time Humphrey was assuming his new duties, USA Wrestling, in conjunction with New York City's Olympic Bid Committee, was hosting the World Freestyle Wrestling Championships in Madison Square Garden. I was president of USA Wrestling. The night before, at the New York Athletic Club, USA Wrestling sponsored a banquet honoring six distinguished individuals and recognized all of the United States' past Olympic and world champions.

The six honorees were Pulitzer Prize-winning author John Irving, former chairman and CEO of Goldman Sachs Steve Friedman, founder of Alcoa Standard Corporation John Vaughan, Speaker of the House Dennis Hastert, Secretary of Defense Donald Rumsfeld, and 1970 Nobel Peace Prize-winning agricultural scientist Norman Borlaug. All received a Lifetime Achievement Award from the International Wrestling Federation.

With all due respect to the extraordinary accomplishments of the award recipients, I was most impressed by modest Norm Borlaug, known as the "father of the Green Revolution." I first met the unassuming Mr. Borlaug at a NCAA wrestling championship and have admired him ever since. Borlaug had refused to accept the idea that the poor and starving in the world were doomed. His tireless efforts to develop drought and disease-resistant wheat helped save millions of lives. Through his work, poor people around the world have been spared famine and are now able to feed themselves.

Of course, wrestling played an important role in his determination. Dr. Kenneth Quinn writes, in his biography about Borlaug, "Norman developed a dogged tenacity from participating in his high school wrestling program—another quality that would play a crucial role in some of his greatest achievements."[7]

As president of USA Wrestling at the time, it was my responsibility to give the opening remarks at the awards ceremonies. I compiled what I wanted to say but still anguished over the presentation. The possibility of forgetting my lines or saying something stupid and making a fool of myself in front of the assembled awardees elevated the normal performance anxiety one gets before delivering a speech.

The master of ceremonies that evening was John Bardis, chairman and CEO of MedAssets—and a consummate host. In his introduction, Bardis told a story about one of USA's first multiple world gold medalists, Lee Kemp, a teammate of his at the University of Wisconsin. Bardis described how accomplished he felt every day after practice when Kemp would only beat him by one point. That is, until he realized, "Lee would only beat his grandmother by one point." It was a great introduction for the audience but also an opening for me.

After Bardis introduced me, I began, "John's story about Lee reminded me of my first major responsibility as U.S. national coach. It was the 1979 World Championships in Mexico City, which also was Lee Kemp's first major international competition. In the early rounds Lee drew several of his toughest opponents, namely the Iranian and the Soviet, and prevailed in close matches. The wrestling world was not yet aware that Lee characteristically would beat the worst wrestler in the world just as he would beat the best guy in the world—by a few points." I continued to set the scene. "There were ten wrestlers remaining going into the next round, but only six wrestlers could place. Under the double elimination format, Lee's next opponent, a Yugoslavian, had to either beat Lee or lose by less than eight points to finish in the top six. I suspect because they realized his chances of beating Lee were slim, the Yugoslavian coach approached me with a proposition."

"He said, 'If Kemp agrees not to defeat my wrestler by more than eight points, my wrestler will allow Kemp to win.' Somewhat puzzled by the proposition, I said, 'We don't do that' and walked away. As I was walking away it occurred to me that Lee doesn't beat anyone by more than eight points."

I continued, "Later that evening Lee wrestled the Yugoslavian and, you guessed it, he won by only a few points. I glanced over to the other corner, and the Yugoslavian coach winked and gave me the thumbs-up sign." In finishing the story I said, "To this day when I see the Yugoslavian coach, now president of the Macedonian Wrestling Federation, he says, 'Stan my friend'—and I cringe at the thought." I heard Hastert and Rumsfeld chuckle and Norm Borlaug laugh. I was at ease.

The next morning, before the World Championship started, I met with Humphrey in Lehman's offices at 49th Street and 7th Avenue, just a short walk from Madison Square Garden. Before replacing Marantz as head of global fixed income sales, Humphrey had been head of credit (corporate bonds) sales. I found him somewhat glib, and we did not always see eye-to-eye. Humphrey had suggested that while I was in New York we should talk. As he put it, "I want to get up to speed on the residual trades."

I am not sure I ever accomplished getting Humphrey "up to speed," but during our conversation a thought kept flitting through my mind: "Humphrey reminds me of someone. I am certain it isn't Norm Borlaug, but I cannot think of whom."

Then in a flash, it occurred to me: "The Yugoslavian coach."

In lieu of detailed product knowledge, Humphrey effectively swayed Lehman's senior management with enthusiasm and optimism. His personality was better suited for working at a hedge fund than as a Wall Street sales-force manager. He lacked the sense of duty that would impel him to confront the trading desks for what was in the long-term best interest of the firm.

Humphrey discovered early in his career the benefits of aligning with trading at the expense of being a monitor of risk taking. Like a politician or motivational speaker, Humphrey was a master at verbal crafting. "Humphrey could tell you to go to hell so tactfully that you looked forward to the trip," someone once mused.

Like Marantz, Humphrey was unwavering in managing his own career while knowing disturbingly little about mortgage securities. Both were ambitious and utterly committed to personal advancement, and as a result neither had time to question the trading desks' risk-taking. As a fellow mortgage salesman offered, Lehman just went from Tweedledee to Tweedledum. Though some seemed to succeed on social skills, it was my opinion that ultimately substance should be the enduring qualification for success on Wall Street. Perhaps I was wrong.

As Lehman's tax department jettisoned its acquired NERD portfolio for a substantial profit, it also returned to each desk the remains of their respective residuals. The mortgage desks were no longer wards of the tax department and the risk was their own. Or so I thought.

After reviewing the remnants of the respective NERD positions, most of the trading desks wanted out. The calls came quickly. "Can you find someone who can manage this stuff?" As emphasized before, when trading NERDs, market pricing convention calculates a transfer once the phantom income reverses into phantom loss. It was rightfully assumed that prudent entities would always recapture the basis immediately as opposed to over the remaining life of the REMIC. Lehman was no exception. It was most profitable and in its best interest to recapture the basis and secure the write-down up front.

With no phantom income remaining, there is no need to pay the acquirer for assuming the tax liability. Yet it is necessary for the owner to continue to file tax returns through the life of the REMIC. Since Lehman recaptures the basis on the transfer date, the next owner cannot report any losses on its tax return. Therefore it is necessary to pay a nuisance fee, as it is called, to compensate the recipient for the cost of both servicing and tax reporting. For example, Lehman paid a nuisance fee of approximately $700,000 for the 116 deals described earlier. Stated differently, Lehman paid the transferee a nuisance fee of just over $6,000 per residual to administer the tax reporting for the remaining term of the REMIC. In return Lehman recaptured tens of millions in tax-basis immediately instead of over the next four to five years; not a difficult decision.

Several traders balked at paying the nuisance fee despite the benefit to Lehman. As Lehman's internal accounting practice had it, when the residual reversed to phantom losses, it no longer charged the desk's ledger. Yet, should the trading desk choose to transfer the NERDs, the nuisance fee was its responsibility. Hence greed took over, and some of the trading desks myopically concluded that if they held the residuals until the issues paid off, their profit and loss account (P&L) would never be charged. True, but when pressed and given the explanation of the overwhelming benefit to Lehman, most willingly acquiesced. The non-agency desk would not listen to reason and chose to retain the residuals that were in the phantom loss phase. "Fuck Lehman; it's my P&L," was the way I remember it being phrased.

Primarily for protocol reasons, my first call was to Michael Glover, then head of Lehman's mortgage sales. Glover joined Lehman in 2000 in the derivatives sales area and had just recently moved to head up mortgage sales, despite his limited mortgage sales experience. In personality, he closely resembled Humphrey—most likely the reason for his promotion. Clearly it was not his nuanced knowledge of the mortgage market.

Though Glover admitted he had limited experience with residuals, he was sympathetic with the concept. Nonetheless, he purported to have no authority over trading and was unwilling to carry the torch. Therefore, I spoke with Humphrey and informed him that the non-agency desk was unwilling to transfer the NERDs because of the nuisance fees. After my conversation with Humphrey, I sensed I was getting nowhere, so I drafted an email to both Humphrey and McDade to explain the overwhelming economic advantage of transferring any residual once it passed into phantom losses. It also pointed out the perverse incentive of Lehman's current accounting. The following are highlights from several of my conversations with and emails to McDade and Humphrey:

> **Because of the cost of transferring the non-economic residuals (mostly a higher nuisance fee) the desk was planning on retaining them. This speaks to the problem I raised last year: Under the current arrangement, the firm is subsidizing the P&L of the CMO desks that**

retain the non-economic residuals and introduces artificial incentives…

The firm pays the taxes on the income reported on the quarterly schedule Qs (10Qs described earlier). When the deals are transferred to a 3rd party or they pay off, the reserve fund is released and taken into income by the respective desk while the firm writes down the basis. Net result: the firm incurred the entire cost of funding the deferred asset. This can be rather significant…

In order to capture the true economics, the amount of the reserve fund should be market driven. The desk would then have to decide at issuance if it were better to transfer the risk to a 3rd party or maintain and manage the risk internally… This assures optimal transfer: whenever the present value of the deferred asset's funding is greater than the inducement fee.

At the very least the firm should debit the various reserve funds for the cost of financing any negative balance. This will come closer to capturing the true cost of the REMIC and align the P&L of the desk with that of the firm…

If I am misinformed please let me know. Otherwise, unless we remedy the inequity, the desks' P&L will not be aligned w/ the firm's and we are subject to divergent profit motives.

Unfortunately McDade, who earlier sprang to defend the accommodative internal accounting policy for residual interest, showed no such zest to rein in the very trading desks that benefitted. What once was a mighty roar to protect the profits of the trading desk was not even a vague squeak from the throne of the global head of fixed income.

Unlike Vanderbeek, McDade did not possess the fortitude for confrontation and had a difficult time managing conflicts or wading into disputes. His reluctance to face controversy contributed to a risk management structure at Lehman that found itself ill-prepared for a crisis. Behind-the-scenes disputes between sales and trading are common on Wall Street; these standoffs, in the most effectively managed firms, are debated until resolved. The open critiques uncover recklessness or weaknesses in the decision process and create an open-minded environment so important in a well managed trading operation.

Lehman's arrangement confirmed my earlier suspicions that it augmented the mortgage desks' profits. Unless Lehman did not have any income to recapture, keeping NERDs that were generating phantom losses did not align with elementary accounting, cost attribution, or risk management. The very desk that benefited the most from the accommodative policies of Lehman's tax department was now unwilling to incur even a small fee, despite the advantage to Lehman.

"The opportunity as well as administrative costs should fully reflect Lehman's economic reality," I argued. Unfortunately McDade did not see it that way. He deceived himself into accepting the practice under the guise that it was in Lehman's best interest. Translation: Sherr's desk had strong trading profits, ergo, he must be right.

Without accurate attribution of costs, risk management becomes impossible. Risk managers have a difficult time keeping abreast of the risk in new market innovations with proper cost accounting, let alone depending on faulty attribution.

If one searches through the resumes of Marantz, Humphrey, and McDade, one finds no sales or operating experience in either mortgage or asset-backed securities. They had little understanding of how the mortgage desk operated—a fundamental weakness and a deeply troubling thought, given the importance of mortgages at Lehman. Sales, trading, and risk managers who spend at least some part of their career in asset-based securities markets naturally have a better understanding of the potential perils facing the business.

Giving McDade, Marantz, and Humphrey the benefit of the doubt, it is possible they may have attempted to corral the risk and were thwarted. I hesitate to place all the responsibility with them. Maybe they were just well-placed spectators, or responsibility was so widespread that no one had any control.

Reining in trading desks is often difficult to pull off politically during times of prosperity, and the task takes a strong personality. As credit spreads contract, over time traders and management assume it to be a new paradigm rather than temporary euphoria. Trading desks become addicted, and delude themselves into thinking the benign markets are a permanent norm and not an aberration.

As an ex-Lehman researcher eloquently described it: A self-reinforcing dynamic leads to excess confidence. Dealers willingly fund large positions with relatively narrow margin requirements, and executing large transactions has little impact on prices. The expansive trading volume generates profits despite slim bid-ask spreads making even inept traders appear talented. Clients become more accommodative, magnifying the illusion of liquidity.

Nonetheless, there were signs during McDade's stewardship that either he did not recognize his shortcomings or that he did not view them as such. Hoping to maintain peace with his direct reports, he failed to encourage those he supervised to establish true teamwork, build a consensus, or deliver controversial news. My understanding was that the partnership between the heads of sales and trading, under the leadership of the head of global fixed income should provide proper risk governance. At Lehman under Humphrey, Sherr, and McDade—"The Three Risketeers" as someone once referred to them—risk governance was woefully inadequate.

McDade and Humphrey were always a step behind when compared to the mortgage trading desk. The combination of Sherr's strong personality and management's lack of understanding of structured securities resulted in a fragmented risk management structure. The trading desk was better prepared for any argument and McDade, with his permissive style of management, acquiesced to their demands. If McDade and Humphrey found it difficult to comprehend NERDs, it is hard to imagine they understood synthetic CDOs or CDOs squared. Though perhaps not as clever as the proverbial foxes, the traders were guarding the henhouse.

It seems naive, but I thought we were supposed to be on the same side. I recall questioning McDade's and Humphrey's decisions, then being accused of unprofessionalism and hurting morale. Pushing back or rocking the boat was no longer encouraged. What should have raised red flags among Lehman's risk managers was routinely dismissed. Instead of advancing more effective risk management that might have curbed market sentiment and a wholesale run on the bank, McDade and Humphrey had chosen to turn Lehman upside down and avoid the foul odor hovering over the structured-product desk.

I had announced my intentions to retire at the end of the year. Yet my frustrations continued to grow as I became torn between a sense of duty and a desire to let it rest. "This soon will be someone else's problem," I would think. Unfortunately, my personality does not allow me to idly stand by in such situations and I knew I would rest better if I followed my instinct. As I mulled over what to do, I remembered a similar circumstance before the 1976 Olympic trials.

Sports Illustrated ran a story by Herman Weiskopf entitled, "Working His Way Up from the Bottom." In the article Weiskopf ordained Wade Schalles, one of my opponents, to make the Olympic team as "the United States' best hope for a wrestling gold medal at the Montreal Olympics." Though I viewed Carl Adams a tougher opponent, Schalles was certainly a formidable foe. Schalles held the NCAA record for the most pins and had just won the prestigious Tbilisi tournament in the Soviet Republic of Georgia. His style of wrestling was remarkably unique. It required his opponents to be keenly prepared. In retrospect, this is something I appreciate.

In his story, Weiskopf conceded that Schalles needed to "outwrestle Carl Adams, two time NCAA Champion and Stan Dziedzic, an NCAA titlist" to make the team and stated "Schalles has split 14 bouts with Dziedzic." Shortly before the edition went to press, *Sports Illustrated*, as practice requires, called to confirm the accuracy of the text.

The more Weiskopf described the content, the more agitated I became. The U.S. team most likely would have a returning Olympic champion, Ben Peterson, a world champion, Lloyd Keaser, and an Olympic silver medalist, John Peterson; yet *Sports Illustrated*'s self-anointed experts were going to decree that Schalles, who had never made a world or Olympic team, was "the United States' best hope for a gold medal."[8]

When Weiskopf turned to verifying the content, he said, "Schalles claimed the two of you have split evenly in fourteen matches."

I said, "You may want to check the record; that's not correct."

He responded, "*Sports Illustrated* would proceed and run the story as is."

"Go ahead," I said. "It doesn't matter."

"Why?"

"Because Schalles isn't going to make the team," I stated emphatically, and hung up.

Now as I approached retirement, I felt that same compulsion to speak out, but for completely different reasons. In 1976, I didn't care if *Sports Illustrated* ran the story. I just wanted the satisfaction of telling Weiskopf, "I told you so." This time, in contrast, I wanted Lehman's senior executives to take action and address the problem. Yet more important, I wanted to avoid saying, "I told you so."

I attempted, in vain, to persuade senior executives to re-examine ways to bolster attribution and risk management in the fixed-income department. Unfortunately, Lehman's most senior management rejected any further discussions regarding the unraveling of Lehman's attribution and risk management models. My trust that the leaders put the firm's interest first, was gone. Lehman's creed of open communication and teamwork were no longer "nonnegotiable." The Three Musketeers' motto of "All for one, one for all" had morphed into "Every department for itself" among Lehman's Three Risketeers. Lehman was losing its risk adverse compass that had been at the core of its original culture, and I was branded a disgruntled rebel.

The key here: The preeminent responsibility of the heads of major divisions should be risk management. A platform and oversight device that encourages debate—from those who daily serve the customers—around the wisdom and quality of risk measures should be constructed, even, if necessary, with lines of communication open to the board of directors. When dissent is not discouraged, there are more than a few highly qualified non-executive employees with the intelligence and experience to help navigate through a crisis.

---

* Janulis was largely responsible for amassing Lehman's vertically integrated subprime subsidiaries. Ouch.

18

LEHMAN'S FINAL CHAPTER

"History repeats itself because no one listens the first time." Anonymous

It would be disingenuous to assign the burden of incompetence for their lack of foresight on McDade, Marantz, Sherr, and Humphrey alone. If failing to be prescient enough to recognize the symptoms is incompetence, why stop there? Nearly all of Wall Street was remiss in predicting the impending implosion. The best and brightest on Wall Street collectively underestimated the risks that real estate posed to the financial markets. Washington touted the percentage increase in the rate of home ownership while government-sponsored enterprises FNMA and FHLMC, directed by the secretary of the U.S. Department of Housing and Urban Development, helped fund subprime mortgages.

BlackRock, which the Fed often sought for advice, made one of their largest acquisitions, Hilton Worldwide, just before the global hotel market went into the worst contraction in occupancy rates since the Great Depression. Ben S. Bernanke, chairman of the Federal Reserve Board, and Henry Paulson, the treasury secretary, also failed to see the gravity of the problem. In the spring of 2007, Bernanke and Hank Paulson reassured the public that the mortgage problems were isolated and continued this optimistic view for months. In March 2007, Bernanke stated, "At this juncture, however, the impact on the broader economy and financial markets of the subprime market seems likely to be contained."[1]

Yet the lesson here is not about being clairvoyant; it is about putting in place a prudent structure that seeks the collective wisdom of interested parties, aligns personal wealth with risk, and provides a credible mechanism to intervene. This should be a framework that fosters forward-thinking solutions for complex issues yet does not curtail the benefits of scale and scope.

Although there is little to offer to exculpate McDade, unquestionably the ultimate responsibility resided with Dick Fuld. Missing the cues that Lehman's risk management was inadequate, Fuld was the architect behind Lehman's demise; he had condoned the untenable leverage and reckless risk management.

A public figure who may help the reader acquire a sense of Fuld's managerial persona would be Vladimir V. Putin; Russia's ex-KGB officer turned prime minister. Fuld, with his stiff demeanor (so common among Soviet-era KGB agents) gave the formal appearance of a totalitarian aristocrat who viewed the competition with deep suspicion. Where Putin sought to restore Russia to its rightful place among world powers, Fuld believed he was destined to restore Lehman to its once-prominent place among the world's premier investment banks.

And appearing as a no-nonsense, strong (but not admired) leader, he nearly succeeded. After all, struggling through several crises, such as Russia's default, LTCM's near failure, Enron's unraveling, and the aftermath of 9/11, Fuld was at the helm as Lehman emerged as one of the largest and most profitable investment banks in the world.

Most saw Fuld as straight-laced, but few, other than his loyal lieutenants, found him fair-minded. His personal characteristics, in sharp contrast to Putin's, were far less flashy. Fuld did not attempt to cultivate a charismatic or colorful image, as Putin did. Though physically solid and an avid squash player, vainly striking a pose, riding bare-chested in public, or stirring up dust on a Harley-Davidson were not within Fuld's character.

Unfortunately, as the press fell over one another to praise Lehman as one of Wall Street's best-managed banks, Fuld became intoxicated with his own greatness. In the end, he believed that only he knew what was best for Lehman. Fuld's inadequacies began to surface and then abruptly came into play during the crises. Along with his neatly tailored suits, Hermes ties, and freshly shined shoes, Fuld preferred loyalty to competency.

One person who epitomized Fuld's boundless trust was Mark Walsh. After graduating from Fordham Law School, Walsh joined Lehman in

1987. Eventually, as a result of a series of prodigious investments, he earned Fuld's confidence and with it an extraordinary latitude to commit Lehman's capital. This was evident long before Lehman's demise.

Shortly after I had been promoted to managing director (MD) in 1996, all of the global MDs were summoned to New York for a weekend of meetings. Although I had received my obligatory letter of congratulations, a Lucite plaque commemorating my promotion, and a vintage bottle of Dom Perignon, this was my first meeting as an MD.

I recall bits of Fuld's remarks praising the acumen of the commercial real estate group, and Walsh in particular. Fuld recalled one of the group's first major investments, a distressed pool of commercial real estate debt from Westinghouse. Fuld, a notoriously awkward speaker, seemed enthusiastic and even confident in his delivery as he stated: "After months of improving the assets, Walsh and his group repackaged the debt into commercial mortgage-backed securities and realized a substantial profit for Lehman."

Then Fuld musingly described a related gamble, the purchase of a landmark building, One Time Square, by Lehman's principal transaction group. He recounted giving Walsh his approval with one caveat: "I do not want to read about this in the papers." Needless to say, the press got wind of the transaction and soon everyone knew. Still, Fuld completed the story praising Walsh's pioneer efforts and the mighty returns Lehman had realized.

It was not the last of Walsh's team's headline-grabbing deals. Seemingly every year the commercial real estate group would do at least one landmark transaction worthy of the press's recognition, including the 1997, $2.24 billion joint conduit transaction with First Union (described earlier in Chapter Ten). With each new profitable venture, Walsh's status grew—as did his authority to risk the firm's capital.

The confidence in Walsh and Lehman's real estate activities was not confined to the executive branch. This optimistic view was widely held within Lehman and throughout the commercial real estate industry. The coordination of the investment banking functions under Ray Mikulich, the securitization process managed by Mike Mazzei, and the principal transaction group led by Mark Walsh provided Lehman with a unique platform in the late 1990s and early 2000s.[2]

Nevertheless, the difficulty Lehman had funding its commercial real estate during Long Term Capital Management's near collapse—something the Atlanta office was keenly aware of—was not recognized for the warning it should have been. For Lehman, the risks had been there for some time, and management should have understood the consequences.

Although it was temporary, Lehman under Vanderbeek's guidance became more cautious following LTCM's near demise and began to look for ways to move some of the funding risk off of Lehman's balance sheet. Lehman had several employee investment partnerships primarily designed as retention vehicles for its managing directors.

Part of Lehman's solution to move some of the real estate positions off its balance sheet was to borrow from those private-equity models and start private real estate funds. Senior management deemed at the time that there were more attractive commercial real estate deals than Lehman had capital.

Curiously, Mark Walsh was chosen, along with Ray Mikulich, to co-head the group. Increasingly, more lines of Lehman's commercial real estate business reported to Walsh. This further consolidated his authority and put Walsh in a unique position on Wall Street. While other financial firms prudently divided those responsibilities among several managers, Lehman consolidated them, ignoring the most rudimentary tenant of risk management. After hearing about the appointment, I recall quipping, "They must be stoned."

Another salesman agreed. "They have to be smoking dope to concentrate that much authority with Walsh. I don't care how smart he is!"

I explained, "I didn't mean Fuld and company were smoking dope; I meant 'Stoned,' as in Andy Stone." Stone, like Walsh, was viewed as both talented and creative and had gained the confidence of Credit Suisse First Boston's senior management after several prescient commercial real estate purchases. Credit Suisse First Boston gave him the authority to go on a buying spree, which eventually strapped the bank with billions of highly illiquid commercial real estate loans and equity. Oops![3]

Some may wonder if Walsh's meteoric rise was happenstance or genius. Best answer: a little of each. To be sure, intelligence, talent, drive, and timing all had a role in Walsh's ascent. While others, like Andy Stone, flaunted their power, Walsh was surprisingly soft-spoken and resisted developing a public persona. Walsh would be easier to cast as a nerd in the film *Revenge of the Nerds* than as Gordon Gekko in *Wall Street*.

The point is not that Walsh was incompetent; quite the opposite. Instead, it is that the confidence in his ability to continually generate profits was such a widely held view among Lehman's senior management. If anyone doubts the widespread trust in Walsh, look at his unchecked powers and the amount of money management invested in the private real estate funds.

Whether the confidence in Walsh was founded or unfounded, it is easy to understand how it materialized. The contribution to Lehman's earning of each new commercial real estate venture further solidified Walsh's credibility among the firm's senior management. Just as Drexel's boundless confidence in Michael Milken during its expansion of the high-yield market led to a lack of supervision and its ultimate failure and LTCM's tremendous confidence that the world's markets would behave rationally led to its demise, so too did Lehman's stupendous confidence in the mortgage and commercial real estate group prove to be its Achilles heel. Lehman's management should never have allowed Walsh's bets to reach such perilous levels.

At the most critical juncture, Fuld and his loyal lieutenants chose to okay the Archstone-Smith purchase, expanding Lehman's balance sheet to untenable levels. The significant losses Lehman incurred from its share of the $22.2 billion Archstone-Smith purchase were most likely the proverbial straw that broke the camel's back. As real estate assets softened, Lehman should have paid the break-up fee and walked away from the deal. This time, Walsh's industry-specific knowledge and his uncanny instinct for good deals were insufficient.[4]

The risks should have been more apparent to Lehman's senior management than to anyone else. Yet for unknown reasons, the aloof and defiant Fuld found it unnecessary to establish prudent boundaries for the exposure to commercial real estate. In retrospect, we can see that many of the signs should have been crystal clear—and would have been if not for Lehman's senior management, who wore rose-colored glasses.

As mentioned earlier, after Lehman's sturdy revival following LTCM's near collapse, Fuld perceived any panic-induced sell-off as a signal to buy. But this time things were different. Fuld's obsessive attention to tracking down and exposing conspirators supposedly wanting to overthrow his kingdom ultimately led to his failure to recognize the extent of Lehman's risk exposure. A trader who had a front row seat pointed out that any reasonably intelligent sales-person would have understood Lehman's risk, but Fuld didn't. Instead of a steward of Lehman's franchise, Fuld saw himself as the owner.

As its yearlong decline unfolded, in a desperate eleventh-hour effort to attract capital and assuage concerns Lehman began providing details to the media of a plan to place its troubled mortgage and commercial real estate assets into a "bad bank."* In a strange paradox, Lehman—which had expanded its commercial real estate efforts with a "good-bank, bad-bank" partnership with Westinghouse Electric Corporation—in the end worked toward a similar solution.

As a result of lax lending policies, in the 1980s Westinghouse had amassed a commercial real estate portfolio of poorly underwritten office, apartment, and hotel properties. In an effort to liquidate one of the largest real estate debacles of the decade, Westinghouse had spun off the assets into a bad-bank partnership with Lehman. Perhaps there was some complacency: because the Westinghouse workout plan was successful, it was believed that Walsh could succeed again this time. Fuld and his loyal acolytes must have thought Walsh had a rabbit up his sleeve.[5]

Unfortunately, the Hail Mary pass came too late in the game and the gamble was much too large. The market demons had already surfaced, ready to pounce on arrogance. Lehman's once-impregnable commercial real estate and mortgage departments faltered. In a throwback to the Glucksman era, Fuld tragically repeated his mentor's mistakes and Lehman grew dysfunctional. This time there was no American Express to rescue Lehman.

Fuld's obsession with outmatching the returns of his peers and his inability to build a consensus or manage conflicts diplomatically was reflected in his inability to request feedback or encourage debate. In Fuld's eyes, Lehman executives other than his few loyal lieutenants were less than capable of proffering informed decisions. The kingdom is mine the gorilla roared!

Fuld should have learned from previous crises that structuring trading desks to a kind of common ownership or partnership, defining the pay-for-performance clearly, and seeking broader participation in conflicts offered the foundation for sound financial risk management.

Lehman should have understood as well if not better than most that a balanced sales–trading partnership functioned most effectively. Preserving the partnership served as a guard rail on concentrated risk and a market intelligence-gathering vehicle. But instead, Lehman's disorganized diversification turned the once focused franchise into a highly leveraged, awkward conglomerate of loosely related fiefdoms.

In defiance of widespread statements from authorities that there was no taxpayers' money or legal authority to bail out Lehman, Fuld did curiously little to reduce risk. As Fuld's loyal Lehmanites continued to give him the reassurance he sought—but not the dissent he needed—Fuld remained stubbornly willing to call the government's bluff.

Clinging to unrealistic valuations of Lehman's commercial real estate and mortgage assets, Fuld held out for a better deal. Even on the eve of destruction, as Lehman stood on the threshold of darkness, the headstrong Fuld and his loyal lieutenants seemed to feel that dawn was near and remained unwilling to acknowledge the impending danger to which they themselves had exposed Lehman.

As certain as it is darkest before dawn, Fuld was confident that the sunrise would bring a buyer. Unfortunately, as the middle of the night approaches, it is also dark and Fuld, desperate to find a rescue plan, ran out of options as Lehman faced a window of darkness. The eve of the inconceivable too soon gave way to the dawning of the inevitable. Lehman, a firm that had withstood previous disasters, had lost itself when it compromised the very risk management it was built upon, and the flame that had burned for more than a century and a half, was extinguished. Fuld—defiantly independent Fuld—had put the legendary Lehman Brothers on the dark side of history.

---

* Generally speaking a **"bad bank"** is formed to remove problem assets from the balance sheet of a struggling financial institution. It is a separately capitalized legal entity created to hold nonperforming or impaired assets.

19

LESSONS LEARNED FROM LEHMAN'S DANCE WITH DELUSION

"In today's complex and fast-moving world, what we need even more than foresight or hindsight, is insight." Anonymous

In the aftermath of Lehman's more tragic than predictable demise, Wall Street will take customary post-crisis actions and install sturdier risk-management controls. It will take initiatives to improve the accuracy of quantitative risk models, tighten internal limits, raise margin requirements, increase the restricted equity portion of bonuses, and require transparency of information from counterparties and managers who oversee the individual desk's risk. Unfortunately, customary measures are more likely than not to be inadequate—as they were for Lehman.

If one reviews Fuld's testimony about the collapse of Lehman before the House Committee on Government Reform, there are signs of what went wrong. Fuld effectively validates his unwavering commitment, "I never sold any shares, and that's why I had ten million left. I believed in the company. I could have sold that stock. But I did not, because I believed we would return to profitability." And in response to questions about what he thought of the bailouts of some of his competitors, Fuld states regretfully, "I would have loved to be part of that group..."

Yet in the end, Fuld offered no mea culpa, no regrets as to what other course he might have taken, and no acknowledgment of mistakes. He never even hinted that Lehman's failure was either preventable or in any way a direct result of his reckless decisions. Instead, with careful rhetoric, striving to avoid any appearance of culpability, Fuld offered, "... What could I have done differently? What could I have said? What should I have done? And I have searched myself every single night. And I come back to this: at the time I made those decisions, I made those decisions with the information I had....."[1]

Apparently, Fuld did not think to ask himself the most important question: What happens if I am wrong? Perhaps his own paranoia hampered his capacity to look ahead and imagine the consequences. Fuld staunchly contended that it was not his own misjudgments that proved to be Lehman's downfall. Instead, he argued that it was the regulators' unwillingness to intercede on Lehman's behalf, the short sellers that bet against Lehman, and the capricious and unpredictable headwinds of the financial markets that caused the firm to collapse.

Assuming that the same misguided confidence in both individuals and markets will not re-emerge, is a mistake. A history of crises cautions us that overabundant greed is a threat. In fact, global financial markets structurally are more prone to develop over-exuberance now. Given the recent consolidation of competition and assets within fewer financial entities, the seeds of another irrational market may have found fertile soil—a breeding ground for another crisis.

Wall Street has long known (but like Lehman, tends to forget) that pricing of even the most liquid assets requires a substantial discount or haircut (a cushion) for the perceived cost of moving relatively large blocks of assets. When assets are marked-to-market, neglecting to consider the size and the relative dimension within its market is simply reckless. Lehman and/or the Financial Accounting Standards Board should have required the commercial real estate division to discount the pricing of its portfolio to make an allowance for moving large blocks of assets–a reversion to reality.[2]

Today policymakers have two unpalatable choices: allow large financial entities like Lehman to go into bankruptcy (and then collectively the country can hold its breath as the financial system races toward the abyss) or put it on the taxpayers' tab. Neither is appealing. In fact, both should be unacceptable.

The Treasury, Federal Reserve, and Wall Street's corporate leaders purportedly could not manufacture a solution allowing Lehman to unwind in an orderly way in lieu of bankruptcy. By all accounts, the Treasury and Fed knew the potential catastrophic consequences of Lehman's insolvency but contend they lacked sufficient powers and were unable to find a better way to contain the carnage. Lehman's failure underscores the need for oversight authority to audit and intervene to force profligate entities into compliance before crises become unmanageable. The elevated uncertainty is the true public enemy.

Lawmakers and regulators may need to think more radically than in the past. There are no *Back to the Future* sequels with time machines or Marty McFlys to bring back an almanac detailing future overheated markets. The policy maker's quest should not be to find a system that predicts but rather one that prevents irresponsible risk-taking that requires taxpayers' money. Even staunch laissez-faire promoters concede that allowing self-interested traders to reap the bounty from risky bets while losses have the potential of being borne by the taxpayer does not support a sound financial system.

The longer managers of trading units wait to fashion disciplined, capitalized structures, the more difficult it will be to make adjustments. Banks and/or regulators can tackle the problem now or sit back and wait for the next subprime fiasco to initiate a vicious cycle that accompanies each crisis and damages the economy at large.

Not that long ago, partnerships understood the concept. As a public company Salomon's management knew the importance as far back as the late 1980s. When Salomon's management wrestled with the issue of introducing a percentage payout for the arbitrage desk, Salomon's CEO Gutfreund must have anticipated that the plan would stir unrest among other key employees and potentially introduce added incentives to risk the firm's capital. In fact, most likely that was the reason Salomon acquired the expertise of Myron Scholes, who in 1977 won a Nobel Prize in economics for his part as co-originator of the Black-Scholes formula for pricing options.

Gutfreund must have understood that any effective pay-for-performance plan needed to accurately account for the amount of risk. What he failed to anticipate was Paul Mozer's contempt and defiance before he could institute the plan.

As alluded to in Chapter Seven, I accidentally stumbled upon the concept when Myron Scholes contacted me when I was a mortgage salesman at Salomon. The reader may be asking why Myron Scholes, who helped create the most widely used pricing formula in the financial industry, wanted to talk with me. The same thought came to my mind. Rest assured it was not because he wanted to know whether the *sigma* in his option equation was unique. He was inquiring about the circumstances that motivated some of my clients in the REMIC residual market.

Why Scholes wanted to speak with me is not important, but his primary duties at Salomon were important. Since shyness is not an attribute I possess, I did not hesitate to ask the question: "Why are you working on such an insignificant issue? Deriving elegant mathematical formulas seem far more interesting." He kindly answered, "As a special consultant to the office of the chairman my challenge was to calculate an appropriate cost-of-capital adjusted for the risk within the various divisions of Salomom. With John Gutfreund's departure, I am attempting to constructively use my expertise during my tenure at Salomon."

I can only guess that John Gutfreund wanted to corral Salomon's arbitrage group. He understood that Salomon's arbitrage desk was a large hedge fund with inordinately cheap funding and with the benefit of cover supplied by Salomon's market dominating trading volume. Gutfreund realized there was no cogent argument that could be made to pay a percentage of revenues without accurately accounting for the cost of capital.

For me, several ideas kept recurring: What if Scholes had solved the elusive issue of the appropriate cost of capital for individual risk units? If the concept gained traction and became part of Wall Street's best practice, it may have averted or at least lessened the severity of global financial crises. The performance-enhanced proprietary trading operations could have been appropriately separated from the customer-focused duties of raising and efficiently allocating capital. A built-in governor to excessive risk!

Determining exactly the appropriate capital levels under such a governance structure is a challenge. Yet just because adequate capital levels are difficult to calculate precisely, it is no reason to abandon the effort. There are more than enough talented bankers capable of calibrating the magnitude of risk and cost of capital.

Establishing secure capital levels among divisions to ensure each has its own source of liquidity in a crisis may prove to be a far easier task than ascertaining the suitable size or appropriate functions for our financial institutions. It is no secret within the industry that there are wide disparities in the amount of risk taken by various trading units. Among the fixed income units, these range from a matched book of U.S. Treasury bills to the proprietary book of over-the-counter (OTC) derivatives.

Regulators have long understood the concept of relative risk. They restrict what assets banks can own, set minimum margin requirements, and adjust capital ratios to reflect risk. For instance, U.S. banks cannot own stocks (per the Banking Act of 1933) nor can they own bonds that are below investment grade, because they are too risky. Also, examiners adjust banks' assets for risk when determining minimum capital ratios.[3]

Unfortunately, capital requirements at the bank holding company apply only to the bank, investment bank, or insurance company subsidiaries and are terribly easy for Wall Street to game (see Chapter Four on gaming risk-adjusted capital). Current regulations do not mandate minimum capital ratios at the individual trading desks such as derivatives, governments, corporate bonds, money markets, or mortgages.

If Lehman's commercial real estate division, as a vivid example, were independently capitalized and were required to increase capital at a marginal rate greater than the proportional rate of asset growth, leverage might have been restrained. If escalating margin requirements were in place as credit spreads tightened, the self-reinforcing price appreciation might have been tamer. If a major portion of the net worth of the group's employees was retained in its division's capital, the calls for a dispersion of risk might have occurred sooner and with greater resolve.

Yet more important, if Lehman's management had continued to ignore the risk, its failure would have been more orderly and far less costly to the taxpayers. When the residential and commercial real estate units foundered, the stakeholders and debt providers would have suffered, but the overall financial entity might have remained intact (if smaller).

The distressed assets could have been placed into a fund administered by a private-public partnership; management could have been replaced; and a lesser, adequately capitalized and more limited Lehman could have continued operating. The vicious cycle that had the potential to cascade until the toxic assets clogged the financial irrigation system could have been held in check, shielding the taxpayer from the trading desk's high-octane speculation.

When the banking system required emergency funding, supervisors would have had the ability to expeditiously isolate the crisis and allow the essential credit supply to continue uninterrupted, ensuring the resilience of the system. By separating the faltering desk and its toxic, hard-to-value assets from the rest of Lehman, the argument continues, confidence would have been restored and the everyday business of the bank maintained—but purged of the irresponsible risk takers. The remaining entity would be wounded and more narrowly focused, but at least understood.

Employees' incentive plans that ensure certain sharing in profits or losses based on the restricted stock and/or options accumulated during their employment, are not unique. Payout plans, in which key employees receive or purchase restricted stock and/or options of a unit within a financial entity based on a deemed value, also exist. Barclay's global money-management division is an excellent example. Upon selling the unit to BlackRock, a number of executives at Barclays received the proceeds from the shares accumulated under such a plan. This type of structure combines the discipline of a partnership within each business unit and provides a market-based balance between risk and reward. Gains and losses are more aligned to the ones responsible.[4]

BlackRock itself started in 1988 as Blackstone Financial Management, part of the Blackstone Group. Ironically, the Blackstone Group was co-founded by Peter Peterson and Steven Schwarzman, both ex-Lehman bankers, following an internal struggle within Lehman between investment bankers and traders, one of whom was the now infamous Dick Fuld. Another example is Pacific Investment Management Company, originally part of Pacific Life Insurance Company.[5]

Wall Street may resist such a structure, claiming it subjects them to the risk of losing their most valued employees. Yet the argument is specious, arguing erroneously that talented risk-takers will rush to hedge funds if we alter the "heads I win, tails you lose" asymmetric compensation model. Offering the hope of compounding one's capital and building a business by taking advantage of the resources within a larger company should attract the most talented and brightest in the industry. Holding out the opportunity to become the next Laurence D. Fink, chairman and CEO of BlackRock, or William H. Gross, founder and CIO of Pacific Investment Management Company, would rival the lure of becoming a partner. Furthermore, fellow risk-takers whose money is at stake will be vigilant crusaders against excessive risk-taking.

Lehman missed the clues and hence the opportunity to institute such changes. Other large financial entities may learn from Lehman's mistakes and take preemptive action to govern risk taking by putting in place measures that harness excessive leverage in performance-enhanced markets. Unless Wall Street banks prefer the government to limit their size and/

or impose straight line fees to discourage risky activities, risk managers may want to introduce a market-based approach, one that borrows from the discipline of partnerships and puts substance behind the multipronged compensation plans they espouse.

Dividing larger banks internally into separate legal divisions with specific risked-based capital, some of which is the interested parties' own restricted stock and options, might also be essential to the solution. When the interests of the suppliers of capital and the risk takers are in harmony, good things seem to happen. Sales and trading are more likely to prudently maintain adequate margins when lending their own money, which in turn may help mitigate the vicious cycle that precedes financial crises. Excessive leverage or insufficient capital-at-risk within Lehman's individual trading units drove its overall failure. The ability to build wealth along with the shareholders will foster a culture of long-term risk management. Think auto claw-back!

What would such a structure accomplish? Like a partnership, it would create wealth on realized profits—net dollars realized in disposition over the price paid in acquisition—not interim marked-to-market gains. It would allow financial innovation to flourish but not stray from the proper course. This would give investors and regulators details about capital levels and make monitoring leverage clearer. It would also make it easier to identify systemic risk and separate funding of the banking and investment banking activities. This structure would make it easier to segregate conflicting duties between originating and distributing. It would create a meritocracy that better corralled risk and retained the most effective talent. It would also end the Fed's practice of rescuing trading desks from ill-advised risk-taking. And, most importantly, it would allow supervisors a credible way to enhance market discipline and close units without breaking up or disrupting the fundamental commercial or utility bank. The benefit that large integrated banks with a worldwide footprint provide in today's diverse global economy would be retained.

What such a structure does not do is immunize markets from panic or prevent banks from taking speculative risks that may lead to failure. Admittedly, mitigating the effect on financial institutions and aligning risk with wealth creation may not totally prevent or obviate the need for government intervention in the next crisis. Segregating risk into divisions will improve and expedite the gathering of data, but structure and expectations of rational behavior, by themselves, are insufficient.

The massive destruction of wealth among LTCM's and Lehman's principal equity holders is evidence. What happened in Long Term Capital Management debunks the idea that structure alone can eliminate any further diligence. A group which arguably contained the most intelligent financial minds ever assembled took risks, which if wrong, could bankrupt them. Why they took a path that risked profound economic disruption, most of their net worth, and a possible catastrophic financial consequence is deeply puzzling, yet nonetheless instructive of the danger in unbounded confidence. Even the most sophisticated models cannot forecast either panic or euphoria.

Certainly there is an argument to be made that says that regulators can no longer wait until risks emerge before reacting. It is incumbent upon supervisors to intervene expeditiously to restore confidence and resuscitate demand. The need for the "pre-eminent regulator" and its oversight committee to intervene to re-establish trust remains a possible solution. When either self-interest or prudence gets out of hand, the "super-regulator" needs to moderate the vicious cycles. Quickly interceding and bypassing malfunctioning markets, similar to its debt purchasing program and the Term Asset-Backed Securities Loan Facility, may be one of the Fed's most powerful tools. The question is: Who should bear the cost when markets need to be stabilized?

Taxpayers will no longer accept a structure in which trading desks create systemic risk and do not pay the cost—nor should they. Neither will they wait until after a government rescue to recoup the cost. Calls for a tax or transaction fee are gaining broader endorsement from global finance ministers. Given what the S&L crisis brought into focus, flat-fee insurance is fraught with problems. There is no better example of how mispriced deposit insurance promoted risk-taking. Wall Street banks, securities firms, hedge funds, and money managers may do well to learn from Lehman and initiate discussion with lawmakers regarding a public–private partnership to determine when such insurance would be appropriate and how to price it.

An infrastructure via the credit default swap (CDS) market has the capacity to price this insurance along with a mature legal framework and evolved market standards in the International Swaps & Derivatives Association (ISDA). CDSs are tradable, over-the-counter derivatives that behave like insurance and provide protection against default. Think auto insurance to cover losses in the event of a default.

A CDS is an efficient medium to transfer risk. It also solves the timing problem. The oversight board no longer must guess about what asset is overpriced and when the end of the bubble is approaching. It only needs to discern which asset class is unreasonably priced. In a standard CDS contract, the purchaser acquires protection to cover the face value loss of the asset in the case of a credit event typically defined as: failure to meet payment, bankruptcy, default, or restructuring for an designated period. The buyer agrees to make periodic payments (insurance premiums) for this protection. Should the asset fail to meet its obligation during the life of the contract, the CDS seller (insurer) is obligated to compensate the CDS buyer for the loss.[6]

Therein lays the rub. Unlike insurance contracts, in the over-the-counter CDSs market, there are no regulators routinely checking the books to make certain that funds are available to cover any claims. (Note: most seem to agree that AIG's capital and funds to satisfy policyholder's claims was sufficiently segregated within the regulated insurance subsidiary.) Credit default swaps trade actively on a variety of indices, sovereign debt, and large individual issuers. The rise in standardized, high-volume CDS indices shows the ability to trade CDSs on exchanges and to clear through a clearinghouse.

As argued in the derivative section (Chapter Three), pushing CDSs to be processed through a clearinghouse increases the transparency, lowers the transaction costs, and most importantly absorbs the counterparty risk, which reduces the potential for contagion. Exporting the technology and structure to trade more indices-such as certain derivatives, subprime mortgages, and commercial mortgages-would provide valuable pricing information. Advanced dealer models might supply the government with practical market-based pricing. As models improve, so too would regulators' ability to price taxpayer risk. An evolution as opposed to a revolution!

Devising a joint solution with the private sector that could harness trading data and information from the CDS market could improve how our free markets function. When markets begin to overreach, the Federal Reserve, within its oversight authority, could act as the seller of CDSs (insurer). The trading desks, hedge funds, insurance companies, or other financial entities sufficiently intertwined to introduce systemic risk would be the buyers of the respective CDS indices, introducing restraint and confidence. Any subsequent intervention could be funded by those market-priced premiums and not by a uniform tax.

The Federal Housing Authority's public–private concept, without the political influence, may serve as a potential model. A self-funded government agency provides the insurance, and, for a fee, pre-approved lenders underwrite the loans. A similar private–public partnership where, for a fee credit default swap desks price the cost of insurance and a self-funded government agency supplies the insurance, may prove effective and worth pursuing. As the risk premium demanded by investors escalates compared to other similar credits or markets, it sends a warning signal to both management and regulators of deteriorating financial conditions.

Under the current system, confidence among market participants builds during benign markets, leading banks to require increasingly lower margins or down payments. In part this pushes marks or values to levels higher than the capital base warrants or where they would be, absent the added leverage. When an unexpected disruption creates market turmoil, this confidence fades and panic often emerges. Market participants flee risk and seek safety in the most liquid government bond markets, causing credit spreads to widen. Lenders demand larger margins. When margins calls are not met, assets are liquidated, further fueling the decline.

Prices fall so quickly that traders build in a cushion when pricing assets. If the ensuing cycle or downward spiral is large enough and beyond fundamentals, government intervention may be required. Under a structure that compartmentalizes the risk when margins and/or capital levels are inadequate, supervisors as well as risk management can recognize the deficiency and intervene in a more timely fashion.

Have confidence–absent an appropriate cost of capital–financial institutions will allocate funding to the desks generating the highest returns, irrespective to risk. This is something a casino manager may desire, but is hardly a strong foundation upon which to build a durable financial system.

EPILOGUE

"The dogmas of the quiet past are inadequate to the stormy present. The occasion is piled high with difficulty, and we must rise with the occasion. As our case is new, so we must think anew, and act anew. We must disenthrall ourselves, and then we shall save our country." Abraham Lincoln, December 1, 1862 Message to Congress.

Most people would agree that the global financial structure does not work and needs repair. Financial entities—or at least parts of them—need to be restructured in order to enable them to fail; and taxpayers should not be held responsible if or when this occurs. The status quo among major banks is unacceptable. Self-correcting markets have been debunked, and Wall Street banks must accept responsibility and make dramatic changes in their risk management structure.

Maximizing shareholders' wealth is not always compatible with the construction of a stable financial system. Collecting the bounty on profitable trades, while sticking the taxpayers with the tab for trading bets gone awry does not comport with market efficiency. Today's crisis requires a new approach. Our nation must build a stable foundation to support a sound banking system for future generations—a system that insulates the risk and protects the traditional banking activities of taking deposits and providing sufficient access to liquidity to make loans.

Had the Federal Reserve not orchestrated emergency measures following Lehman's bankruptcy, the nation's entire banking system would have been at risk. Without the Fed's intervention, it is plausible that no major financial institution would have survived. Though some still reject the idea, Wall Street should concede that all the large investment banks could have failed if the government had not interceded following Lehman's failure. By waiving the rules and allowing both Morgan Stanley and Goldman Sachs to become bank holding companies, the Fed probably protected them from suffering the same fate that met Merrill Lynch, Bear Stearns, and Lehman.[1]

Wall Street, which vigorously defends the merits of a pay-for-performance structure, should support paying the taxpayers for their contribution. Otherwise, Wall Street bankers are indeed the greedy ingrates that taxpayers make them out to be. And Wall Street's so called meritocracy is malarkey. At some juncture (hopefully soon) and at their own accord, Wall Street bankers will accept responsibility. There appears to be inexorable political will calling for action against what is widely perceived as speculative excesses. An imperative for change!

Should Wall Street fail to take measures to govern cavalier risk-taking, policymakers may reinvent the financial private sector in a mode that stifles innovation. When faced with the choice of overregulation or the possibility of another crisis in several years, lawmakers will attach to the anti-banking sentiment and naturally opt for the former, for reasons of national interest.

In the recent crisis, misguided regulations were more often the problem than deregulation. Those who refer to the limitations of markets were in many cases describing the limitations of risk managers, policymakers, and supervisors, rather than to less-constrained markets. Market accomplishments remain. Though less-constrained markets may not have done as much as some hoped—and certainly less than most wanted—nonetheless, free markets have accomplished a great deal more than many expected. Losing sight of robust, free-market ideas as mainstream policy is akin to throwing out the champagne with the cork when the champagne is still bubbly. The financial crisis was not an indictment of free markets or capitalism, but rather a failure of supervision and risk management.

Let us hope it is not too late to curtail excessive government intrusion in financial sector governance. Given the level of resentment the current recession spawned, it is understandable that many feel government restrictions are a sort of poetic market justice that Wall Street should incur for the bets paid off by the government bailout. Yet for our nation's economy, creating de facto government-sponsored entities and allocating capital under political pressure is dangerous and could lead to disastrous repercussions. Providing Congress the avenue to shove banks as it did FNMA and FHLMC to politicize the lending process is not fiscally prudent and exposes the taxpayer to unconscionable risks. The thought of our financial system besieged by requests from Congress should make one cringe.

To deflect public outcry, Wall Street banks may temporarily redistribute the split of revenues between shareholders and employees, increase the percentage of restricted stock and options in employees' bonuses, introduce claw-back provisions, and extend the time it takes for deferred compensation to "vest" (become eligible to trade). Such changes are necessary adjustments. They are steps in the right direction. However, these fall short of restraining what outsiders rightly consider to be extravagant bonus packages following a government-funded rescue.

It is no surprise that surviving Wall Street banks balk at suggestions that they account for all their benefits, and that they do not wish to fully repay the taxpayer. After all, Wall Street concedes, we take our money seriously. Nonetheless, Wall Street must be challenged or embarrassed (if that is possible) into taking responsibility and abiding by the very meritocracy that it espouses.

Wall Street could start by repaying the taxpayers for the portion of profits it realized from the oodles of cheap funding supplied by government guarantees. Next, the federal government should calculate the cost of the carnage that would have occurred among derivative counterparties if it had not rescued AIG from bankruptcy after Lehman's collapse—perhaps hard to compute, but an estimate or ballpark number would suffice. The lien on future profits quickly mounts. At the least, retaining the windfall as a capital cushion in lieu of compensation seems responsible.

Maintaining a meaningful portion of employees' restricted equity and options within their division's capital in lieu of the firm's equity solidifies partnerships among employees and lessens the temptation to take excessive risk. At the same time it would appease many of Wall Street's most talented employees. Sources of steady low-risk income and competent investment bankers providing valuable advice to key clients, for example, may be happier campers under such a structure, especially if they have input into the capital allocation process.

The market may show that when the risk-takers are on the hook and incur the full costs of their freewheeling activities, their appetite for risk may diminish. They may find returning to some of the habits that precipitated the current crisis too costly.

Risked-based capital is exceedingly complex, thus it is easy for Wall Street wizards to game or rework in a fashion that masks the true amount of capital. One of the primary reasons the global financial system approached the possibility of apocalypse was careless risk management and misperceived leverage on individual trading desks and hedge funds. And Lehman was the poster child. Policymakers need an effective structure that eliminates the government backstop from non-deposit-funded businesses, one that allows the marketplace to determine the pricing and effectively allocates capital. The first line of defense is controlling leverage, margins, and capital at its source, where decisions to allocate capital are made.[2]

Under the current scheme, the greatest costs of failure are borne by the lender of last resort: Main Street. The taxpayer would not care if the losses incurred were only those of the bankers. Few begrudge (and most applaud) the long-term investment returns of astute investors such as Warren Buffett. Why? Because his own money is at risk and he takes full responsibility for his investment decisions. Wise investing, not irresponsible speculation, should be rewarded.

More than twenty years on Wall Street has led me to conclude that divining systemic risk may be impossible. It seems beyond our collective intellectual capacity to precisely foretell the next financial crisis or tailor a foolproof structure to assure the stability of global financial markets. Crafting a financial system to avert or forestall all future financial crises is wishful thinking. Yet an oversight committee that stands ready to moderate irrational prices and a banking system that governs risk-taking at the desks' level (where bubbles emerge) may be resilient enough to contain the turmoil and maintain requisite confidence.

A more contained structure, in which each desk maintains its own capital and debt, requires well-trained, well-equipped, and keen-eyed supervisors. Increasing leverage and margin ratios as positions approach systemic risk levels, and the introduction of credit default swaps as insurance to intervention when necessary, are valuable tools for supervisors in carrying out their regulating responsibilities.

Markets, as we should all understand by now, are capricious and do not always work as originally assumed or planned. Market participants can quickly become leery of markets that appeared bulletproof only days before. It is essential that super-regulators have the mechanism and authority to cross business lines and intercede if failure is deemed to pose a systemic hazard. Redrafting our financial model to expand the power of regulators to allow them to unwind individual risk units without requiring the holding company to claim bankruptcy provides a more orderly disposition process. This authority alone should give potential risk-takers pause.[3]

Training supervisors capable of making the distinction that markets are approaching systemic risk levels raises a serious challenge. Separating the wheat from the chaff and unraveling indications of a growing bubble are difficult. Yet regulators, in concert with market intelligence, may be capable of recognizing the warning signals that indicate markets are overextended and present systemic risk. The task requires supervisors to specialize and become fully conversant with the latest financial instruments. It also requires that they have the authority to impel trading desks to comply. The training level and/or supervisory structure are not currently advanced enough for them to keep abreast of evolving markets and complex financial instruments. The antiquated and outmoded infrastructure needs updating and the capital structure simplified. It is far too easy for Wall Street to game the current risk-adjusted capital requirements (see Chapter Four).

The mimicking of innovations that occurs on Wall Street is an essential component leading to irrational markets. Those at the vanguard of innovation are rewarded handsomely, which draws imitators seeking to capitalize on the same profits. Global firms build businesses to keep abreast of competition, subjecting each to like risks. These entities provide funding to each other as well as many of the same institutional customers causing complex connectivity and contagious consequences. When these entities sense a problem, they understand the dynamic of first-come-first-served. In lemming-like fashion, everyone rushes to the cliff's edge and a cascade of defaults ensues.[4]

To withstand future financial disasters, pricing must be more visible and the derivatives markets' capital structure must be reshaped. It is painfully clear that liberating the full force of market discipline on the global banking system could have catastrophic consequences. Given the struggle following Lehman's demise, no central banker in the industrialized countries should be willing to test this theory and allow the financial system to explode. Pretending otherwise will only serve to exacerbate the next panic.

It is a formidable challenge for regulators and Wall Street to compromise on a solution that reins in risk without stifling innovation. Derivative markets have grown from an obscure, over-the-counter interest rate swap market used by thrifts to lengthen their liabilities into a global business. The Long Term Capital Management crisis and Lehman's demise demonstrate the uncertainty and destabilizing potential of the web of interdependency in an over-the-counter derivatives market. Wall Street's management needs to understand it is in its own best interest to improve transparency.

Derivatives deepened the severity of the recent crisis, drawing scrutiny to a need for greater transparency. The near collapse of the financial system after Lehman's downfall placed a spotlight on the potential risks of opaque markets. Whether you feel the scrutiny of Wall Street was justified or was just a search for a scapegoat, clarity will benefit everyone. Widening the collection of trading data and trading of standardized contracts on an exchange is safer. Standardized derivative contracts processed through a clearinghouse reinforces confidence and hence, credit. A financial institution that stands between member firms to guarantee that each clearing firm honors its obligation enhances liquidity. The process would improve pricing and trading information and attract a larger group of investors.

In a timely manner, unique OTC trades need to find as many standardized features as possible. Until customized, OTC transactions are standardized to adequately process them through a clearinghouse; larger margins and timelier marking-to-market are necessary to cushion markets against potential taxpayer losses and retain confidence in our financial system.[5]

The combination of large profits for innovators with the ability to shroud leverage and arbitrage regulatory requirements proved too tempting for the industry to regulate itself. Measures taken thus far reconfirm Wall Street's inability to comprehend the message. Unless Wall Street installs a system that penalizes excessive risk-taking, regulators must outline the consequences of misguided risk-taking.

When the Federal Reserve pumped billions into the financial system, its balance sheet ballooned. This action was taken to jump-start residential and commercial real estate markets; fund commercial paper of large companies; support life insurers; and guarantee money-market funds when faced with the possibility of breaching the mythical dollar mark. Whether one defends or decries the government's massive intervention, most agree that the Fed's capacity to calm markets is diminished and that those responsible should be held accountable.[6]

Our financial system like an old, wobbly table teetered towards collapse. Ben Bernanke and the other central bankers found more thoughtful, if not tardy, solutions than just using folded dinner napkins and temporarily propped it up. They located a sweet spot and the table appears balanced and stable. However, a more permanent solution is required. The uneven base needs repair. More durable footings must be designed and placed on solid ground to support a new structure. Otherwise, when the props are removed the table may wobble and our financial system will exceed the limits of deflection, and collapse.

Free-marketers may wish markets would remedy themselves, but a more vigilant role for market regulators seems unavoidable. If the table tilts far enough, Wall Street's favorite French tipple may spill. Let us hope the wine spills in their lap and not on the floor where the waiter is left to clean it up. The victims of misguided risk-taking cannot be asked to pay the cleanup costs again.

The characteristics of normalcy should not provide a sense of complacency. As Lehman's experience demonstrates, financial managers learned more about the past, but not necessarily about the future. History has been an unreliable predictor. Although common mistakes are often repeated and many lessons are lost, every financial crisis has been unique. An exogenous incident takes on a life of its own, forms an unconventional response, and ignites a chain of events previously deemed implausible.

It is crucial to remind policymakers and risk managers about Lehman's history as they seek a sturdier financial structure. Financial innovations and consolidation of assets amplify financial assets' price volatility. The extent of the damage caused by the current crisis demonstrates this dynamic and underscores the vulnerability of a global financial system, thus emphasizing the importance of recalibrating volatility. There is no reason to think volatility will not increase with consolidation.

Policymakers have not implemented structural changes that will prevent us from repeating the mistakes that will lead to another crisis. Most of the rhetoric about legislation only states that regulators promise to "do better next time." This is not particularly comforting. Aside from a few minor changes in Wall Street business practices, nearly three and a half years have passed since the crisis struck—and our legal and regulatory infrastructure is virtually the same as it was before the crises. Unless regulators successfully contain leverage, it is not likely that central bankers will lessen the exuberance-prone global financial markets.

It is the responsibility of policymakers to implement dramatic changes in the policies that govern the structure of taking risk, if they are to reach their goal of a financial system that is flexible enough to foster innovation yet adequately governed against losses that will burden the taxpayer. Otherwise much of the benefit from the Fed's action to save the too-important-or-interconnected-to-fail entities in our system will be realized by those prone to repeat the same mistakes.

The world waits with its fingers crossed as policymakers wrestle over the shape of the most extensive financial reform since the Great Depression. The future of the financial system worldwide and our nation's prosperity largely depend on policymakers' formulation of a new financial architecture. Let us hope that lawmakers have the foresight and acumen to make the meaningful changes that are necessary to strengthen our archaic regulatory structure.

This is not to sound bleak. On the contrary, the global financial system has more political will and intellectual capacity focused on a solution than ever before. The same wisdom that spared us financial Armageddon has an opportunity to bring reliable restraint to the unhinged exuberance of Wall Street and to put in place an effective, vibrant financial structure that instills confidence that the funding mechanism will remain stable.[7]

Even though at times it may not seem like it, the goal in writing this book is not to advocate or prescribe solutions or patent remedies, nor is it an attempt to offer suggestions for a risk utopia. Rather, it is to provide anecdotes that illustrate where Lehman's and other financial entities' ill-conceived incentives and wrong-headed risk management contributed to this crisis, then to step aside and allow policymakers, market participants, and Wall Street management pick up the debate. The purpose is to open the dialogue on plausible solutions that are distinctly different from the conventional after-the-fact approach that authorities currently use to muffle or reduce the cost that mark financial crises. This book is meant to be a constructive use of lessons lost on Lehman to spur debate among financial experts in the government and private sector that prevents a repeat of the recent calamity.

<u>A Survey of the Debates Facing Policymakers and Risk Managers as They Strive to Design a More Durable Financial Structure:</u>

"Reality looks much more obvious in hindsight than foresight. People who experience hindsight bias misapply current hindsight to past foresight. They perceive events that occurred to have been more predictable before the fact than was actually the case." Hersh Shefrin

The saga of Salomon Brothers, the thrift industry, Long Term Capital Management, and Lehman Brothers weaves a narrative replete with lessons. The following is an ex post facto account or survey of the debate with the profound benefit of hindsight.

Issue # 1: Although the process of securitization was maligned, policymakers who call for restrictions and burdensome regulations must deliberate carefully.

As the process of securitization advanced, an assortment of complicated structures with dubious value emerged. This evolution led to a combination of complicated mortgage choices that confused even the savviest of borrowers. The complications helped to mask the moral failures of lenders, borrowers, and underwriters. Eventually these mutations provided limited to no efficiencies, weakened the trust of investors, and promoted perilous leverage.

An apt example of the effects that escalate when complicating and expanding the possibilities available through a security is a collateralized debt obligation (CDO): the first in a sequence of increasingly more convoluted securities (followed by synthetic CDOs and CDOs-squared). CDOs are a type of structured security created by establishing a "special-purpose vehicle" to hold an interest in a grouped pool of assets. The assets packaged in CDOs vary and in many cases include riskier, lower-rated, thinly traded classes of other securities. Subprime-mortgage classes were often the primary ingredient.

A large batch of subprime mortgages often rated triple B or lower, for example, were packaged, carved into classes, and then sold to investors around the world. The senior class and first-in-line to receive the cash flows collected from these bonds were anointed a triple A rating, the highest credit rating. At the height of the delusion, triple A-rated classes of CDOs were judged so safe they traded at interest rates only slightly above the comparable maturity U.S. Treasury notes.

The alchemy lay in the fact that the ratings for the package as a whole exceeded the sum of its individual parts. This mistake was rooted in the rating agencies' erroneous belief in the power of diversification. Wall Street convinced the rating agencies that the sum of a diversified pool was inherently less risky when bundled and sliced into pieces.

By combining an increasingly greater number and types of financial entities offering loans, with a complicated assortment of selections, the mortgage industry created an avenue for the unscrupulous to pilfer the uninformed. The risk of manipulation increases and some conflicts of interest are introduced when one entity hosts the underwriting, securitizing, and distributing duties.

Though the costs may have exceeded the benefit in the recent "great recession," forgetting that securitization has permitted borrowers access to global funding that was previously unavailable to them could prove to be a mistake. Securitization inextricably links the world's capital markets and continues to serve as a conduit between banks and investors around the world.

Up until the late 1980s, banks were primarily structured to gather deposits and originate loans. Starting with mortgage loans, financial assets once confined to the balance sheets of banks were packaged into marketable securities. Then they were sold and traded in global capital markets. Soon, the technology of pooling mortgage loans was exported to other asset classes. Credit card receivables, home equity loans, auto loans, aircraft leases, commercial mortgages, and even sovereign debt were packaged to form securities. Funding, which in many cases had been a function of capacity in the banking industry, was now a global issue. Viable projects now had access to the worldwide credit markets.

Innovative structures enable those who need funding to match the investment preferences of capital-market investors. As a result, the amount of money available to fund viable projects is greater and the cost lower than otherwise would be the case. Stymieing the securitization process will make our financial system less efficient.

Now the challenge is to harness the potential of securitization without stifling innovation. The quest should be to devise a balanced structure within the banking system that assures transparency rather than introducing regulations that fail to govern as intended. Consumer choice and honest competition are the cornerstones of an effective global financial system. When the music is bad, one doesn't smash the instruments; one tunes them or replaces the musicians who play them. Market participants must demand detailed data underlying each loan. The primary purpose of securitization is to provide vehicles to efficiently allocate capital, not to supply cover and mask the risks.

Issue #2: Liquidating assets from insolvent thrifts should demonstrate to policymakers that managing large asset disposition is best done in a public-private partnership in which taxpayers maintain a sizeable ownership.

Early in the disposition process, the Resolution Trust Corporation (RTC), woefully understaffed and poorly trained, quickly realized they were at a substantial disadvantage, so they engaged the private sector. The RTC realized that consolidating and partnering with experienced private-sector managers was a more cost effective method to manage the inherited portfolios of distressed assets.

To accomplish more favorable execution, the RTC pioneered what they referred to as equity partnerships, allowing the taxpayer to retain a sizable interest in the assets. The remaining interest was acquired by a private-sector partner, who directed the management and sale of the assets.

Largely the RTC acted as a conservator of failed thrifts by contracting out much of management and disposition of assets to its private-sector partners. The partners supplied valuable experience in managing and disposing of distressed assets and capital. The profit-sharing structures of these private-public partnerships assured an alignment of incentives.

Issue #3: Policymakers had an inadequate understanding of the risks being taken by the institutions they were supposed to regulate.

The thrift episode demonstrates that federally-insured deposits should be restricted from making proprietary bets in an attempt to boost profits. Regulators would like us to believe that the demise of the thrift industry was a result of inept management. Though the industry had its share of less-than-competent managers, the problem was largely structural: federally insured deposits should not be used, either alone or commingled, to fund relative-value trading bets.

Bureaucratic forbearance, new investment powers presented by the Garn-St. Germain Act, and the deregulation of deposit gathering in the early 1980s presented a perverse incentive for insolvent thrifts to gamble their way to solvency. Allowing technically-insolvent thrifts to continue to accept new deposits in addition to a number of other ill-conceived regulations resulted in unintended consequences that exacerbated the problems.

The method of pricing deposit insurance, meager capital requirements, forbearance, and relaxed asset restrictions increased risk taking by teetering Federal Savings and Loan Insurance Corporation-insured thrifts. The moral hazard of flat-fee deposit insurance was an expensive undertaking for the taxpayer. Introducing a flat fee in response to the recent economic meltdown may just set the stage for another congressionally induced catastrophe.

Issue #4: The government is an undependable business partner and is ill-equipped to make prescient decisions—absent political influence—regarding individual financial institutions.

When political tides change, the whim of the government can quickly shift. Politically popular policy is much easier to deliver to constituents and often motivates a politician's or policymaker's decisions. Lehman and other large financial institutions should have understood that the government is prone to interpret ambiguous market information as validation of their decisions, when political calls for scalps are popular.

Apparently the consequences of financial excess and a subsequent abandonment of the thrift industry proved not to be indelible enough to prevent Lehman's management from repeating the same mistake. If Lehman's senior management did not know then, it knows now that lawmakers are inherently reactive rather than proactive. Congress rarely revisits regulations of the financial markets frequently enough to stay abreast of the evolution of markets. Only a crisis prompts action. Policymakers are content to enact post-crisis legislation that suffices for a decade or so, or until another disaster elicits a response.

Today, economic populism guides policymakers to demonize Wall Street banks as they exonerate their own complicit policies. It is much easier than foreseeing change and appropriately reshaping regulations.

Issue #5: The ability of debt issuers to shop for the most advantageous ratings from the government-anointed rating agencies

introduces a potential conflict of interest and overly optimistic ratings.

The stir that rating agencies would face tougher rules has subsided somewhat. Proposals that restrict the practice of shopping for the best rating, impose higher liability standards, and improve accountability among the rating agencies that inflamed the meltdown has found little traction. Critics who argue that the rating agencies gave overly optimistic ratings to win business brought warranted scrutiny to the custom of issuers paying the rating firms.

This focus instilled a sense of fear among issuers. Mortgage-backed security issuers on Wall Street have fretted for some time that the racket of shopping among rating agencies for the most favorable rating would be exposed. Issuers most fear a confidential process where information is broadly disseminated and investors choose the rating firms.

To restore public confidence that their ratings represent an unbiased view of credit risk, rating firms may do well to introduce a system that strengthens transparency and independence. If regulators fail to address these government-blessed arbiters of risk (Standard & Poor's, Moody's and Fitch), whose DNA was found everywhere among the rubble, investors might seek a more reliable measure of credit risk. Lessening the agencies' favored status falls short of strengthening their quality and independence.

The prevailing thought among investors' remains: Rating agencies are still in connivance with the same issuers that led to the crisis. And this only serves to reinforce the notion that rating providers have not made significant revisions to their rating approach to instill needed confidence in their assessment of credit risk. Their most important audience is the market participants who judge their ability to provide investors with a reliable assessment. As long as issuers can shop for ratings and there is a direct, commercial relationship between the issuers of debt and the rating firms, their opinions will remain suspect. Unless policymakers overhaul the issuer-pays model in order to curb the potential conflict of interest and refashion transparency and accountability, investors might seek a way to bypass the rating agencies and liquidity will suffer.

How would one view the results of an Olympic wrestling match if one of the wrestlers chose and paid the referee? In a charitable assessment, I would find the outcome tainted.

Issue #6: In the long run, trading the lion's share of derivatives through a clearinghouse is in the market's best interest.

Most should agree that derivatives play a vital role in the efficient allocation of funding and are a valuable tool to manage risk. Absent new derivative innovation, our financial system runs the risk of restricting access to capital and dulling an effective hedging tool in the global capital markets. At the same time, it is naive for Wall Street risk managers to think that self-interest will not cross the line into unfettered greed.

Innovators strive to limit price discovery and maintain a profit advantage for as long as possible. The challenge for risk managers is to move customized contracts onto listed markets as soon as possible. Lehman's failure has focused attention on how much global finance has changed and the potential risk of contagion. The potential catastrophic consequence of a financial meltdown, when counterparties of privately-traded derivative contracts go under and initiate a cascade of related failures, was averted, but at significant cost. Immediately after Lehman was allowed to fail, the Treasury and Federal Reserve decoupled the viral web of OTC derivatives and bailed out AIG. This helped to stave off a financial collapse. The risk that one default produces a chain of interconnected failures is patently destabilizing.

Underwriting counterparty's risk, calculating daily marks, and managing margin accounts are cumbersome tasks that are more efficiently administered by a clearinghouse. The benefits from a central clearing body that provides transparency and takes away counterparty risk—which prevents markets from seizing up as they did when Lehman failed—are overwhelming.

Trading derivatives on exchanges is not a new concept; it dates back centuries. The world's oldest continually operating exchange, the Chicago Board of Trade, was established in 1848. It is now part of the Chicago Mercantile Exchange. Primarily formed to address the concerns of the agricultural community, it was the first to list an exchange-traded futures contract. Options and futures exchanges have flourished as the primary trading, settlement, and clearing vehicle.

The essential reason for financial innovation remains to find solutions for complex business problems and expose inefficiencies in the allocation of capital. It is not an excuse to flout the rules or to conceal risk. Financial institutions may be wise to see the advantage and institute a disclosure process to assure full transparency.

Clearer pricing and a greater variety of contracts traded on an exchange will produce more inexpensive avenues for market participants to manage risk. Improvements include providing more information about trading exposures and requiring larger margins. However, these are not enough. In the long run, trading the lion's share of derivatives through a clearinghouse is in the world's collective best interest.

Issue #7: The potential for miscasting investment properties or shrouding risk is magnified as securities become more complicated.

Even a talented and diligent supervisor could hardly be expected to remain abreast of or possess the capacity to dissect all of the innovations devised by Wall Street's rocket scientists. Drawing from Lehman's failure to heed the warnings and engage the experience of its personnel, supervisors might be wise to acquire timely information by improving their dialogue with the private sector. A clever supervisor could share information among market participants and still provide oversight that introduces the requisite restraint. There is a strong incentive for risk managers, trading desks, hedge funds, and other market participants to cooperate and share information, especially regarding broader systemic matters. An astute and independent supervisor could bring market participants to recognize that less volatile markets are in their own best interest.

Configuring a sustainable structure that stymies financial failure does not require a clairvoyant or intrusive supervisor. Optimistically, we may believe that financial exuberance can be eliminated but realistically, that is wishful thinking. The objective of mitigating the severity of these excesses is ambitious enough.

Thus independence for those responsible for overseeing systemic risk in our too-important-or-interconnected-to-fail institutions is of paramount importance. Under our current structure, regulators do not have access to information or the apparatus and authority to restrain risk taking. A super-regulator requires sufficient authority and independence.

Issue #8: Marked-to-market accounting to calculate capital needs to be reconstructed.

Some basic background: It is reckless to ignore the size and relative dimension of the assets within their respective markets when marking-to-market. Wall Street has long known it is irresponsible to believe that each day's closing prices are reliable indicators of fair value.

A clear example to dramatize this point is a closed-end fund. A closed-end fund is similar to a mutual fund; however, its size does not change with net purchases or redemptions. Instead, it sells a fixed number of shares and uses the proceeds to purchase stocks, bonds, or other assets.

A mutual fund meets redemption or purchase orders at the closing net-asset-value (NAV) each day. To satisfy a mutual fund's requested redemptions; it only sells assets if the net amount required exceeds the cash reserves: a kind of margin account. In contrast, the number of closed-end fund shares remains constant and trades in the open market on exchanges. Consequently, the price of closed-end-fund's shares often deviates materially from the NAV. During the times when markets are in distress, these discounts can be substantial.

To recover the discount of a closed-end fund, the sponsor's choices are to buy back shares or collapse the fund and liquidate the underlying assets. Even when the most liquid assets are held, market participants require a substantial discount for the lack of liquidity and perceived cost of moving relatively large blocks of assets.

In a normally functioning market, with the exception of meager amounts of highly liquid listed equities and on-the-run U.S. Treasuries, few marks offer valid pricing for anything but a small trade, certainly not for the increasingly concentrated portfolios of today. Yet these marks form the foundation to measure risk, determine pay-for-performance, and derive profit and loss statements. Think opinion not fact!

For more complex, illiquid instruments, calculating the price usually requires a trader to make more assumptions. Slight differences in their assumptions may result in radically different prices. This puts in question the validity and/or the probity of the process. In crisis conditions, demonstrated by the consequences of Russia's default and the recent subprime pandemic, markets seize, rendering mark-to-market pricing worthless. When a lemming-like dash to the precipice ensues, valuations are meaningless. How can one mark an asset to-market when there are no "bids" or buyers?

To comport with market realities one must incorporate increasingly larger discounts as the scope and complexities of the assets grow. A lack of faith in the veracity of Lehman's marks on its disproportionate residential and commercial real estate holdings, compounded problems and led to its undoing.

The concept of fair-value accounting is compelling. Our current system puts far too much of the onus of judging the integrity of marks on the investor and regulator. Because investors rely upon the integrity of a reported balance sheet, they depend on the veracity of independent and transparent accounting. Confidence in capital levels goes hand in hand with accurately measured asset pricing. Our independent accounting standards play a vital role in making U.S. capital markets the envy of the world.

It is time to implement a better system to mark assets, one that tempers destabilizing valuation swings. A system that discounts pricing to reflect the haircut for moving large blocks of assets in propitious markets but makes allowances for fire sale estimates in a collapsing market. A reversion to reality!

The Financial Accounting Standards Board (FASB) should exercise independence and install a more reliable judge of valid prices. More than bankers' compensation hangs in the balance. The smooth functioning of the global banking system is at stake.

Issue #9: Viewing the ability of the financial system to withstand crises from a historical perspective rather than from a prospective view is not prudent.

Lehman's near-death experience during the LTCM crisis compelled its management to put in place a sturdier risk management structure. Lehman required larger margins; lengthened debt terms and exposures were aggregated and priced in a more timely fashion across trading desks. As Maureen Miskovic, Lehman's then chief risk officer, aptly put it: "Models designed to foretell risk will be viewed in a different context. A .5 percent chance of occurrence will no longer be perceived as unlikely or remote; instead it will be interpreted to mean, be prepared for it to occur once every two hundred days."

Equally important adjustments were made to the way trading desks hedged their positions and viewed market-making. Conventionally, when bond traders took inventoried bonds and put the firm's capital at risk, they shorted the like-duration treasury as a hedge. A Lehman mortgage trader recalls that shorting treasuries protected the price movements associated with interest rate moves, but left us exposed to adverse credit-spread changes.

As the volatility and historical relationships of credit-spreads changed during the LTCM crisis, mortgage trading desks altered their hedging strategies. At that juncture, shorting assets whose credit spreads would likely move in tandem quickly became the norm. The diminished profitability resulting from the higher hedging costs, however, persuaded Lehman and others on Wall Street to reduce the amount of capital allocated to the market-making business and devote more capital to proprietary trading.

Today the prevalent thinking seems to hold that our current financial crisis is a once-in-a-lifetime event. But conventional wisdom may prove narrow-minded and have dangerous consequences. Lehman's major mistake and lesson lost was to only calibrate the risk models to withstand the new extreme introduced in 1998. Authorities may do well to learn from Lehman's failure to heed the lessons from Russia's default and the subsequent LTCM collapse. The ability to endure financial crises should be viewed prospectively instead of from the perspective of the most recent crisis. In the future, increasingly greater volatility should be expected.

Issue #10: In the midst of tumultuous times associated with a financial panic, no one can determine with any confidence when a financial entity is "too-important-or-interconnected-to-fail."

The Federal Reserve's litmus test for too-important-or-interconnected-to-fail remains: Will the shock of failure jeopardize the entire financial system and hence the broader economy? The very contention that the government's recent intervention will lead these larger banks to take more risk has led many central bankers and government officials worldwide to the conclusion that limiting the size and scope of banks is the best way to protect taxpayers.

One proposal gaining strength among policymakers would give regulators the authority to preemptively dismantle healthy institutions they deem too big, and also to separate commercial banking from investment banking. Legislating large, interconnected global banks to unilaterally reduce their size and become small or "not-connected-enough-to-fail" just might push our economy back into the Dark Ages of the S&Ls. Of course, banks can shed businesses that are nonessential to their core function and simplify their organization. But to whittle down sprawling franchises is a different story, one that ignores the advantages of economies of scope and scale that large, diverse banks provide in today's global economy.

The current globalization of financial markets requires a myriad of banking activities. The role that large, integrated banks play in the financial irrigation system of the global economy serves a vital commercial function.

The benefit of foreign exchange services and access to global capital that accrues to customers of a global financial institution are key examples of integration leading to economies of scale.

To overlook the benefits of large banks to provide expedient global processing of currency and other commercial payments and transfer transactions seems short-sighted. Imposing restrictions may reduce these efficiencies and will significantly handicap the ability of U.S. banks to compete against their foreign competitors. In today's economy, large corporations and equity, fixed income, commodity, and foreign exchange markets operate on a global scale. This requires the same global scope from financial institutions.

The levees that separated banking and investment banking began to erode well before the repeal of Glass-Steagall in 1999. The evolution of securitization and derivatives had blurred the lines that divided the financial service industry. Aside from underwriting equities and bonds, there were few things that large banks did not do, even before the repeal. This expansion process was part of a global economic evolution, not a change in ideology.

The firewalls that were installed to segregate bank subsidiaries from non-bank subsidiaries in a holding company structure could easily extend to individual risk units. Lehman's non-bank subsidiaries were easily separated and sold—in several cases, to existing management—when it failed. Lehman's structure allowed regulators, for example, to extricate the money management and private-equity units from the failed entity. If similar firewalls with individual capital had been in place for the trading units, Lehman's failure may have been more orderly and significantly less costly.

As policymakers struggle to design changes so that future crises do not require taxpayer money nor disrupt the broader economy, a restriction to limit size might not prove to be the best answer. One problem with imposing boundaries on the size of financial entities is that no one has the faintest idea of what the boundaries should be. It is as much a function of how interconnected these financial institutions are, as it is of size. It is possible to solve the problem without dismantling large financial institutions.

Lehman's assets totaled less than $700 billion at the time it filed for bankruptcy protection. The turmoil created in the aftermath of this event should provide evidence of the fragility of our financial system. Policy heads and bank managers may do better to learn from Lehman's demise and focus on structures that subdue vicious cycles. From now on, the prudent assumption should be to expect increasingly more violent price swings unless irrational asset prices are moderated.

Issue #11: Make no mistake; the same misguided confidence in individuals and markets will reemerge.

If one reviews Dick Fuld's testimony about the collapse of Lehman before the House Committee on Government Reform, there are clues. Fuld effectively validates his unwavering commitment: "I never sold any shares, and that's why I had ten million left. I believed in the company. I could have sold that stock. But I did not, because I believed we would return to profitability." In response to the bailouts of some of Lehman's competitors, he said, "I would have loved to be part of that group...."

In the end, Fuld offered no regrets as to what other course he might have taken and did not acknowledge his mistakes. He never even hinted that Lehman's failure was either preventable or in any way a direct result of his reckless decisions. Instead, with careful rhetoric, he asked, "What could I have done differently? What could I have said? What should I have done?" and continued, "At the time I made those decisions, I made those decisions with the information I had."

Apparently, Fuld did not think to ask himself the most important question: "What if I am wrong?" Perhaps his own paranoia hampered his capacity to look ahead and imagine the consequences. Fuld staunchly contended that it was not his misjudgments that proved to be Lehman's downfall but the regulators' unwillingness to intercede on its behalf, the short sellers that bet against Lehman, and the capricious and unpredictable headwinds of the financial markets.

Wall Street will take the customary post-crisis action and install sturdier risk-management controls. It will take initiatives to improve the accuracy of quantitative risk models, tighten internal limits, raise margin requirements, increase the restricted equity portion of bonuses, and require transparency of information from counterparties and managers who oversee the individual desk's risk. Unfortunately, customary measures are more likely than not to be inadequate—as they were for Lehman.

Irrational behavior of market participants should be expected. Assuming that the same misguided confidence in both individuals and markets will not reemerge, is a mistake. Our quest should not be to construct a system that predicts but a system that prevents irresponsible risk-taking from requiring taxpayers' money and spilling over into the economy at large.

Risk managers and regulators need to think differently than they have in the past. The best preemptive measure to accomplish discipline may be leverage. To require increasingly larger margins and risk-based capital within individual financial units where risk is now taken may be the best tool.

Issue #12: Executing a macro-economic rescue program to stem a calamitous financial system collapse differs from designing meaningful and comprehensive supervisory reforms to avoid repeating the great economic meltdown we experienced over the past three and a half years.

While I am not suggesting that the Federal Reserve is ill-suited to oversee systemic risk, the point should be emphasized that the super-regulator, whoever it may be, requires independent authority and the expertise to regulate all large financial institutions. The rescue of LTCM, AIG, FNMA and FHLMC made it clear that systemic risk is not confined to large commercial or investment banks. It includes hedge funds, insurance companies, government sponsored entities, and any financial entity able to impose systemic risk.

Today, to arrive at an assessment of systemic risk, whoever is responsible for the supervisory function must rely on a sketchy supervisory system too disjointed to discern systemic risk. The challenge of sorting through reporting data from various agencies complicates efforts of any new super-regulator assigned this task. Likewise, the ability to arbitrage regulator restrictions compounds the problem. When risky units are deemed to require additional capital to restrain systemic risk, altering ownership structure (regulatory arbitrage) does not lessen the risk and needs to be deterred.

The argument for independence of the resolution agency to impose restriction harmoniously among all large financials entities is compelling. Lawmakers and the executive branch may consider setting strict directives that give the super-regulator discretionary authority to access financial information and make principled recommendations. The circumstances and uncertainty surrounding Lehman's demise, and the subsequent bankruptcy proceedings, highlight the need for a super-regulator to have full statutory powers and a clear path to intervention, in due process with its oversight committee.

A regulatory structure that offers no credible alternative to intercede, as we head toward a collision course with financial Armageddon, seems enormously irresponsible. The conclusive possibility of some sort of conservatorship or receivership might reintroduce the discipline that eludes our current structure.

Few deny the need for an oversight body responsible for system-wide risk. The debate is where it should be lodged. Of the various federal agencies, the Federal Reserve appears to have the most compelling argument to host the oversight and supervisory group, even if it may consolidate more authority under the Federal Reserve. The Fed's responsibility as the institution in charge of maintaining the safety and soundness of the financial system as a whole, argues for its comprehensive involvement in the oversight and supervisory functions. The authority may prove vital for the Fed to guide the economy when reacting to the next financial panic.

Issue #13: Retaining the right to defend against Congress's infringement on the Fed's ability to manage monetary policy without political interference is central to the market's confidence.

Worldwide central bankers are patting themselves on the back. Commonly one hears the claims: *The financial officials of the world's biggest economies acted quickly and forcefully. The programs we launched have successfully diffused a rapidly deteriorating and potentially dangerous situation. We averted a panic almost miraculously.* And proudly they offer the formula: *Collectively following the collapse of Lehman Brothers we committed ourselves to prevent any other large financial institutions from failing. We instituted a litany of bold programs, including purchasing mortgage-backed bonds and debt issued by FNMA and FHLMC, guaranteeing debt for several large banks, opening the discount window for select at-risk investment banks, and providing rescue capital to faltering financial institutions such as Citigroup and AIG, to restore frozen credit markets.*

Naysayers argue that more could have been done and that some policy choices were mishandled. But even if a less tardy response or a more orderly failure of Lehman may have saved taxpayers billions of dollars, few have reason to argue with the central bankers' assessment or can offer superior alternatives to those orchestrated by worldwide central banks in the recent crisis. History is replete with the adverse consequence of politicizing the Federal Reserve System. It is paramount to retain the Fed's coveted independence.

Issue #14: Another lesson that seems to fade along with financial crises: Requiring large banks to hold a greater amount risked-adjusted capital at the holding company level is not adequate.

The financial industry is far too creative and imaginative in finding ways to mask leverage, and hence, risk. The evolution of increasingly more complex securities, off-balance-sheet fiascos, and creative capital structures that disguise leverage illustrate this well. History provides ample examples of expanded leverage attributed to creative masking and an influx of product innovation. But none furnishes a better case study than Japan's fondness for excessive leverage in the 1980s and the subsequent episode of massive deleveraging within Japan's financial system.

In 1988, the leading industrial nations, referred to as the International Monetary Fund's Group of 20, met in Basel, Switzerland. The group agreed to a set of rules for global bank regulators. The accord, called Basel I, set risk-based standards to instill confidence in the solidarity and soundness of the global financial system. The group devised complex formulas that assigned measures of risk for what it believed were the gamut of bank investments. In spite of the noble efforts of these international regulators, the accord did little to ensure prudent capital levels among global banks.

Japanese banks consistently boasted about excess risk-based capital. Unfortunately, Japanese banks' extravagant leverage fueled easy credit and contributed to a significant overvaluation of stocks and real estate in its market. Increasingly, the Japanese made riskier loans to speculative buyers and pushed prices to illogical levels that could only be justified by assuming indefinite growth rather than cash flow fundamentals.

Japan's adventure shows that relying on risk-adjusted capital opens the system to potential gaming, especially during prosperous times. It would be unwise to ignore Japan's struggles. Remember, at quarter-end on August 31, 2008, Lehman reported nearly three times the required core capital and a Tier 1 capital ratio of 11 percent. Only two weeks before filing for bankruptcy, Lehman's capital still looked good.

Although the impact of Japan's meltdown was relatively small outside of Japan, the lessons of masking excessive leverage and the cost of subsequent deleveraging are nonetheless instructive. As one might imagine, the potential to miscast investment characteristics and to shroud risk are magnified as securities become more complicated.

Today, markets seem to presume that central bankers retain a limitless capacity to print money. If we fail to solve the conundrum of curbing asset bubbles, the world just may have an opportunity to test that capacity.

Issue #15: Pressing the government's social agenda and market policies through the private banking system helped fuel the crisis and does not comport with a sound financial structure.

In 1992, the Federal Housing Enterprises Financial Safety and Soundness Act was designed by Congress to force the government-sponsored enterprises FNMA and FHLMC to acquire affordable housing loans. To comply with the law's requirements, FNMA and FHLMC subsequently provided Wall Street with a ready market for irresponsible mortgages. This dovetailed with another federal law, the Community Reinvestment Act (CRA). The CRA pressured financial institutions to boost lending in low- and moderate-income communities. The CRA generated aberrant demand: in this case, a voracious appetite from FNMA and FHLMC for mortgages that qualified to meet low-income lending mandates.

When the supply of worthy borrowers was exhausted, lenders relaxed underwriting standards to increase CRA lending. To meet FNMA's and FHLMC's turbo-charged demand, Wall Street eagerly produced increasingly risky assets. When combined with a secular decrease in mortgage rates— from roughly 10.5 percent in the spring of 1990 to 5.5 percent in 2004— the United States developed an unprecedented housing bubble, which provided the fodder for the subsequent subprime-induced panic.

By the summer of 2006, subprime mortgages skyrocketed from just 5 percent in 1994 to roughly 20 percent of all mortgages originated. The rate of homeownership escalated alongside the increase in subprime lending. Between the mid 1990s, when lawmakers strengthened the CRA to reduce red-lining (discriminatory lending against low-income neighborhoods) and 2006, U.S. home ownership increased from approximately 64 percent to over 69 percent.

The increase in the percentage of people owning homes did not reflect lending reality. Too many borrowers simply could not afford the houses they purchased. Few predicted that the increased amount of substandard loans would result in our financial system teetering on the verge of collapse, but many recognized the driving forces behind the deterioration of subprime mortgages. The flawed congressionally-induced demand loosened underwriting standards.

When housing prices advance at a rate faster than the average income, larger not smaller down payments are prudent. Instead, the number of mortgages with both below par equity and credit standards escalated under the guise of advancing home ownership. Mandates that require private institutions to facilitate affordable housing or that promote a government's social agenda for financial entities do not comport with sound financial management.

If Congress chooses to enact lending mandates to achieve political agendas, government agencies are much better suited to fill this role. The FHA's public–private partnership is an example of using a government agency as a vehicle to remedy what policymakers deem social inequities. GNMA's advantage of a government safety net provides an inexpensive funding source for low- and moderate-income homeowners. Together, the two provide a clear accounting for the cost and a much easier way to measure the success or failure of the program. The taxpayer can then see how much of their money goes to support the housing market and judge if this is the way they want their dollars spent.

Issue #16: The preeminent responsibility of the heads of Wall Street banks' major divisions should be risk management.

Lehman missed the red flags that should have told them that their risk management was inadequate. The fixed-income management at Lehman should have known from experience that structuring trading desks to a kind of common ownership or partnership, defining the pay-for-performance clearly, introducing conflict resolution mechanisms, and seeking broader participation to modify potential risk lays the groundwork for sound risk management. Lehman should have understood that a balanced sales–trading partnership functions most effectively. Preserving the partnership served as a guard rail on concentrated risk and a market intelligence-gathering vehicle.

Reining in trading desks is difficult to pull off politically during times of prosperity and requires a strong personality. As credit spreads contract, traders assume it is a new paradigm rather than temporary euphoria. A self-reinforcing dynamic leads to excess confidence. Dealers and investors willingly fund large positions with relatively narrow margin requirements. The expansive trading volume generates profits despite slim bid-ask spreads and makes even inept traders appear talented.

It would be disingenuous to assign the burden of incompetence to Lehman alone for this lack of foresight. If failing to be prescient enough to recognize these symptoms is incompetence, why stop there? Nearly all of Wall Street was delinquent in predicting the impending implosion. The best and brightest on Wall Street collectively underestimated the risks that real estate posed to the financial markets.

But the lesson here is not about being clairvoyant. It is about putting in place a prudent structure that seeks the collective wisdom of interested parties, aligns personal wealth with risk, and provides a credible mechanism to intervene. A framework that fosters forward-thinking solutions for complex issues yet does not curtail the benefits of scale and scope.

A collaborative and inclusive platform and oversight mechanism that encourages debate around the wisdom and quality of risk measures should be constructed to muffle the cycle. There are more than enough highly qualified frontline managers in the trenches daily and willing to pursue the issues, especially when a major portion of their own net worth is at stake.

Issue #17: Management's new challenge is to design a compensation structure that is risk adjusted, aligns personal reward with realized–not interim–marked profits, and compartmentalizes the risk.

Even today's investment banking management acknowledges that the method used to pay sales, trading, and banking encouraged excessive risk-taking and contributed to the crisis. Disagreements about adjusting warped incentives are not about the goal but about the most effective method to accomplish it. Government-imposed restrictions or pay caps may create a real risk of an exodus of talent—by those not responsible for the losses— to unrestricted financial entities and potentially grave, albeit unintended consequences for taxpayers.

Likewise, the notion that bank executives or even traders wittingly gambled the destruction of their firm for the sake of annual compensation either remains a mystery or makes little sense. Lehman's and Bear Stearns' employees held among the highest percentage ownership on Wall Street. As Fuld testified to Congress, "I could have sold that stock [ten million shares]. But I did not, because I believed we would return to profitability."

The decline in value of their restricted stock and/or options holdings for most of management and senior traders on Wall Street far exceeded any annual pay package. In most cases, a large portion of the net worth that employees accumulated over their lifetime was at risk. Management may have been ignorant to the extent of the risk their firms were taking, but deliberately jeopardizing destruction because of compensation is a difficult argument.

The typical partnership's earning distribution structure offers insights and lessons into aligning the consequences of risk-taking with the risk-takers. Over time, a major percentage of a partner's net worth is retained in the equity of the partnership. Each partner receives his or her portion of the firm's earnings, which aside from a small cash payment, remains as equity in the firm. Generally, a partner is not allowed access to his or her equity before retirement. And then the equity is usually distributed incrementally over time. Under such a system it is easy to imagine how intensely the partners focus on risk and wealth creation.

Both Lehman and Wall Street understood the concept of a partnership and in an attempt to replicate the discipline required management to emphasize the importance of relative performance, teamwork, and client relationships in their annual compensation evaluations. And more importantly, the best performers on Wall Street were compensated with sizeable portions of restricted stock and options. Unfortunately, Wall Street missed the mark wretchedly.

The clarity with which to assess performance requires accurate marking-to-market to measure and manage risk and a correlation with realized, not just accrued, earnings. Wall Street is replete with inflated egos that dramatize the need to measure performance accurately—an area where Lehman's fixed income management increasingly faltered.

The asymmetry in the current system does not exist within partnerships. Forming partnership structures within individual financial units might provide a vehicle to lessen the vicious cycles. Lehman's mistake of letting one department bring down an entire firm is unacceptable. More than bankers' compensation hangs in the balance: Smooth functioning of the global banking system is at stake.

Issue #18: Absent an appropriate cost of capital for each division, firms allocate funding to those generating the highest returns, irrespective of risk. This is hardly what a financial system wants to encourage.

There are no better examples to illustrate this point than the thrift industry's episode with risky investments and Lehman's perilous bets by its residential mortgage and commercial real estate groups. For different reasons, both sought the highest returns with seemingly little regard to the risk. Some in the thrift industry chased the higher return potential of high yield bonds and commercial real estate to survive. On the other hand, it was Lehman's unbounded confidence in the mortgage desk's and the commercial real estate group's ability to continually deliver outside returns. Yet in both instances, supervisors were unable to recognize the risk.

Determining secure capital levels among divisions may prove to be an easier task than ascertaining and defining a suitable size and discerning how interconnected the balance sheets among our financial institutions are. It is not a secret within the financial industry that there are wide disparities in the amount of risk that various trading units take. It will be a challenge to accurately determine the appropriate capital levels among various risk units. Fortunately, there is no shortage of talented bankers on Wall Street who are capable of calibrating the magnitude of risk and the cost of capital.

Regulators have long understood the concept of relative risk. They restrict what assets banks can own, set minimum margin requirements, and adjust capital ratios to reflect risk. U.S. banks, for instance, cannot own stocks (per the Banking Act of 1933) nor can they own below-investment-grade bonds because they are too risky. And examiners adjust for a bank's risky assets to determine its minimum capital ratios.

Wall Street may resist such a structure and claim it subjects them to the risk of losing their most valued employees. But the argument simply reflects a false fear that talented risk takers will rush to hedge funds if we alter the "heads I win, tails you lose" asymmetric compensation model. The offer of compounding one's own capital and building a business by taking advantage of the resources within a larger company should attract the most talented and brightest in the industry.

Unfortunately the current capital requirements apply singularly to the bank, investment bank, or insurance company and are terribly easy for Wall Street to game. Regulators do not have the authority at this time to mandate minimum capital levels for individual trading units such as derivatives, governments, corporate bonds, money markets, or mortgages. When risk is accurately priced by the marketplace, financial entities may decide that the most efficient capital structure is to sell or spin off the most risky units. When confronted with a real risk of failure, and no subsidized funding, they may conclude that the ownership stakes in these entities is less attractive and that their capital can be deployed more efficiently elsewhere.

ACKNOWLEDGEMENTS

I discovered that writing a book, much the same as training for the World Championships or the Olympic Games, takes a great deal more time and assistance than I first imagined. When preparing for a World Championship or the Olympic Games, talented workout partners, expert coaches, advanced scouting reports, and state-of-the-art training facilities are vital. The wrestler, of course, supplies his physical capabilities, his wit, and most importantly, his will to win. Similarly, content suppliers, copy editors, constructive critics, and literary experts contribute their expertise when preparing a manuscript. The writer puts the puzzle together, and supplies the narrative and the passion to tell his story.

Then there is the matter of time, not just your time. The time of those former colleagues and clients who so graciously provided their insights. I hesitate referring to our dialogues as interviews, since as friends we engage in conversations on a regular basis. In these particular instances, however, the discourse centered more on the anecdotes and the role Wall Street's—and particularly Lehman's—management (or lack of management) played in the recent crisis. Finally, there is the inconvenience and nuisance that writing a book imposes on your friends and family and others who share your immediate sphere.

Let me start by acknowledging the instigators. A source of passion, I suppose, would typically remain unmentioned. Yet in this case, I felt Richard S. Fuld Jr. and his loyal lieutenants deserve specific acknowledgement. Without their hubris and reckless risk-taking as a motivator, I would neither have started nor completed this project. The times when I struggled and felt like abandoning my efforts, it was my visceral anger at Fuld and company's failure to ensure Lehman's viability that kept me going. At times when my passion was drained, it was the thought of their risk malpractice that elevated my spirit. As I said in the preface, I would rather not be telling this story.

My greatest appreciation goes to Ted Gilley, my daughter Jodi, Gloria Navarro, and Ted Reese for their editing expertise. Unique anecdotes, in-depth insights, and a bird's-eye view are not enough to capture and maintain the attention of the reader. An appealing exposition is required if an author is to effectively present his message to his audience.

The publishing editor Ted Gilley's suggested edits, deletions and word changes that improved the quality and clarity of the narrative.

My daughter Jodi supplied twin talents: compositional skills and the bluntness often necessary to produce clarity when dealing with complex anecdotes. While editing, Jodi had no inhibition about noting in the margin, "Dad, I don't have a clue of what you mean here." And her suggestions regarding sentence structure have resulted in a style I believe will benefit the reader.

Gloria Navarro had the advantage—or perhaps the misfortune—of having heard many of these anecdotes countless times in our regular dinner group gatherings, including the indelible wrestling stories that influence my very nature and inform the Wall Street tales of hubris and excess. A lifelong educator, Gloria's doctorial review proved useful in the editing. Her ever-patient and insightful reflections supplied a view from someone outside of the business community.

Ted Reese's background as an international wrestler and coach and his keen literary mind made him uniquely qualified to edit this text. The combination of his rich international wrestling experience and his excellent command of the English language instilled a sense of confidence in my work. Ted wrestled at Yale while earning a bachelors of arts degree in English. After serving in the Marine Corps, Ted continued his formal education, receiving a master's degree from Harvard before ultimately being awarded a PhD in English from Brandeis. Yet it was Ted's detailed understanding of wrestling and his diligent and thoughtful editing that proved most invaluable. For all who know Ted, when I say, "His editing was much more than exceptional," the image is clear.

During my careers in both wrestling and Wall Street, I have been fortunate to have worked on a daily basis with some of the most dedicated, talented, and driven people in the world. The experience has been enriching. To those former clients and colleagues at both Salomon Brothers and Lehman Brothers who so willingly assisted me in reconstructing anecdotes and provided inspiration, I am particularly grateful. Re-establishing the timeline and retracing the sequence of distant events was a challenge, even with my voluminous and detailed notes and correspondences. Their reflection and guidance illuminated some of the nuances often overlooked during my review. Without their recollections and counsel, the book would not have been as thorough.

Some of the clients and colleagues mentioned in these accounts—in particular Ivan Ross, Don Arndt, and Don Uderitz—generously gave of their valuable time to review parts of the content and give me their advice. As I struggled with the delicate balance between my tendency to consider the audience and my tug toward unfettered expression, they tactfully pointed me in the right direction. Others—and there are many—wish to remain anonymous, and I do not want to jeopardize their trust. What I stated in the introduction still holds for all of them: They are talented, qualified, and intensely devoted individuals who I count as friends and whose confidence I wish to keep.

Of course, any author who fails to mention his family would be remiss. The total preoccupation and the countless hours spent researching, planning, pondering, writing, and re-writing was selfish on my part and required enormous patience from my family. I owe the deepest gratitude to my children Emily, Tommy, Katie, and Jodi, and especially my wife Arlene, for persevering during the two-year effort of completing this book.

NOTES

Preface

1. Frank Partnoy, *Infectious Greed: How Deceit and Risk Corrupted the Financial Markets.* New York: Times Books, 2003.
2. Michael Lewis, *Liar's Poker.* New York: Penguin, 1989, p. 9.

Introduction

1. Jon Hilsenrath, "Fed Debates New Role: Bubble Fighter." *The Wall Street Journal*, December 2, 2009.
2. L. Gordon Crovitz, "No Such Thing as Riskless Venture Capital." *The Wall Street Journal,* August 10, 2009.

Chapter 1

1. Adam Smith's *Wealth of Nations,* London: W. Strahan and T. Cadell 1776.
2. Paraphrased from Salomon's 1984 Training class, *"The Mortgage Securities Reference Manual,"* Salomon Brothers, 1984.

Chapter 2

1. Peter G. Brown, Thomas A. Zimmerman, and K. Jeanne Person, "Introduction to Mortgage and Mortgage-Backed Securities," Salomon Brothers, September 1987.
2. Michael Waldman and Steven Guterman, "Mortgage Securities: 1972–84," Salomon Brothers, March 1985.
3. Henry Kaufman, *On Money and Markets.* New York: McGraw-Hill, 2000.
4. Joseph Hu, "The Multifaceted Revolution in Securitizing Residential Mortgages," Salomon Brothers, October 1983.
5. Judy Hustick and Mary McDaniel, "Major Developments in Housing and Mortgage Finance in 1985," Salomon Brothers, January 1986.
6. Interview with the author.
7. Nick Timiraos and James R. Hagerty, "High-End Homes Frozen Out of Budding Housing Rebound." *The Wall Street Journal,* August 3, 2009.
8. Sarah N. Lynch, "SEC Criticized on Raters." *The Wall Street Journal,* August 29-30, 2009.

9. Serena Ng, "Moody's Compliance Head to Testify." *The Wall Street Journal,* September 30, 2009.

10. "The ABCs of Collateralized Debt Obligations and Credit-Default Swaps." *ERate,* October 9, 2008.

11. "Protecting the Credit Raters." *The Wall Street Journal*, October 1, 2009.

12. Interview with the author.

13. Interview with the author.

Chapter 3

1. From a sales training presentation by Gioia M. Parente describing her research report, "What Drives Interest Rate Swap Spreads," Salomon Brothers, September 1987.

2. Robert M. Stavis and Victor J. Haghani, "Putable Swaps," Salomon Brothers, March 1987.

3. "What's a clearinghouse?" *The Economist,* April 22, 2010.

4. Mark Mitchell, "Did the Markit Group, a Black-Box Company Partially Owned by Goldman Sachs & J. P. Morgan, Devastate Markets?" Market Rap, November 17, 2009.

5. Randall Smith and Sarah N. Lynch, "How Overhauling Derivatives Died." *The Wall Street Journal,* December 28, 2009.

6. www.wikinvest.com/wiki/Chicago_Mercantile_Exchange_(CME) (accessed November10, 2009).

7. Interview with author.

Chapter 4

1. Natasha Brereton and Stephen Fidler, "BOE's King: Big Banks Should Get Broken Up." *The Wall Street Journal,* October 21, 2009.

2. Frank J. Fabozzi and Steven V. Mann, *Floating-rate Securities.* New York: John Wiley and Sons, 2000.

3. Michel Crouhy, Dan Galai, and Robert Mark, *The Essentials of Risk Management.* New York: McGraw-Hill Professional, 2006.

4. Joseph P. H. Fan, Masaharu Hanazaki, and Juro Teranishi, *Designing Financial Systems in East Asia and Japan.* London: Routledge, 2004.

5. "To Lose One Decade May Be Misfortune ..." *The Economist,* January 2, 2010.

6. Leslie Scism and Randall Smith, "Wall Street Wizardry Reworks Mortgages," *The Wall Street Journal*, October 1, 2009.

7. Ibid.

Chapter 5

1. Based on a synopsis of her research report: Barbara T. Alexander, "Will 1990 Signal the End of a Demand-driven Housing Market?" Salomon Brothers, January 20, 1990.

2. Describing his research report: Joseph Hu, "Housing Finance in a Deregulated Environment," September 1984.

3. Ibid.

4. "His Personal Piggy Bank." *Time*, March 12, 1990.

5. http://en.wikipedia.org/wiki/Collateralized_mortgage_obligation (accessed September 2. 2009).

6. Judy Hustick and Mary McDaniel, "Major Developments in Housing and Mortgage Finance in 1985." Salomon Brothers, January 1986.

7. Ellen Evans and Gioia M. Parente, "What Drives Interest Rate Swap Spreads." Salomon Brothers, September 1987.

8. Ibid.

9. Ibid.

10. Michael Waldman, Mark Gordon, Thomas A. Zimmerman and K. Jeanne Person, "Interest Only and Principal Only STRIPS." Salomon Brothers, May 1987.

11. http://www.fdic.gov (accessed September 4, 2009.

12. http://en.wikipedia.org/wiki/Drexel_Burnham_Lambert (accessed September 8, 2009.

13. Ibid.

14. Jerry W. Markham, *A Financial History of the United States, vol. III.* Armonk, NY: Sharpe, 2002.

15. Timothy Curry and Lynn Shibut, "The Cost of the Savings and Loan Crisis: Truth or Consequences" FDIC Banking Review 13, no. 2:26-35, 2000.

16. Henry Kaufman, "On Money and Markets" New York: *McGraw-Hill, 2000.*

17. Jerry W. Markham, 2002.

18. Donald R. Fraser, "On the Wealth Effects of Supervisory Goodwill Controversy." *Journal of Financial Research* (March 22, 1999).

19. Ibid.

20. Ibid.

21. As quoted in the *American Banker,* June 27, 1989.

22. Donald R. Fraser, *Journal of Financial Research* (March 22, 1999).

23. Lee Davison, "Politics and Policy: The Creation of the Resolution Trust Corporation." *FDIC Banking Review* 17, no. 2 (2005).

24. Timothy Curry and Lynn Shibut, "The Cost of the Savings and Loan Crisis: Truth or Consequences" FDIC Banking Review 13, no. 2:26-35, 2000.

Chapter 6

1. Rob Alford, "What Are the Origins of Freddie Mac and Fannie Mae?" History News Network, 2003.

2. Alex J. Pollock, "Why Canada Avoided a Mortgage Meltdown." *The Wall Street Journal*, March 18, 2010.

3. "The Next Fannie Mae." *The Wall Street Journal's Review & Outlook,* August 11, 2009.

4. Deborah Solomon and Jon Hilsenrath, "No Easy Exit for Government as Housing Market's Savior." *The Wall Street Journal*, September 15, 2009.

5. Edward Pinto, "Acorn and the Housing Bubble." *The Wall Street Journal,* November 13, 2009.

Chapter 7

1. Mark Waldman, Mark Gordon, Thomas A. Zimmerman, and K. Jeanne Person, "Interest Only and Principal Only STRIPS." Salomon Brothers, May 1987.
2. M. D. Youngblood, "CMO Equity: The Influence of Structure and Collateral on Return." Salomon Brothers, August 1987.
3. M. D. Youngblood, "The Evolution of CMO Residuals: Economic, Accounting and Tax Issues." Salomon Brothers, November 1987.

Chapter 8

1. "Buffett's 1991 Salomon Testimony." *WSJ MarketBeat*, May 1, 2010.
2. Joseph Wechsberg, *The Merchant Bankers.* New York: Pocket Books, 1966.
3. John N. Ingham, *Biographical Dictionary of American Business Leaders.* Santa Barbara, CA: Greenwood Publishing Group, 1983.
4. "Hutton-Shearson Deal Announced." *New York Times*, December 4, 1987, http://query.nytimes.com.
5. Ralph Waldo Emerson, "Lectures on Success" from *The Complete Works of Ralph Waldo Emerson* (first published: 1903). http://www.rwe.org.

Chapter 9

1. Charles R. Geist, *The Last Partnerships.* New York: McGraw-Hill, 1997.
2. Internal memo entitled "Lehman Announces Strategic and Organizational Developments," April 2000.
3. http://www.iiioffshore.com.
4. "Foreign Affairs, March 4, 1979 to January 20, 1981." American Public University, http://www.u-s-history.com.
5. Christine Brennan, "25 Years Later, Olympic Boycott Gnaws at Athletes." *USA Today,* April 13, 2005.

Chapter 10

1. Peter J. Wallison, "The President's Bank Reforms Don't Add Up." *The Wall Street Journal,* March 21, 2009.
2. "First Union Capital Markets Corporation Names Williams Managing Director of Fixed Income." *PR Newswire*, April 12, 1996.

Chapter 11

1. Jon Hilsenrath, "Central Bankers Breathing Easier." *The Wall Street Journal,* August 22-23, 2009.
2. Damian Paletta and Paul Glader, "Fed's Next Job: Figuring Out Just Who Is Too Big." *The Wall Street Journal,* June 19, 2009.
3. Jon Hilsenrath, "Revamp Could Hurt Central Bank, Warns Head of Philadelphia Fed." *The Wall Street Journal,* July 28, 2009.
4. Alan Binder, "An Early-Warning System, Run by the Fed." *The New York Times,* July 26, 2009.

5. Sudeep Reddy, "Official Warns of Threat to Fed's Independence." *The Wall Street Journal,* July 10, 2009.

Chapter 12

1. Robert Pozen, "Stop Pining for Glass-Steagall." *Forbes Magazine,* October 5, 2009.
2. Peter Eavis, "Sizing Up the Big Issue for Banks." *The Wall Street Journal,* September 11, 2009.
3. Charles Calomiris, "In the World of Banks, Bigger Can Be Better." *The Wall Street Journal,* October 20, 2009.
4. Jon Hilsenrath, "Fed Debates New Role: Bubble Fighter." *The Wall Street Journal,* December 2, 2009.
5. Edward Pinto, "Acorn and the Housing Bubble." *The Wall Street Journal,* November 13, 2009.

Chapter 13

1. Mark Whitehouse, Betsy McKay, Bob Davis, and Steve Liesman, "Bear Tracks: In a Financial Gamble, Russia Lets Ruble Fall, Stalls Debt Repayment ... " *The Wall Street Journal,* August 18, 1998.
2. "Review & Outlook: Decade of Moral Hazard." *The Wall Street Journal,* September 25, 1998.
3. John M Berry, "A Tap on the Gas." *The Washington Post,* October 18, 1998.
4. Lehman Earnings Memorandum.
5. Interview with author.

Chapter 14

1. Richard S. Fuld, "Where Vision Gets Built." Lehman Brothers Annual Report, 2000.
2. Richard S. Fuld, "The Art of Client Services." Lehman Brothers Annual Report, 2003.

Chapter 15

1. Mike Martindale, "Silverdome sale price disappoints." *The Detroit News,* November 17, 2009.
2. David Yermack, "Keeping The Pay Police At Bay." *The Wall Street Journal,* October 10-11, 2009.
3. Statement of Richard S. Fuld before the U.S. House of Representatives, March 2009.
4. Benjamin G. Rader, *Baseball: A History of America's Game.* Champaign: University of Illinois Press, 2008.

Chapter 16

1. Bob Davis and Jonathan Weisman, "Nations Agree to Vet Each Others' Policies." *The Wall Street Journal,* September 26-27, 2009.
2. Craig K. Elwell, The Dollar's Future as the World's Reserve Currency: The Challenge of the Euro." CRS Report to Congress, July 2007.

3. Philip Hersh, "Chicago's Early Exit Should Be USOC Wake-up Call." *The Baltimore Sun,* October 4, 2009.
4. Ibid.
5. Julia Werdigier, "Britain and U.S. Clash over a Financial Tax to Insure Against Bank Crises." *The Wall Street Journal,* November 7, 2009.
6. Peter Mandelson, "We Need Greater Global Governance." *The Wall Street Journal,* June 19, 2009.

Chapter 17

1. www.investorglossary.com/phantom-income.htm (accessed October 8, 2009.
2. M. D. Youngblood, "The Evolution of CMO Residuals: Economic, Accounting and Tax Issues." Salomon Brothers, November 1987.
3. Ibid.
4. William Perez, "Foreign Tax Credit or Deduction." http://taxes.about.com.
5. IRS Revenue Procedure 2001-12. The Alternative Asset Test.
6. Ibid.
7. www.wrestlinghalloffame.org/news September 14, 2009.
8. Herman Weiskopf, "Working His Way Up from The Bottom." *Sports Illustrated,* May 10, 1976.

Chapter 18

1. Benjamin S. Bernanke, "The Economic Outlook." Presented to the Joint Economic Committee of Congress, March 28, 2008.
2. Steve Bergsman, "Let's Make a Deal." *RETAILTRAFFIC,* March 1, 1998.
3. Devin Leonard, "Andy Stone's Big Hangover: After Lending Binge, Mogul Fights for C.S. First Boston Bonus." *The New York Observer,* November 7, 1999.
4. Dana Rubinstein, "Mark Walsh, Lehman's Unluckiest Gambler." *The New York Observer,* September 30, 2008.
5. Ben White and Jenny Anderson, "Lehman Weighs Split to Shed Troubling Loans." *The New York Times,* September 5, 2008.

Chapter 19

1. Statement of Richard S. Fuld before the U.S. House of Representatives Committee on Oversight and Government Reform, October 6, 2008.
2. Henry Kaufman, *On Money and Markets.* New York: McGraw-Hill, 2000.
3. George J. Benston, *"The Separation of Commercial and Investment Banking: The Glass Steagall Act Revisited and Reconsidered,* New York: Oxford University Press, 1990.
4. See Vidya Bhaktavatsalam and Christopher Condon, "Blackrock to Buy Barclays Fund Unit for $13.5 Billion." *Bloomberg,* June 12, 2009.
5. PIMCO Web Site, "History." http://europe.pimco.com.
6. "How Does a Credit Default Swap Work?" GE Asset Management, White Paper Series, Spring 2005.

Epliogue

1. David Wessel, "Government's Trial and Error Helped Stem Financial Panic." *The Wall Street Journal,* September 14, 2009.

2. Mark Whitehouse, "Crisis Compels Economists to Reach for New Paradigm." *The Wall Street Journal,* November 3, 2009.

3. Sanford I. Weill and Judah S. Kraushaar, "Six Steps to Revitalize the Financial System." *The Wall Street Journal,* October 26, 2009.

4. Ian Bremmer and Nouriel Roubini, "How the Fed Can Avoid the Next Bubble." *The Wall Street Journal,* October 6, 2009.

5. Kara Scannell, "At SEC, Scholar Who Saw It Coming." *The Wall Street Journal,* January 25, 2010.

6. Andy Kessler, "The Bernanke Market." *The Wall Street Journal,* July 15, 2009.

7. Carter Dougherty, "I.M.F. Calls for Complete Redesign of Bank System," *International Herald Tribune,* October 1, 2009

www.ingramcontent.com/pod-product-compliance
Lightning Source LLC
Chambersburg PA
CBHW071412170526
45165CB00001B/246